Side Saddle on a Comet's Tail

The Life of Frances Dana Gage

Dr. Sandra Parker
Professor Emerita
Hiram College

Smile for the things that made them glad.

Robert Frost

I have an almost complete disregard of precedent and a faith in the possibility of something better. It irritates one to be told how things have always been done … I defy the tyranny of precedent. I cannot afford the luxury of a closed mind. I go for anything new that might improve the past.

Clara Barton

Table of Contents

Acknowledgments v

Introduction 1

Chapter One—Riding the Comet's Tail, Gage's Life 10

Chapter Two—"Go It Darkey," Gage the Abolitionist 49

Chapter Three—"A Moveable Feast," Gage the Women's Advocate 103

Chapter Four—"Devil's Broth," Gage and Temperance 145

Chapter Five—"The Riled and Turbulent Cup," Gage the Writer 177

Epilogue... 207

Works Cited 216

Frances Dana Gage*

Acknowledgements

In 1982, at Hiram College I was asked to join a National Endowment of the Humanities grant called "Regionalism in the Humanities." This supported faculty research into a unique area of northeast Ohio known in the nineteenth century as Connecticut's "Western Reserve" or "Fire Lands." Yankees first knew this part of America as the Northwest Territory; Ohio was then America's western frontier and attracted ambitious, self-conscious, and literate New Englanders. Their pioneer experiences in the Western Reserve led some writers to preserve the quickly fading culture of the frontier.

Following our College Archivist's tips, my initial focus was strictly the Western Reserve where a number of distinguished authors wrote about their part of Ohio. Then my inquiries extended further into the state, and I discovered other Ohio authors. A number of these, like Alice Cary, gained national prominence. Yet, a good case can be made that on the national stage a pioneer woman named Frances Gage was the most influential Ohio women writer of the nineteenth century. She was born in a log cabin in 1808 as Frances Dana Barker and raised near the mouth of the Muskingum River. Her life became more cosmopolitan and occasionally included visits to Cleveland; she expressed admiration for the Western Reserve's style and beauty. For instance, in 1854 after visiting family members in Iowa, Gage praised the landscape by commenting that it felt as if she were "traveling through the best portions of the Western Reserve." Some of this connection was aesthetic, some experiential, some familial because Frances Dana Barker Gage was highly conscious of being descended from New Englanders and was proud of this heritage. She saw its reflection in the early settlers known in her childhood who first entered the wild lands that became the state of Ohio.

Frances Gage's life experiences were infused in her writing. She created reams of work in many genres, some typical of the limits of a pioneer housewife, like letters, poems, and stories written for regional journals. Eventually this success led to her polemical essays, speeches, and novels. In her contemporary world, Frances Gage built an intimate relationship with her readers. Her name will usually appear here as "Frances Gage," but during her childhood she was known as "France," a family nickname. She often called herself "Frances Dana Gage," integrating her maiden surname or its initial as a tribute to the Dana family's heritage. Finally, in many essays and Clara Barton's 1892 tribute to women who sacrificed in the Civil War, she is called by the "pen name," "Aunt Fanny."

Locating Gage's extensive writings has been complicated by such matters. Often she was published in obscure sources, so the included bibliography represents pertinent poems, essays, letters, and tales that provide resources for tracing her life. My deep appreciation must be extended to Hiram College for getting me started on this research topic, especially its grant director, Professor David Anderson. The college's librarians, led by Archivist Joanne Sawyer and Director, David Everett, were invaluable. Gratitude also should be extended to the many colleagues who helped me think and write more clearly, especially Kenyon Professor Joyce Dyer.

A number of historical societies and museums have aided my research. For helping with Frances Gage family inquiries, I would like to thank the following: Philadelphia's G. A. R. Museum and Library; Parris Island's South Carolina Museum, Steven Wise, Curator; County Historian Larry Roland and Dr. Chester DePratter; Marietta College, Dawes Library Special Collections, for "Written by Hand" Catharine Barker autobiography; Bentley Historical Library, University of Michigan, Ann Arbor for Dr. Wilcox advertisement; Diana Dretske, Collections Coordinator Lake County Forest Preserves, Discovery Museum, Wauconda, Illinois—research on Midwestern Gage family members; Jennifer Brathovde, Librarian, Manuscript Division, Library of Congress, Washington, D.C. for Barton Correspondence; Lisa Long, Reference Archivist, Collections Services Division, Research Services Department, Ohio Historical Society, Columbus, Ohio for "memoir of FDG" in Janney

Family Papers and James L. Gage research; Simpson Country Library, McConnelsville, Ohio, for Nettie T. Hennery, typescript from *Morgan County Herald*; Cornell University Library, Division of Rare and Ms. Collection, Carl A. Kroch Library, Fowler Family Papers; Susan M. Jellinger, Librarian II, State Historical Society of Iowa, Dept. of Cultural Affairs, Des Moines, Iowa for Catharine *Barker, Journal of Recollections*; Scott Sanders, University Archivist, Antiochiana; Olive Kettering Library, Yellow Spring, Ohio for tracing Gage children.

On the personal level, I must convey my ongoing gratitude to Maxine Keene who for decades has tolerated my absentmindedness and distraction. Her sustained emotional support made it possible for me to pursue scholarly travails while obsessively writing about Ohio's early women authors.

The Ohio Cultivator used this cover graphic It was a journal she edited ad wrote for as "Aunt Fanny

INTRODUCTION

Thomas Wentworth Higginson quipped late in the nineteenth century that American women writers found "their passage into literature by first compiling a cookery book."[1] That observation epitomized the dilemma of many women who first validated their domestic competence, so they could rise above its constraints and commit themselves to professional writing. The devastating germ of truth in Higginson's observation can be best seen in Lydia Maria Francis Child who in 1829 published *The Frugal Housewife, Dedicated to Those Who Are Not Ashamed of Economy*, which went through 35 printings before 1850. She was a brilliant New Englander who went on to impressive literary accomplishments. Child and Higginson shared commitments to abolition, social reform, editing, and writing. He was a prominent reform leader— Harvard educated, an officer of freedmen in the Civil War, and advocate for abolition, temperance, and women's rights. Higginson saw himself as a colleague to many celebrated women, for instance he composed a biography of Margaret Fuller and supported Emily Dickinson's poetry. But, he cannot have fathomed how difficult any of his accomplishments would have been if he, like Child, were born into a female body.

The crux of the matter was that women who wished to achieve in the public realm often sought domestic approval before daring to become viable reformers or writers. It was a matter of navigating treacherous waters, and many gifted figures like Margaret Fuller did not live to achieve fulfillment in a safe harbor. Frances Gage did. Her essays were not recipes but taught women how to be efficient home managers; this was the foundation from which she broached her reform interests. In an 1862 poem titled "I Live Two Lives," she expressed her recognition of the dual and irreconcilable centers of her own being." This poem described the stress wrought by living alternately in private and public worlds. A modern critic has ably traced these contradictions in her "Two Lives."[2]

Fame began coming her way late in the 1840s when she was middle-aged. About the same time as the Seneca Falls Women's Rights Convention occurred in New York State in 1848, Frances Dana Gage entered Ohio's reform movement as an opposer of slavery and intemperance. She quickly garnered a reputation as nurturer and idealist who wielded a competent pen. Eastern reformers' reactions to Gage were somewhat complicated; some, like Amelia Bloomer, treasured her as a colleague; many admired her bravery as a Union military worker who helped freedmen. Progressive liberals of the day, like William Lloyd Garrison and Henry Ward Beecher, recognized her as having a place among a cadre of speakers at countless meetings where she attacked slavery and intemperance, while supporting women's rights. Yet, the different reputations Gage won faded after her health faded in 1867. Occasionally someone recalled as Olympia Brown did in her 1911 autobiography that, "Aunt Fanny Gage was really one of the ablest women we have ever had in this country. She was strong and true and original."[3]

Gage was proud of her British ancestry through a Yankee father, Joseph Barker, who in 1788 joined Revolutionary War veteran Col. Rufus Putnam's Ohio Company. This was America's first group of settlers in the Northwest Territory, and the family survived the Indian Wars. In 1808, he sired Frances Barker She and her elder sisters assisted both her mother inside their log cabin home and her father on their farm. "France" was a hard worker who sought praise, but she was also a dreamer, reader, and writer. Her educated father set an example by writing, but discouraged her scribbling. This unconventional "cabin maiden" never lost her desire to write. Her lifetime spanned three generations of American history; she was an Ohio Valley pioneer, then a Buckeye matron during prebellum conflicts, and a noted Civil War journalist whose work was included in leading abolition and reform-minded publications and like Horace Greeley's *New York Tribune*. After the war, Gage's professional career entered a fourth phase when she was sidelined by reformers and resorted to publishing a volume of poetry, three novels, and several collections of children's stories.

Frances Gage's initial audience was regional farmwomen in the Ohio River Valley who affectionately recognized both her name and pen name she adopted, "Aunt Fanny." During these early adult years, she created an "in print" identity that was represented by various names. She never included her father's patronym "Barker" or her husband's "given name," "James." She always retained her first name, "Frances" or initial, "F," and often included her maternal family's name, "Dana," of which she was very proud.

The repudiation of her father's family name and husband's first name stressed her choice to be seen as a woman who was not reliant on men. Furthermore, her maiden surname, "Barker," carried associations she did not embrace—amoral violence, assertion of dominance at all costs, and smug, self-righteous, unquestioning belief in a hierarchy where might makes right. If Frances Gage saw some of herself in this inheritance, she attempted to root it out and worked steadily for the underdog.

She adopted the following authorial signatures: Frances Gage, Frances D. Gage, Frances Dana Gage, F.D.G., as well as the pseudonym "Aunt Fanny." Her early identification as nurturing Ohio wife and mother grew quickly to include a second voice, the regional watchdog that attacked the 1850 Fugitive Slave Law. Later in that decade, her reputation expanded as she began to participate on national platforms. As her older sister commented, the family saw young "France" as a girl who wanted to attack injustices, which she grouped together as her "triune cause"—slavery, intemperance, and women's second-class citizenship. Frances Dana Gage, her big sister complained, wanted to "get her side saddle on a comet's tail."[4] As an old lady, she was proud to think of herself as a trailblazer who, for example, fostered Sojourner Truth, crossed swords with Harriet Beecher Stowe, and helped launch the Republican Party.

The most fundamental influences on her life came from the time and place of her birth. The "Frontier Thesis" of influential historian Frances Jackson Turner defined pioneers as shaped by the concept of free land and westward expansion. Turner valorized frontiersmen's self-reliance. In fact, his final scholarship regretted only the loss of forests. Another generation of western historians later criticized the narrowness of his thesis. For instance, scholars like Patricia Nelson Limerick and Glenda Riley pointed out Turner "overlooked the ladies." Researchers like the thoughtful John Mack Faragher more closely examined the social history of places like nineteenth century Ohio in terms of matters like class, gender, and environment.

Frances Gage's reform career was indebted to the trajectory of another contemporary idea, the romantic ideal that promoted morality and social vision. She perfectly represents what historians Lance Banning and Marvin Mayers describe as the "Jeffersonian Persuasion," a philosophy which embodies Thomas Jefferson's political ideal of equality. This theory of developing opportunities for personal growth argued that intellect is a neutral domain and open to all.5 This extends the Enlightenment philosophy that rejected legal dependency and promoted individual autonomy in civil and political matters. The "common man," regardless of wealth, was guaranteed citizenship, the franchise, and right to participate in government. Females were excluded because custom limited females to domestic roles centering on piety and purity. Yet, America's political climate led women to argue that home virtues should be reflected in public deeds. Why couldn't domesticity be extended into redemptive and regenerative action? Hence Jeffersonian America generated a "distinct social type" of newly intellectual women who felt empowered to comment upon politics.6 Frances Gage was among these thinkers and once commented that she felt "caged" in her Ohio domicile. Unsurprisingly, she broke out of that cage. As Jeffrey E. Smith recently commented, "Gage came of political age, so to speak, in a time marked by the rhetoric of democratic participation . . . in the political process."[7]

Amongst the obstacles to women's entrance into public discourse were American male leaders, whether preachers, politicians, or authors, who articulated protests against female participation in public justice issues. During the era, male authority initially seemed to be reinforced by industrial, urban, and professional developments. Women's authority was restricted to a separate gender sphere that allowed them to be domestic and isolated to the homosocial hearth and quilting bees. Fortunate women escaped from isolation by education and fellowship with others of like mind. Some, of course, found a remedy by bonding with a congenial husband, such as Frances Barker found in James Lamson Gage. He rejected the notion that women were locked into "the fixed orbit of the domestic circle, [where] woman was the complement to man,"[8] and the couple's romantic liaison was cemented over discussions of abolition. Indeed, the anti-slavery movement which defended African Americans' rights was a "selfless" cause that permitted women to step beyond the boundaries of their thresholds. Women saw in slaves' plight a condition of parallel injustice to their own limited legal identity. In discussing slaves' benighted condition, American women generated ideological solidarity.

For numerous American women, the ideals of the "Jeffersonian Persuasion" led to budding reform sentiment or, at least, a justification for independent action, especially when they ventured away from the North East. Consider two disparate writers, Caroline Kirkland and Caroline Lee Hentz; each was adventurous, idealistic, literate, and groundbreaking. Kirkland commented on a utopian Michigan settlement, while Hentz was an apologist for southern slaveholders. Despite such contrasting ideological positions, they were both nontraditional women who entered the world of letters via appropriation of traditional male subject matter—controversial public dialogue. Both women were intelligent, educated and brave, expressing atypical viewpoints that combined domestic values and social issues. Each one's ideas were, one might say, their own excuse.

Frances Gage, too, sought philosophical support for women's reform work. Its endorsement of tolerance, diversity, and open-mindedness supported invaluable role models. Her integration of these values can be seen, for instance, when she met a "delightful" and admired author, Sarah Josepha Hale, who supported women's teacher training colleges and medical schools, but not women's rights. Frances Dana Gage wrote, "I feel no disposition to find fault with her . . . [she] sees thing from one standpoint, I from another."[9]

This tolerance was exceptional in an era when contention was popular. Nineteenth-century scholar Karen Kilcup champions reprinting "lost authors and long out of print works" that deserve critical recovery.[10] Recently, Elaine Showalter in her history of American women's writing, *A Jury of Her Peers,* offers another impetus to such "recovery" and restoration of forgotten writers.[11]

Nina Baym is, perhaps, America's most definitive researcher on women writers of the nineteenth century. Her decision to examine women writers of the American West covered it as a line that moved beyond the Appalachians after the 1830's. Although she commenced her study west of the Mississippi, her reclamation project still provides a valuable framework for considerations of pioneer Ohio. She asks: how did women writers make lives for themselves, how did they represent their unique region, and how did they represent women in their work? Among the "many different Wests" she describes ought to be the Ohio River Valley with the story of its history, landforms, and climate. She may have believed Ohio lacked the color and referential history of the Plaines and southwest. Perhaps she thought Ohio was too familiar since it was populated by Anglo women descended from English forbears. Indeed, pioneer women in wild Ohio country after the turn of the nineteenth century were merely fortunate to no longer have to fight native Americans. But Frances Gage proved in her biographical writing and *Elsie Magoon* that the challenge to women's agency on the frontier remained a riveting concern.

Gage claimed her history book was a contribution to the record of western settlement. I believe, as Nina Baym clarified in her study of our country's women western writers that it is unnecessary to rank authors according to some ideal of literariness.[12] The books themselves simply contribute to the overall project of getting women's experiences into the record.

Historical analyses often build upon a series of dates. In this sense, a brief overview of nineteenth-century America's three reform movements appears as a sequence. Abolition reforms grew from violent episodes that climaxed in the Thirteenth Constitutional Amendment in 1865; temperance reforms extended over time and were more subtle, leading to the Eighteenth Amendment in 1919; women's rights, starting last and having fewer supporters, edged forward on a state-by-state basis until the Nineteenth Amendment was granted in 1920.

Chronologies can be traced in public records. The persons generating these movements could also be visualized as if part of a collage. The idea of understanding an era based on its influential personalities was employed by Englishman William Hazlitt in his 1825 S*pirit of the Age: or Contemporary Portraits.* His collection of biographical vignettes offered readers a new perspective, a kind of visual collage of the Romantic era. For example, his figures shaping the century's ethos included Thomas Malthus, William Wordsworth, S. T. Coleridge, and Sir Walter Scott. If someone like William Hazlitt were to have gathered essays about America's *Spirit of the Age* in the 1850s, the roster would constitute another wonderful collage, including such figures as Susan B. Anthony, Clara Barton, Henry Ward Beecher, Amelia Bloomer, Salmon P. Chase, Lydia Maria Child, Lloyd Garrison, Horace Greeley, Abraham Lincoln, Lucretia Mott, Elizabeth Cady Stanton, Harriet Beecher Stowe, and Sojourner Truth.

Adopting a similar perspective, one could imagine a visualization of abolition's "face"—in its center would be a large portrait of William Lloyd Garrison, and radiating out from his presence would be a myriad of male and female associates who were complementary editors, writers and speakers. A temperance collage would look quite different, perhaps more resembling a mosaic, because sharing its space would be many small men's and women's faces. A woman's rights collage would have a central focal point— two, large figures, Susan B. Anthony and Elizabeth Cady Stanton. Circling their forms would be a variety of smaller women's faces, a few older like Lucretia Mott, but mostly contemporary, such as Amelia Bloomer and Lucy Stone. An approach to history from this sort of visual perspective would emphasize more than reform battles and suggest the significance of character as a determinant shaping events. Consider for a moment what might have happened differently if the respective central collage figures, Garrison, Stanton, and Anthony, had faltered in their dedication or altered their views.

One face that would appear in all three collages was that of Frances Dana Gage. In these simplified terms, her lifelong hatred of slavery and intemperance earned her respect from national leaders who valued her work as author and speaker. Her justice preoccupation easily translated into woman's rights commitment. However, her face on the woman's rights collage might have been placed toward an outer edge because in the 1860's she claimed independence from the tutelage of the forceful Stanton and Anthony. In this way, vagaries of personalities affected contributions to America's reform movements, as the following study will demonstrate.

A quarter of a century ago, I read *Elsie Magoon, or the Old Still-House in the Hollow, a Tale of the Past* by perusing a micro card copy of her 1866 novel. Later this detailed account of pioneer activities in the Ohio Valley became available online at the University of Indiana's Wright American Fiction Series. Today it is easily available on computers. I was interested in Ohio women writers, and discovered that Frances Gage was the most nationally prominent. Her pioneer beginning, lack of a formal education, and progress to Washington and the ranks of leaders on the East Coast, marked this writer as a remarkable and distinguished person.

She was kindly and loveable, every woman's ideal older friend, yet only in her personal correspondence with Clara Barton is this element apparent. She wrote little about family concerns and nothing about her own travails. Cut off from her Ohio roots in 1853, she identified with reformers, though in 1867 Gage was unexpectedly abandoned by woman's rights leaders. A few years later in 1878, knowing she could not recover her strength, Gage moved to Greenwich, Connecticut and lived among her memories.

Introduction

Notes

1. Thomas Wentworth Higginson quoted in Helen Gray Cone, "Women in American Literature," *Century*, 40, no. 6 Oct. 1890): 923.
2. Carol Steinhagen, "The Two Lives of Frances Dana Gage," *Ohio History* 107 (Winter-Spring 1998), 22-38.
3. Olympia Brown, *Acquaintances Old and New Among Reformers*, (Milwaukee, Wisconsin: S. E. Tate, 1911), 10.
4. Catharine Barker, "Written by Hand," Dawes Library, Special Collections Marietta College, Marietta, Ohio, 14.
5. Lance Banning and Marvin Mayers, *The Jeffersonian Persuasion,(* Ithaca: Cornell University Press, 1980) 22.
6. Susan Phinney Conrad, *Perish the Thought* (New York: Oxford University Press, 1976, 22.
7. Jeffrey E. Smith, "Frances Dana Gage: "Turning the World Upside Down," *Feminist Frontiers, Women Who Shaped the Midwest*, Yvonne Johnson, ed. (Kirksville: Truman State University Press, Missouri, 2010).
8. Conrad, 25.
9. Frances Gage, "Letter," *The Lily* (vol. 3, no. 5) (May 6, 1851).
10. Karen Kilcup, "Anthologizing Matters," *Symploke* 8.1-2 (Winter-Spring 2000), 36.
11. Elaine Showalter, *A Jury of Her Peers*, (New York: Alfred A. Knopf, 2009), xiv.
12. Nina Baym, *Women Writers of the American West, 1933-1927,* (Urbana, University of Illinois, 2011).

Chapter One

Riding the Comet's Tail, Gage's Life

The last surviving person with the surname "Barker" passed away in Washington County, Ohio in the middle of the twentieth century. The first man with that name, Joseph Barker arrived on November 1, 1789 from Amherst, New Hampshire. His party emigrated 700 miles on foot and in oxcarts through the states of New York, New Jersey, and Pennsylvania. Then flatboats took them on a wild ride down the Youghiogheny, the Monongahela, and Ohio Rivers until they arrived at a tiny western settlement begun in April 1788 by Rufus Putnam. Joseph Barker was recently married and accompanied his father-in-law's family group. They came to southeast Ohio Country to share the pioneers' dangers— winter, wild animals (especially bears, panthers, and wolves), food shortages, epidemics, and Indian Wars. [1]

The pioneers' leader, Rufus Putnam, is known as "The Father of Ohio." His contemporary fame grew out of a series of heroic and patriotic activities. He served three years after 1747 in the French and Indian War and began as a Lieutenant Colonel in the War of Independence. He was George Washington's second chief engineer and considered to be remarkable for his practical resourcefulness. For example, Putnam laid out several fortifications at West Point, and its Fort Putnam was named after him. In 1779, he served under Major-General Anthony Wayne, and in 1783 was commissioned Brigadier-General. After the war in 1786, Putnam co-founded the Ohio Company of Associates which purchased western lands. The following year, Congress completed the grant to the Ohio Company, and he was appointed its Superintendent. In 1788, Rufus Putnam used his surveying skills to lead a small party to the southern banks of the Ohio River where they founded Marietta, Ohio, the region's first settlement. Here they began a fortification known as the Campus Martius.

During the remaining 36 years of his life, the hearty Putnam took on many frontier roles. He was a judge for the court of the Northwest Territory between 1790 and 1796, United States Surveyor-General from 1796 to 1803, and member of Ohio's first state Constitutional Convention in 1802. The Ohio Company dissolved in 1796. His fame continued after his death. At the outbreak of the Civil War, Marietta area men volunteered to be part of the "Putnam Brigade" by enlisting in Ohio's 62nd Regiment which became distinguished for its outstanding performance. Two centuries later, his name still lingers in the form of a Rufus Putnam Visiting Professorship at Ohio University.

Putnam's family line was from Buckinghamshire, England. In 1634 John Putnam immigrated to Salem, Massachusetts. Similarly, the Barker and Dana families had deep English roots. Joseph Barker was a fifth generation American with ancestral roots in Suffolk. His father was born in New Hampshire; he was born in Newmarket in 1765 and was a skilled cabinetmaker and homebuilder who was known as Deacon Barker. His son, Joseph, was bright, energetic, and played practical jokes, like white washing an unpopular neighbor's horse. Needing to be taught discipline, young Barker was sent away to Exeter Academy for several years and then apprenticed in his father's trade, carpentry, and studied architecture. He married into the Dana family in September 1789 after courting "Affectionate Eliza" Dana."[2]

Her lineage goes back two centuries to Norfolk, England. The Dana name is Celtic for" bold." The Dana family's Puritan ancestors left Manchester, England in 1638 to settle in Cambridge, Massachusetts. Their descendants became known for their contributions in literature and law, especially reform interests such as antislavery. Her father, Captain William Dana, was a successful officer in the Revolutionary War. In late 1788, he left New England with two sons and trekked westward to see Rufus Putnam's Ohio Company that was carving out a settlement from the Northwest Territory. Putnam's original group of 48 men left Hartford Connecticut on Jan. 1 and arrived on April 7, 1788 via old Fort Du Quesne in Pittsburg. Their permanent settlement at the confluence of the Ohio and Muskingum Rivers was named Marietta after the Queen of France. This was wild country, but Capt. Dana, arriving in May, liked its prospects and felt confident his extended family could start a new life in the West. He returned to New England and brought his family to join Rufus Putnam's Ohio Company—his wife, Mary Bancroft Dana, who was raised in Pepperell, Massachusetts, their six sons and three daughters, as well as his new son-in-law, Joseph Barker.

The pioneers knew George Washington took this land from Indians, French, and English, and in 1787 named it the Northwest

Territory, a huge expanse that ran from the Appalachian Mountains to the edge of the western plains. Congress in 1792 granted vast acreage along the northeast corner of the Ohio Company of Associates' territory. The Indians, who never meant to give the land away, fought to keep it, and Rufus Putnam's early settlers paid the price. In January 1791, twelve Ohio Company settlers were slaughtered by Indians at Big Bottom, and the Indian Wars were underway. For seven years, until 1798, Putnam's settlers blockaded themselves in Marietta's blockhouse or fort. Peace did not come with the 1795 Treaty of Greenville, but it did follow the Battle of Tippecanoe in 1811 when William Henry Harrison defeated Shawnee and Creek forces led by the Prophet. Indian warfare was totally over by 1813 when Tecumseh was dead, and the meddling British were defeated at the Battle of the Thames on Lake Erie. So between General "Mad Anthony Wayne's defeat of the Algonquin at the Battle of Fallen Timbers on the Maumee River in 1794 and the prolonged interracial violence of 1811-1815, pioneers were at risk. President William Henry Harrison called for a "war of extirpation," putting the seal on a brutal chapter in American history.[3]

    General Rufus Putnam's settlement was established near native American mounds, called "ancient works and fortifications" at the confluence of Elks' Eye and La Belle Riviere, names given in the native's language and by earlier French settlers for the Muskingum and Ohio Rivers. The eastern pioneers claimed land the Iroquois called "Ohio" or beautiful. Steadfast Gen. Putnam lived there until he was buried in Marietta's Mound Cemetery in 1824 when Frances Dana was 17.

    In the sense that the word "pioneer" is derived from French and signified, as John Mack Faragher points out, foot soldiers that clear the way for an army, the metaphor is apt. It was to happen repeatedly on the continent—dispossession of the Indians was a prerequisite to Anglo-American settlement on the trans-Appalachian frontier. Thus the first pioneers were paramilitary occupiers, wresting the Northwest Territory's lands from Indians in order for the initiation of Anglo-American agricultural development.[4]

    Though Putnam's Marietta was a dangerous place for its first quarter of a century, its excitement engaged the imagination of two descendants who preserved the era in prose. The first was born in Putnam's settlement in 1794. Julia Corry, whose father, Ebenezer, was among those killed by Indians, was taken by her mother to be raised in safety near Albany, New York. With a married name, the young woman returned to Ohio in 1812; Julia Dumont became famous for romanticizing Ohio River Valley heroes.[5] The second birth of a future writer in Putnam's settlement was a girl born in 1808 as Frances Barker.

    Contemporary historian W. D. Gallagher described the Indian War challenges settlers faced. He described settlers, like Joseph Barker, who "sallied" out of their garrisons "where they had been more or less closely confined for five years." He called their worst challenges "famine, sickness, deaths . . . smallpox and putrid sore throat." Nonetheless, Marietta's garrison life "saved the pioneer settlements from being entirely broken up.[6] In 1795, the Barker family was burned out of their first cabin and returned to the village blockhouse for safety where they lived for a total of seven years. Joseph Barker's father-in-law, William Dana, settled his extensive family further south, in Belpre; this was adjacent to the Ohio River and across from the slave state, Virginia. The Dana clan was a second family base for France Gage. When several smallpox epidemics swept into Marietta, Elizabeth and the children were sent to Belpre for safety, but the second time she caught the disease and was badly scarred.

    Joseph Barker was named sergeant in the local militia and was placed in charge of Marietta's blockhouse at "Point." In December 1814, he was rewarded for service in the Indian Wars with 100 acres that extended over both sides of the Muskingum River north of Putnam's settlement. Joseph Barker's one hundred acres of free land was known as #1 in the Donation Tract. This was the beginning of the Barker farm that he later extended to 600 acres. He led his family to Wiseman's Bottom seven miles north of Marietta on the east shore of the Muskingum River where he built a log cabin. Frances was born there, the fifth daughter and next to last child of Joseph Barker. She was six years old when peace was secured on the frontier. The Barkers were one of the first white families to settle in the area which later was referred to as Union, Ohio. He received fruit tree grafts from neighbor Israel Putnam and planted an orchard of Roxbury Russets (or so-called Putnams) that were slow growing but pest resistant. Years later, he joked that planting seedlings during the war was a matter of "holding his scalp with one hand while he dug holes with the other."[7] Towards the end of the Indian War, Joseph Barker occasionally left the Marietta fort to clear his overgrown orchard and start building cabins. His first

16' square cabin became a utility shed when he moved the family into a larger hewed log house with a brick chimney. Then the first structure burned, destroying his corn crib and releasing hogs from their enclosure. That sent Barker back to work, and he also did carpentry work in Marietta to earn cash for the family. Before long, he balanced farming and building.

Barker became Colonel of the militia, a title he always relished as he did diverse challenges—whether building houses, extending his farm, surveying, or serving as a community leader. He was named a Justice of the Peace in 1799 and judge of Washington County's common pleas court from 1830 to 1842. Known in his own era as an able architect, builder, and shipbuilder, posterity appreciates the fact that his manuscript, "Recollections," is a valuable resource. It was primary source material for two early historians, Samuel Prescott Hildreth's *Pioneer History of the Ohio Valley (*1848) and Martin Andrews' *History of Marietta* (1902).

The winter of 1797 placed Joseph Barker in the middle of a controversial episode in American history. A new British immigrant came to Marietta with his young wife. His name was Blennerhasset (1764-1862) and he was an aristocrat descended from King Henry III. This man was schooled at Westminster, Trinity College Dublin, and was a member of the bar. Blennerhasset was scouting for land to develop into a plantation, and, because he wished to employ slaves, it would have to be located south of the Ohio River that was the boundary of the slave holding south. In 1798, the aristocrat bought the northern section of an island two miles from Belpre, where the Dana family lived, and near Parkersburg, Virginia. His family moved into the island's Indian Wars blockhouse, and he began planning construction of his estate. Harmon Blennerhasset was friendly with the Putnam settlers, opened a dry goods and hardware store in the area, and wisely employed experienced local builders, including Joseph Barker.[8] The mansion's construction took two and a half years since it was to be the "grandest building west of the Appalachians" and "one of the most beautiful and extravagant of its time." It became a sort of feudal estate that provided the "premier social attraction of the Ohio Valley."[9] In 1800, when the Blennerhassets moved into the mansion, Putnam's pioneers, including the Barker family, must have been extraordinarily proud of the neighborhood's island becoming a prestigious showplace.

After a few glittering years, the edenic dream began unraveling. Rumors flew of disgrace in Ireland—Harmon Blennerhasset had illegally married his niece, sold his inheritance, Castle Conway, and fled Great Britain in shame. His plan was to redeem himself in the New World on the Ohio River Island. Blennerhasset was courted by many. Among them was Aaron Burr, a prominent politician from New York State who ran for President in 1800. Burr lost the Presidency to Thomas Jefferson by a vote in the House of Representative's Electoral College. This made Burr America's third Vice President, and he served from 1801 to 1805. In 1804, Burr ran for the Governorship of New York State and lost. An argument between Burr and a longtime political rival, Alexander Hamilton, led to a duel on July 11, 1804. It left Hamilton dead and Burr disgraced. He went to the West the following year and set about charming the naïve Harmon Blennerhasset. In later years, it was said that Aaron Burr wanted to attack Mexico; some believed he wanted to secede from America. Whatever Burr's scheme, the Irishman wanted to participate and allowed Blennerhasset Island to be used as a "staging area."

In the spring of 1806, Marietta area residents believed Aaron Burr's activities were government sanctioned, and Joseph Barker was asked if he would accept a commission as Colonel. He was told they were preparing for war with Spain and his militia should learn French maneuvers. All seemed on the up and up, and two of Barker's brother-in-laws signed up to join Burr's forces. In September, Joseph Barker received an order for fifteen large "bateaux" or boats. Two months later on November 20, Blennerhasset arrived at Barker's Muskingum shipyard to see the boats and explain how one was to be named after his son, "Dominic," and fitted for his and Burr's private use. He said the boats would be launched at night on December 10. For the first time, eyebrows were raised. On November 27, President Jefferson issued a proclamation declaring that no war with Spain was eminent and warning Aaron Burr to cease and desist. Ohio's Governor, Edward Tiffin, within four days authorized the seizure of Burr's boats and supplies. Water traffic on the Muskingum and Ohio Rivers was stopped. Ten of Joseph Barker's boats were intercepted, though several unfinished boats remained at his shipyard. This was the end of what pioneers jokingly called "Burr's flotilla." One of the original Ohio Company leaders, General Edward W. Tupper, in November 1806 composed a mock-heroic poem to commemorate the event, "The Battle of Muskingum, or Defeat of the Burrites." It joked about the mooring of Burr's boats providing an excuse for local men to take the supplies and "gorge" on whisky and peach-brandy at the blacksmith's shop.

Aaron Burr sailed one boat down the Mississippi River toward Natchez. Though disguised as a frontiersman, he was captured in Mobile, Alabama. Meanwhile, Harmon Blennerhasset went into hiding when Jefferson's orders were being enforced. His wife was visiting friends in Marietta so escaped the Virginia Militia that came to the mansion and ransacked it. The family escaped, although Blennerhasset was quickly detained and locked up in the Virginia State Penitentiary. He was tried as a co-conspirator with Aaron Burr. Both men were released due to insufficient evidence and remanded for trial in the District of Ohio. Instead of facing that indignity, Burr fled America for Europe where for some time he continued his political machinations.

Harmon Blennerhasset, the gullible aristocrat, was never convicted of anything. Nevertheless, the Virginia Militia returned to the island in 1811 and set fire to the mansion. Gone was the "impeccable island paradise [that was] the toast of the Ohio Valley."[10] The stubborn Englishman and would-be slave owner subsequently bought a small plantation in Mississippi Territory and lost it due to bad crops and low cotton prices. Finally, Blennerhasset slunk away from the New World and died of apoplexy on another island, Guernsey, off England's southeastern shoreline. The entire affair was an American scandal of high visibility and became fodder for commentators like historian and author W. H. Venable whose version of the significant melodrama was fictionalized in an 1840 novel, *A Dream of Empire, Or, the House of Blennerhasset.*[8]

Joseph Barker was wiser for the experience. Aaron Burr had already paid him $1,319 for 11 completed boats. The unlaunched boats were seized by President Jefferson, and local creditors, like Joseph Barker, waited to receive reimbursement from the Blennerhasset estate's assets. This disturbing scenario left Putnam's settlers shaken and stunned by the prospect of treason in the Ohio River Valley; they were embarrassed about their neighbor's shameful trial. Of course, the notoriety died down after the embers of Blennerhasset cooled, and local residents who worked for its hapless owner remained free of taint. No bad consequences followed for the patriarch Joseph Barker. He was not what Hildreth labels "an aspiring man," and continued to work—farming, building, and serving as County Commissioner, Common Pleas Judge, and State Legislator. In 1828, Barker supported Andrew Jackson's successful bid for the presidency and often was the speaker at patriotic events.

 Joseph Barker's values—industry, enterprise, economy, morality, and perseverance—were transmitted to his children. He sired four boys (one drowned at age 3) and six daughters. All but one of his children married, giving Elizabeth and Joseph a total of 63 grandchildren, eight of whom belonged to Frances Dana Gage. His oldest offspring were born in Marietta's fort. The Barker's "starter home" was a log cabin where Frances, arrived on October 12, 1808. This baby inherited the advantages and disadvantages of being an infant in a large pioneer family. She proudly called herself a "cabin maiden," and enjoyed revisiting their early log cabin. However, the house where she really grew up was a Federal styled brick building built in 1811 by her father when she was seven. Picturesquely located overlooking the Muskingum River, it had an impressive Adams doorway with sidelights, recessed brick arches on the second story, a slate roof, and sandstone foundation. Inside it was adorned with fancy woodwork; its beauty led her father to be considered a master architect and builder. Even in the twenty-first century, this home is described as a significant example of early architecture in south eastern Ohio. Descendants and owners have kept the Col. Joseph Barker homestead in a good state of preservation. In 1978 it was designated a "historic site on the National Register of Historic Places," and it has a plaque saying it was the home of "activist Frances Gage."

 She and her siblings received limited education at the district school where grammar and geography were taught. A contemporary and life-long friend of Frances Gage, Rebecca Janney, wryly commented that their elders believed, "higher branches of study were a kind of mental food too highly concentrated" to be allowed.[12] Joseph Barker was a community leader and considered to be learned; sometimes he taught school. In 1830, France's father helped establish a Ladies Seminary in Marietta. On many evenings at home, the patriarch read to his family by the fireside. He allowed his young daughter who had a "grasping mind" to borrow books. On the thriving Barker farm, theirs was a subsistence economy where all hands were occupied. The farm's production included apples, peaches, milk, butter, cheese, corn, potatoes, and pork.[13] All of Joseph Barker's daughters milked cows, fed the stock, gathered fruit, and gardened, even plowed fields alongside their brothers.

The farm work was harder for France because she had an early physical infirmity. A late autobiographical entry explains, "An accident in my infancy injured my entire left side and lamed me somewhat for life . . . [it] affected and arm and lower limb." She found that her body grew stronger from stretching her muscles with farm work, including picking fruit and gathering nuts. This regime, she wrote, "nearly recovered my force and natural health before I was ten years old . . . [though I was] still lame and my left hand and arm was smaller and weaker." Despite this infirmity, France tried to "do as much as anybody."14 Lameness affected her value in the kitchen where her five sisters complained she let things fall, did not do things nicely, and was cross. Their consensus expressed to mother that she should go with "father and the boys." Gage explained in a late autobiographical fragment that her disability led her to become inventive. For instance, when corn was to be planted and she could not walk well, she would "hop from furrow to furrow with the golden grains in my apron." Pain, she also admitted, sometime made her a "cross and fretful," so when she could not work at all, the child would escape into the woods with a book.

Solitary thinking also led to some unusual enterprise. For instance, wanting cash when she was 10 years old led France to earn her first fifty cents by washing apple seeds from the apple mill and selling them to a French traveler. This initiative enabled her to buy paper from which she made a book in order to "begin my scribbling" which had to be hidden from her disapproving father. He only saw this "book" when she was 20 and lived with her husband. She also paid attention to the skills of nursing and wrote in 1876 that it disciplined her not to give in to an early propensity to be impertinent, petulant, quick tempered, and impulsive.[15] Catharine Barker, Frances' elder sister, noted that she grew resourceful, perhaps the family thought, too much so. Occasionally, France's precocious spirit evoked paternal disapproval, as when she assisted a visiting cooper. Her father was stung by how good she was at it and punished her; France was sent indoors to her "proper sphere" and heard her father comment, "What a pity, she was not a boy!" In an 1867 speech, Frances Gage honed an earlier account of this episode, explaining that it led to her belief in inborn abilities that are not limited by gender: "I was born a mechanic, and made a barrel before I was ten years old. . . My father looked at it and said, 'What a pity that you were not born a boy, so that you could be good for something. Run into the house, child, and go to knitting.'"[16]

She was angered through the years by such insults and taught her philosophy to readers, "thousands of girls are born with mechanical fingers. Thousands of girls have a muscular development that could do the work of the world as well as men; and there are thousands of men born to effeminacy and weakness." The following year in *The Ohio Farmer* Gage returned to this sensitive topic in an essay, "Women's Sphere and Duty"[17]; she asked why women should not cultivate their inherited paternal aptitudes, such as interest in being a mechanic, scientist, or doctor. This postbellum essay reinforces her argument by adding that God's gifts ought to be celebrated in women as well as men, lest, like a caged eagle, the gifted woman withers because she cannot spread her wings and be "true to herself." Frances Gage warns that ignoring birth's gifts lessens a woman's potential and diminishes her from being man's equal partner.

Her essay "Looking Back" in the first issue of *The Woman's Advocate* in 1869 continued the theme. She recalled an episode when her father discovered her covertly reading *Blackstone's Commentaries on the Laws of England,* dated 1765, and he observed, "If you were a boy, I would send you to College." Her lack of a formal education always rankled since frontier girlhood was painfully circumscribed by demands that restricted her. Worse yet, her father's insult that females could not be "mechanical" implied that any female who had mechanical talents was defective, unnatural, and, being unfeminine, was "masculine." At age 15 "France" was hurt by family criticisms that labeled her "strange" and "blasphemous." As she turned into a successful old woman, Frances Gage's anger only grew because she saw more damage being done to other women who weren't able to escape narrow gender prescriptions. She came to recognize the irony of her father unwitting turning her into a feminist; in her words, "I was outspoken forever afterward."[18]

Though Joseph Barker demonstrated family and community leadership and let her borrow books, she was able to appreciate his strengths as well as regret her weaknesses. Writing about him with humor offered respite. In 1850 in *The Lily* and the *Pittsburgh Saturday Visiter,* the 46 year-old matron wrote a humorous account of how a farm girl's feminine "sphere" could be broken into pieces. Gage provided five examples of its dissolution on the Barker farm. When she was eight, her father placed his youngest and last child in a sidesaddle and "bade me plough." She remembered its being "glorious and exciting to ride before the plough out in the open." As well, the girl learned how to saddle and harness their horse, plus run their mill. Once, when no male worker was at hand, she chopped a hole in one-inch thick ice in order to water 50 cows and horses. This was the point where the girl supposedly saw the "last part of her sphere slipping under the ice" to be gone forever. France decided to create her own "sphere" based on "the platform of usefulness." Her most impressive sphere-destroying event was saving her five-year-old nephew from a vicious horse. Frances Gage confided to the reader, I "rushed in resolutely and saved the child's life." After one of these episodes, her outwardly stern father, "patted my sun-burned locks and told me I was 'really good for something.'"[19]

So, Frances Barker was an exceptional child and, despite her "oddities," a valued person on the farm. She found another positive image of women's value in family stories about female bravery. Putnam's pioneer fighters included women like Grandmother Dana and Mother Barker who during the Indian Wars loaded muskets and stood guard in the Marietta fort. The girl was sorry to have missed this excitement and wished she, too, could have confronted marauding natives.[20] Another essay Gage wrote for *The Lily,* similarly called "Woman's Sphere," was about her typically "feminine" mother who also departed from the limitations of woman's sphere when she "trudged" over the Alleghenies. During the Indian Wars, Elizabeth Dana Barker spent years with "all manner of privation."

After being freed from that constraint, the young wife took her children and went to the Barker's log cabin where Frances was born in 1808. Joseph Barker was often away doing building projects in Marietta that left his young wife alone with their children. During this time, she loaded rifles and stood sentry duty while wolves and panthers howled. Young France recognized she must have been a burden and later puzzled over the question—how did frontier life reflect woman's sphere?

During France's youth, of course, there was plenty of opportunity for courage, especially as related to slaveholders on the south side of the Ohio River. This boundary divided two cultures; on the north were transplanted Euro-American settlers from New England who repudiated slavery and tended to be political liberals like the Dana clan. South of the river were plantation slaveholders who, protected by Henry Clay's 1820 Missouri Compromise, defended slavery in states like Virginia and Kentucky. The Ohio River was a constant and permeable reminder of slaves' proximity, and over it, countless slaves traveled to escape their chains. Many fugitives fled across the Ohio River from Parkersburg, Virginia. They needed rest, food, and protection. Aiding them was dangerous, civilly disobedient, and illegal. To be avoided were the mercenary slave catchers who followed slaves in order to gain cash rewards for kidnapping them.

The Dana family assisted escaping slaves. One time Frances Barker and her mother, Elizabeth, paddled a canoe 14 miles down the Muskingum and Ohio Rivers to visit Grandmother Dana in Belpre where she received "her first lesson in anti-slavery from holding a candle for my mother—in a dark cellar—while she bathed the whipped back of a black woman." Often the girl listened to these relatives verbally attack human bondage, and she was horrified to watch fugitives being pursued by slave catchers who passed through the area.

Though Barker girl's schoolmates mocked her slave sympathies, she never regretted these experiences. It was part of her identification with the "underdog" that fueled Gage's lifelong passion for helping the disadvantaged. The worst abolition outrage she experienced was described in 1852. Gage published an account of seeing her seven-year-old playmate, Fanny, kidnapped by brutal slavers. In 1869 she wrote about it again, shifting the significance away from the screaming and manacled Fanny to her own reactions to the scene. It increased her horror that some blood relatives refused to intercede and help. This was a double outrage.

France Barker had another memorable experience in Belpre that subtly influenced her adult attitudes. She was taken across the Ohio River to visit Blennerhasset Island, the desecrated but once "splendid strip of property" which her father helped to build in 1800. The girl learned the infamous tale of Harmon Blennerhasset and viewed the remains of the grandiose house burned down by local militia. He stood accused of deceit and disloyalty, and his "paradise lost" was a colorful if homegrown morality tale.

The Barkers and Danas could not know that two hundred years later in 1973 the Blennerhasset mansion's foundation would be rediscovered. Its original construction was researched, and the mansion was rebuilt in 1984 at a cost of two and a half million dollars. The center structure is a large, federal styled home and wings attach two smaller buildings, like welcoming arms. In the words of historian Michael Burke, this "architectural masterpiece" was "restored to its original splendor." Today the building her father helped build is listed in America's National Register of Historical Places.

Of course, the Barker women's lives were not ordinarily violent. Frances Gage's poetry describes herself as having been a "free and fearless child" with "unbraided locks." Rebecca Janney remembered her as an impetuous girl who was "independent and energetic" with "wild habits and impulsive nature [that] subjected her to severe criticisms" from teachers and companions who called her a "fool." This friend's biographical sketch underlines the Barker family's dynamic. France's love of nature was "stifled by the ridicule and criticisms of family and friends." Her overworked mother insisted France imitate feminine role models, while her authoritarian father was preoccupied and did little parenting, except to criticize. Hence Frances Barker was not "close" to either parent. Years later, Gage's "Song of the Dreamer" expressed her love and sympathy for Elizabeth Dana Barker, in spite of her stinging disapproval: "E'en my loved and sainted mother/ But seldom on me smiled; / She called me oft her "trouble"/her restless, dreaming child." Yet this childhood led to what historian W. T. Coggeshall described a poet who was "earnest, moody, and romantic."[21] France as a child saw herself as "plain featured to ugly" and hence not beloved.

However, on Jan. 1, 1829, this Barker child married a lawyer, James Lamson Gage, and moved away from the Barker farm to McConnelsville, 20 miles north of Marietta and 68 miles from Ohio's capitol, Columbus. Her parents lived long enough to see her happily married and beginning to publish. On July 3, 1835, when Frances was 27, her mother died. Joseph Barker did not remarry, and when he passed away eight years later there was a massive Marietta funeral. Five of her siblings remained in Morgan County. Joseph Barker, the eldest son, took over the Barker manse on the Muskingum River and his father's place in Ohio's State Legislature.

She carried with her an inherited sense of duty to imitate her father's commitment to community service, leadership, and politics. Like him, she wrote occasional verse, though once her father had called hers "childish rubbish." Throughout her life, she appropriated the phrase and jokingly referred to her poetry as "rubbish." Frances Barker's reading included everything she could lay her hands on from *Sinbad the Sailor*, to Alexander Pope's *Iliad* and *Odyssey*, from Shakespeare to Milton, and the *British Encyclopedia*. Her late essay, "Looking Back" cites early love of Addison, Johnson, and Sterne. Above all, she claimed what made the greatest impression was *Blackstone's Commentaries* which taught her about Common Law and married women's loss of legal existence. Rebecca Janney's remembrance was that Frances Barker's preferred authors were Shakespeare, Cowper, Pope, and Thomson. She perceived her friend's reading to be a compensation for lacking "advisers, friends, comforts, and treasures," and cited France's "remarkably retentive memory." At age twelve, the pioneer girl could memorize "everything that struck her fancy." In Janney's words, books were "ever her silent companion," whether France was heading into the woods or entertaining herself while working flax at the spinning wheel.

The transition from bookish farm maiden to a hectic lawyer's wife provided added opportunities of unanticipated sorts. She was embarrassed when her children began asking questions that she could not answer. This led her to confer with the woman principal of the village's academy to develop a plan of study that included tutorials. She felt this did not interrupt the rhythm of wifely and motherly duties. As her father had done in Marietta, in McConnelsville Frances Gage began providing 4th of July odes, obituary notices, political songs and squibs. Her public grew as she made contributions to the greater community. The village residents provided an audience, sympathetic neighbors who she sought to organize. They said, she later commented, that she could take her hands out of the washtub, to hold a baby in her lap and rock two others in the cradle with her foot, so that she could write. The abolitionist did village legwork, such as gathering petitions, holding meetings, writing letters, and petitioning legislators. Some people urged her to submit material to Lady's Books and Magazines, but she complained that was too easy. Gage wanted her thoughts to be published in political and agricultural papers directed to women and children and men in County and State papers that "go into every family." Thus Frances Gage targeted an audience in "agricultural, educational, antislavery, and temperance papers." These publications discussed things that were practical and true, she argued, as well as copied far and wide. It was flattering being known as Aunt Fanny and receiving letters "asking for advice and counsel."

Gradually, her reform acquaintanceships extended beyond Ohio's boundaries because she shared epistles with other persons, including eastern reformers like Amelia Bloomer and Susan B. Anthony. Such supportive friendships raised the woman's self-esteem, enlarged her social network, and brought her into a more cosmopolitan sphere.

Her marriage to James Lamson Gage was the most important decision of Frances Dana Barker's life. As Anya Jabour explains in *Marriage in the Early Republic*, there were several forms of matrimony. The traditional style of pioneer marriages like that of Gage's parents' narrowly defined wives' sphere with traditional women's home labors freeing their husbands to roam away from the domicile. Frances Barker did not want to replicate her parents' marriage. Her first step was escaping her patriarchal father's power by becoming someone's wife; she emerged from the pioneer cocoon into larger "bonds of womanhood." She and James were equally committed to a looser kind of union. These abolitionists anticipated some of the next generation's values, especially a different style of marriage from their parents with new conventions that stressed companionate mutuality, love, and respect. For instance, James Gage encouraged her on-going education, wherever it took her. Each had a lifelong commitment to reform activities, whether abolition, temperance, or women's rights. During the 1840s Frances Gage survived an attack of typhoid fever that impaired her memory and health for a number of years and, yet she later called the decade the happiest years of her life.

James Lamson Gage was born on April 8, 1800, in Litchfield, Tioga County, New York State. His parents, James Gage and Polly Drury, raised eight children, four boys, and four girls. They were descended from ancestor John Gage who in 1633 came to Boston with Governor Winthrop from County Suffolk, Britain. The immigrant became a freeman who owned land in Ipswich. Some of his descendants settled in Litchfield, New York where they farmed and operated a wheel making shop. This was where James Lamson Gage was raised and explains his second "career" plan to produce train wheels. Several of his siblings went to Illinois, including Sarah, Esther, Leonard, and Ambrose. George Gage founded Gages Lake, Illinois, while Jared and John helped found the Village of Wilmette, Illinois. In 1864, John Gage moved his family east to Vineland, New Jersey where his widowed sister-in-law, Frances Gage, later lived for several years. James and John's siblings, George, Leonard, and Esther, settled in McHenry County, Illinois; joining them were their parents, James Gage and Polly Drury Gage, who immigrated from Litchfield, New York. The family's patriarch lived with George, Leonard, and Esther until he died in 1889; his wife passed away in 1903.

James Lamson Gage was named after his father. He left Litchfield to study law before settling in Morgan County, Ohio. On June 20, 1826, he paid cash for 12 square miles of land in McConnelsville,[23] a village settled in 1817 and named after Revolutionary War General Robert McConnell. During his years of residence, the town was booming. For example, in 1840, there were 957 residents; six years later the town had five churches, fifteen stores, two newspapers, two flourmills, and a woolen factory.

When he was 28, James Lamson Gage married the 20-year-old Frances Barker and between 1831 and 1842 sired eight healthy children. Political liberalism united the progressive couple who were leaders in McConnelsville.[24] James Gage practiced law there from the late 1820s to the early 1850's. He was the village's prosecuting attorney from 1828 to 1831 and between 1836 and 1840. After McConnelsville's 1839 incorporation, James Gage served as a village Trustee and Assessor in 1840 and 1841. Three years later, he became an Associate Judge between 1844 and 1847. Frances' husband, like her father, was a community leader in his village. Less fortunately, James Gage's eventual plunges into speculative career advancements as a "self-made man" were unsuccessful.

James Gage's income came from his law practice, elected offices, and an iron foundry he built in 1839. It was constructed at the southern terminus of McConnelsville's Main Street on the Muskingum River bank. His son Charles was attracted to the business, and their foundry produced such local necessities as kettles for salt and maple sugar production. It seemed to be very successful. Historians James Gaylord and Charles Robertson note James was a Universalist and active in abolition activities.[25] He was occasionally mentioned in regional media, for example, the *Daily Ohio Statesman* in Feb. 16, 1850 carried a report on his attendance at an abolition committee meeting where he condemned "in manly tone the malignant spirit of a false and cowardly conservatism" and called for racial justice.[26] The same publication on June 12, 1851 reported that "James L. Gage, Esq. of Morgan County, a Whig lawyer and politician of influence" was supporting the new Ohio

Constitution which proposed judicial reforms.[27] In August 1852, he attended a state Convention in Columbus of the Free Democracy organization where Salmon P. Chase was encouraging opposition to slavery.

Yet a few months later in April 1853, family members were startled to learn that James Gage wanted to leave Ohio and take them to a new life in St. Louis, Missouri. His motives were never made clear by his wife. Evidently beneath the surface of his enterprising professional life James Gage experienced financial reverses in McConnelsville. A Morgan County historian commented, "He was a lawyer of fair ability" whose foundry "did a good business for a time, but [was] unsuccessful."[28] James Gage sold off his mortgaged home and business. He wanted to leave Ohio and had read that there were rich mineral deposits in Missouri where railways were going to be built. James knew this site would require foundries.

Perhaps, too, he was restless and experienced the fever for "pushing on," or as Horace Greeley famously said, "Go West young man." What they left behind was the family's home base in McConnelsville and Belpre. Their imposing Federal style home on a bluff overlooking the Muskingum River James had built a decade earlier. In many ways, this home resembled the impressive home her father built in Marietta. The couple named their new home Mount Airy, and it was her domestic haven with breezy rooms that were used by traveling church preachers and boarders. In its Ball Room, Frances Gage hosted local abolition and women's rights meetings. It had a wonderful garden and always represented her edenic ideal. For Frances Gage, losing this property was the worse wrench. James Gage's move took them and many of their children into slave-holding Missouri.

Their eldest son George was born in 1831 and was 22 when they left McConnelsville. Then the children were separated by two-year intervals; Charles 1833, Mary 1835, and a double birth in 1837 when both Ambrose and Sarah were born. John arrived in 1839; James appeared the next year, 1840, and the last "baby," Joseph, arrived 1842; he would have been 11 in 1853 when they migrated to Missouri. The older children who were uprooted from village life lost their extended network of Barker and Dana kin in Washington and Morgan Counties, and all their friends. Not long after the Gages broke up housekeeping, the older boys began to "leave home" and strike out on their own. The only other family member who had left Ohio at this point was Frances Gage's elder sister, Catharine Francis Barker, who recently moved to Iowa. She urged the Gages to come there, but farm country was not part of James' economic plan.

McConnelsville represents an important stage in Frances Gage's life. Here she thrived as matriarch of her nuclear family. Here she tested the waters by experimenting with leadership skills and inventing a literary persona, "Aunt Fanny," that demonstrated her domestic knowledge. She escaped isolation by inventing familial ties with readers, who she called "nieces." One example, for instance, of how to efficiently sequence kitchen tasks came in the form of one "Letter" that taught proper use of "saleratus," or sodium potassium bicarbonate or baking soda. Aunt Fanny's non-condescending advice probably helped buoy her up when she left Ohio.

Her letters to farm journals described the family's move and softened painful events with self-deprecating humor. As she had read in Ralph Waldo Emerson and Margaret Fuller, women as well as men need "self-reliance." Her balance between domestic life and public service shifted during the Missouri years. Frances Gage never lost James Gage's moral support. However, Missouri absorbed his energies and sapped his resources.

Practical assistance was provided by their daughters. [29] Mary and Sarah helped their mother with the weight of Gage domicile maintenance and child supervision. Six demanding Gage boys required shepherding, and their sisters became caretakers who ran the home when their mother was away.[30] Family friend Henry Ward Beecher once described the challenge of raising the Gage sons, noting that Frances Gage "brought up six unruly boys." He estimated an aggregate height her sons would form a column of thirty-six feet, all voting the Republican ticket, and eschewing tobacco and alcohol.[31] Even the dour Jane Swisshelm, editor of the *Pittsburgh Saturday Visiter* and sometimes a prickly woman's advocate, appreciated Frances Gage's humor about her boisterous sons; Swisshelm at a Women's Rights Convention in 1852 repeated an anecdote about Frances Gage trying to quiet a noisy audience by pointing out that it should be quiet—just like her rambunctious sons should and to whom she would say, 'Quit behaving yourselves.'" This domestic joke "brought down the house."[32]

When the Gage family in 1853 arrived in St. Louis, Missouri they found it to be raucous and uncivilized. "Aunt Fanny," bravely described their squeezing into a small rental house that came with a trash-filled and sere 20' by 40' backyard. Within a month, Frances Gage converted this into a "pocket of greenery." She brought in topsoil and planted a colorful flower garden that bloomed from early spring to late summer. It included pansies, verbena, roses, heliotropes, mignonette, nasturtiums, convolvulus, and cypress, attracting birds, butterflies, hummingbirds and bees. However, this garden was not to be enjoyed long because James Gage soon moved the family to a larger home outside St. Louis. It was located on a bluff overlooking the Mississippi River, and Frances Gage dutifully named this house "Mount Airy No, 2." She recommenced decorating and gardening, but it didn't compare to the original Mount Airy.

    The move into a slave state forced Frances Gage to reassess her reform career in the triad causes—temperance, abolition, and women's rights. The 41-year-old Buckeye matron facetiously asked her friend, Rebecca Janney, "Can I live in a slave state?" but did so for five years. Her contentment depended upon continuing to do reform work with a new rural audience. She recommitted herself to a series of speaking tours that Middle Westerners received with unabated enthusiasm. In this sense, the mid 1850s were glory years for Frances Gage, the reformer, who visited small towns in Iowa, Indiana, and Illinois. For instance, on Jan. 28, 1853 Gage wrote an ecstatic letter to *The Lily* from Illinois describing her first course of lectures in Indiana. In Alton and Jerseyville, two towns where the Sons of Temperance had a foothold, she presented both temperance and woman's rights talks. She referred to this work as "our mission," and her audience included clergymen. The 1853 tour consisted of 25 lectures in churches, schoolhouses, and private homes. Residents who enjoyed her presentations generously filled the offering basket, which augmented the Gage family's slender income. She wrote Amelia Bloomer that one day in Fairfield, Iowa the sale of women's rights papers was quite lucrative. The elated Frances Gage celebrated, "reformers together—all working for good."[33] She promised to keep *The Lily* readers informed about "this great western world." Eighteen months later, Gage continued the theme and applauded Iowa for its law restricting liquor sales and consumption. Literary historian Jeffrey E. Smith comments that Gage was fulfilling her Jeffersonian ideal—rural, small-town life that was superior to the city where rancid butter was sold for high prices.[34]

On the other hand, the western move led only to frustration for her husband. The *Missouri Republican* on Sept 3, 1854 published James Gage's essay, "American Iron for Railroads." This expressed his initial optimism over the state's need for railway provisions. He argued the site had ideal topographically for railways and prophesied "the real Pacific Road [will last longer] than the Pyramid of Egypt, or the Chinese Wall."[35] The idea was that new Missouri foundries would employ the state's native pig iron in order to create wheels for the coming railways. Missouri historians credit his prescience; John Gage started the first wheel foundry west of the Mississippi.[36] But his investment depended upon promises embedded in Missouri's Legislative Charter of March 13, 1851. In 1854 James L. Gage's Foundry at Second and Palm Streets, St. Louis, Missouri was listed as having descended toward the bottom of the *Journal*'s long list of competing local foundries. In 1855, several railway companies ordered Gage's car wheels that would be made from Iron Mountain Iron as described in *The Western Journal and Civilian*.[37]

However, things went wrong with James Gage's plans. Contracts went to competing foundries that might have had better St. Louis contacts. Also the Ohioan was an abolitionist in a slave state. There was a major economic downturn, called the Panic of 1857. Ironically, his competitors who won these coveted contracts were to be disappointed since delays dragged on. The project was still incomplete half a dozen years later when Civil War broke out.

St. Louis, Missouri's pro-slavery and alcohol tolerant environment was unhealthy for the Gage family. Thus James Gage's prospects declined, and 1857 was an odd year for the Gage family. James and Frances Gage sent Ambrose, John, Joseph, and their sister, Mary or half of their children out of Missouri for a year to attend Antioch College in Yellow Springs, Ohio. She chose this institution for their children because she saw Antioch as America's only college giving "equal privileges to students of both sexes."[38] James, Frances, Joseph, and Mary left Antioch at the end of the year. The college was a place where Frances Gage lectured on women's rights. Antioch opened in 1853 with Horace Mann serving as its President until his death in 1859. A student, Olympia Brown, in 1860 invited Antoinette Brown Blackwell to lecture at the college, and these two religious women shared frustrations about America's sex segregated ministry. Brown completed her B.A., entered the ministry, and became a leader of reform in Wisconsin.

In Missouri, it was clear after five years that the wheel foundry had produced only economic failure. There were elements in the city who deeply resented the elder Gages' liberal political positions. Hostility increased, and the crowning blow was three fires, probably the work of arsonists who attacked their house and threatened the Gage family. Their eldest son, Charles, took over his father's foundry and remained politically discreet. He renamed the business Gage and Horton, ran the foundry with a partner, and produced stoves. The business thrived until 1880 when the foundry burned down.

James and Frances Gage fled from St. Louis in 1856 and moved near Carbondale in Jackson County, Illinois. James Gage's health was broken and he was unable to ever work again. For the first time in her life, Frances Gage experienced poverty. Her writings humorously describe how adversity challenged her to make the most of new opportunities. Their rental house in Illinois was cheap, run-down, and owned by an unpopular man who distilled and sold "ardent spirits." His filthy house required substantial renovation, so the Ohio matron rolled up her sleeves to scrub, paint, paper, patch, and repair. A July 1860 letter to *The Ohio Farmer* gives a sanitized version of their affairs. During this challenging period, the indefatigable reformer still felt free to pursue her reform interests and kept remarkably busy lecturing. The best thing that happened to her at this period was receiving an invitation from her brother-in-law John Gage to join his group and visit the West Indies. She did. Soon in 1860 James, Frances, Joseph and Mary left Illinois to return to the known comforts of anti-slave Ohio. Frances Gage wanted to help Hannah Tracy Cutler and Elizabeth Jones expand married women's property rights. Their Senate testimony helped to pass a law protecting women's property and wages.

However, the Gage's financial situation was dire. Frances Gage was not a person to complain about her husband's financial misjudgments and their consequences. Her maiden sister, Catherine Barker, kept an *Autobiography* that traces Frances Gage's on-going concerns about her husband's debts.[39] Both women's writings paint a positive portrait of James Lamson Gage. Even Elizabeth Cady Stanton wrote that James Gage had great humanity and moral integrity. As early as 1853, Frances Gage joked with *Ohio Cultivator* readers about her "tall husband" and her having "no fears of his fealty." She joked about scratching out the eyes of any female who set her cap for James.[40] Frances Gage was unquestioning about his abandonment of law, his whisking the family off to a slave state, and his determination to become "an Iron Man—living, moving, and having his being in stoves, plows, engines, and car wheels."[41] However, the effect of these decisions can be seen in an undated poem describing his wife's waiting in their Illinois garden for James to arrive with slowed steps and locks "grown gray." [42]

His physical decline meant that Frances Gage was called upon to "go to work" because their financial reversals justified an atypical arrangement—she must support the family. Of course, in the 1830s and 1840s she cared for Mount Airy and raised a brood of demanding sons. Gage once wrote complainingly to her sister, Charlotte, in Iowa that, without a serving girl, she took in boarders and did the "washing baking brewing frying basting roasting all my self-scrubbing sweeping stewing whipping scolding toasting" [sic].[43]

The still energetic wife shifted gears to move beyond the roles of part-time reformer and writer. Exigency led to her next identity, journalist. She negotiated a full-time job at the *Ohio Cultivator* in Columbus, Ohio. Nonetheless, the couple's marriage was never regretted. His unexpected death in May 1863 ended their 55 year "companionate marriage." Even in old age, Frances Gage reminisced about his youthful courage "on the border of slavedom" that made him a "picket guard upon the outpost of Freedom." She always believed that James Lamson Gage's boldness on the Ohio frontier matched that of William Lloyd Garrison, New England's abolitionist leader.[44]

There was a late public flicker of James Gage's passion for anti-slavery appeared in a letter he sent to the *National Anti-Slavery Standard* from Illinois in March 1863, two months before his death. Denouncing "Slave Power" and criticizing "the rebellion that convulses our land," he blamed Abraham Lincoln for mismanaging the Civil War. His source was General McClellan's published claims that the President had prevented his winning battles. With religious fervor, James Lamson Gage accused the Republican administration of being on Satan's side.[45]

When the move back to Columbus, Ohio only two children were living with James and Frances and, and they were helping to support their parents. Her youngest son, Joseph, and Mary, each took jobs in the city as teachers. The four Gages took up domicile at 147 East Long Street between North High and Third Streets. Thus the house was nearly empty when James Gage learned about the need for workers in South Carolina.

The *Standard* on March 1, 1863 printed Edward L. Pierce's essay proposing South Carolina's Port Royal Experiment. His follow-up essay appeared on June 28. Pierce's call was for volunteers to care for the freedmen in South Carolina. James Gage also read correspondents' reports in such papers as *The New York Times, the Evening Post, the World, the Tribune,* and *The Herald* in which Yankee reporters colorfully theorized about the risks involved with abandoned slaves left in the Sea Islands. One reporter claimed disloyal slaves were being shot by their white owners. They predicted Commodore Du Pont's gunboats were ready to "suppress any excesses," until Charleston was retaken by "The Blow that Would Settle the Contest." James Gage urged his wife to apply for a role in Pierce's "Experiment," and she leapt at the opportunity to join the fray. James was too weak to live alone, so he left Columbus with Sarah and went to a Gage family compound in Illinois. Frances Gage and son George left Ohio in October 1862 for the east coast where they joined a ship going south. Its destination was Port Royal which was north of Charleston on South Carolina's mid-Atlantic coastline. Her eldest daughter, Mary, saw to their affairs in Columbus and soon joined her mother and brother in the Sea Islands.

It seemed as if Frances Gage was inadvertently groomed for this new job. Her domestic, rural, and reform initiatives led to her growing sense of independent competence. It helped that in 1859 she had traveled with her brother-in-law, John Gage, to spend four months in the West Indies and in 1862, James urged her to leave Ohio and help freedmen on Parris Island in South Carolina.

She spent the next 13 months living in an abandoned planter's house on the tip of Parris Island where she supervised freedmen and ran field operations that returned profitable cotton crops. Her poem "A Voice from Parris Island" published on the front page of the *Standard* on Jan. 31, 1863 voiced the Gideonites' passion for helping these abandoned souls. Using the plural pronoun "we," the Buckeye celebrated freedom for the blacks, imagined Southerners regretting the rebellion, and revealed freedmen's buoyant, ecstatic jubilation. However, when she learned that James Gage was dying in Illinois, Frances Gage's mood was darkened. She got in a canoe and paddled away from Parris Island.

Three months later the dispirited widow returned and reentered the war zone that had finally ignited. War casualties were mounting. Then the news arrived that Abraham Lincoln's government was ending the Port Royal Experiment. Starting that fall, the Union was selling off the Sea Islands' plantations. Exhausted, discouraged, and disillusioned, Frances Gage left South Carolina before this process commenced. It was December 1863. The interlude, an apex of intensity in her life, was crystallized in missives about the exotic coastal enigma where so much ugliness and beauty were intertwined.

Being widowed in 1863 was a shock. James' death in Illinois removed any incentive for returning to Ohio, so after visiting his grave and the Gage relatives in Illinois, she paused to lecture and gather support for freedmen and injured Union soldiers. She spoke almost nightly at Soldiers Aid Societies, and when she returned to Parris Island discovered that the Sea Islands experience was ending. There were decisions to be made. Before this, male relatives determined her domicile. From 1808 to 1832, she resided at her father's Muskingum River homestead. Between 1832 and 1853, she lived with her husband in McConnelsville, then briefly near St. Louis, Missouri. Now she must be independent. First Gage went south to Fernandina, Florida and then resumed a lecture circuit. In September of 1864 her carriage crashed near her friend Dr. Edward Beecher's Congregational Church in Galesburg, Illinois. Injuries included broken ribs, a damaged left lung, shoulder, and spine that led to an extended recuperation in St. Louis at her son's home. This was a difficult time and she told "the womanhood of the country" that parents should remain independent from their children.

She was contacted by Mary Barton in Washington, D. C. and asked to participate in a campaign to fund the missing soldiers' project. After this, the weakened woman for whom being "single," was an imposed freedom, took her two daughters east in March 1865 and moved into a rental property in Lambertsville, New Jersey.

In terms of her public reputation and reform career, the Civil War had raised Frances Dana Gage into the position of being a uniquely valued speaker because she could address abolitionists and feminists at post-war conventions. In 1866 Gage was involved with the plan to join anti-slavery and pro women's rights forces into a new organization called the American Equal Rights Association. She was hired to work for the group and Gage planned to continue her temperance concerns with salaried lectures for the Good Templars. Disaster struck on July 26, 1867 when she was paralyzed by a stroke. This abruptly halted her plans for helping shape Reconstruction. Gage's descent was meteoric since she was dropped from the programs of upcoming conventions and given titular acknowledgment as "Vice President," an honorific title. For years, Frances Gage's letters were read into the records.

To Aunt Fanny's flattered surprise, the national media that had printed her essays and poems now fulminated about her collapse. Newspapers like the *Cincinnati Daily Gazette* on March 18, 1868 described Frances Dana Gage's collapse, writing, "The *St. Louis Democrat* on the authority of a son [Charles] of Mrs. Frances D. Gage denies the report which is in circulation that Mrs. Gage is in "reduced circumstances pecuniarily." Three weeks later, on April 3, 1868, *The San Francisco Bulletin* reported, "The authoress has by the death of her husband and a stroke of paralysis fallen into a needy condition . . . a sale of her books, and to this end a special agency has been established in Cleveland." Washington, D.C.'s *Critic-Record* stated on December 30, 1869 that Frances Gage was in feeble health and living in Brooklyn. Regional media, such the *Cincinnati Daily Gazette* repeatedly commented upon her travails and treatment at the Swedish Movement Center in New York City

She was moved to New York City for medical treatments and lived in her daughter's apartment. Mary Gage lived first on Willow Street, then at 17 East 12th Brooklyn Heights, and later on 6th Avenue. After three years of living under Mary Gage's roof, Frances Gage in 1870 moved to Vineland, New Jersey to reside at a hydrotherapy establishment owned by Dr. Lucinda Wilcox. Gage had long been interested in progressive medical developments. Among her eclectic reading was the *Water-Cure Journal*. In September 1852, she wrote to its editor, Dr. Jackson, joining a debate on the benefits of vegetarianism. She supported the "water cure," saying, "if we must have a *pathy* let it be hydropathy," which was a method for internal and external cleansing of the body.[46] In Feb. 1854, she wrote the journal to praise technology's freeing women from drudgery and allowing them to use their minds. The following year, another Gage letter-praised hydropathy, saying, "The use of water is everywhere gaining ground . . . homeopathy, too, is doing great work."[47]

Such, nontraditional medical subjects were popular amongst social reformers like Frances Gage and her reform-minded friends. The pages of reform publications, such as *The Lily,* were larded with advertisements for "Water Cures." Contemporaries sometimes mocked medical fashions as in a popular poem, "Barnyard Rhymes" that parodied *Aesop's Fables*. It presents a turkey, goose, and duck debating "schools" of medical treatment. The turkey called himself an "allopath," while the duck identified as a "homeopath." The common sense goose, said: "I use them all in time of need .... We see that each one has its day, and, like the fashions, pass away. The new Electro-Galvanism . . ." He is interrupted by the irritated duck that halted conversation by warning, "every doctor is a quack."[48]

After her first stroke, Frances Gage did not put herself in the hands of a quack.[47] She initially sought out Dr. George H. Taylor in New York City; he in 1858 went to Sweden to study Per-Henrik Ling's (1776-1839) technique of massage and rhythmic movement that led to modern physiotherapy. Dr. Taylor authored an influential work, *Exposition of the Swedish Movement Cure*, and his treatment improved Frances Gage's mobility. Her letter to *The Ohio Farmer* on Jan 4, 1868, praised the "Swedish Movement Cure" for improving her circulation by using steam driven machinery to move her limbs and joints. Her testimonial concluded, "To see and know is to believe."[51] The result was that for some time Gage was able to walk, and feed herself. Her final 17 years were slowed by diminished health, although periodic recuperations allowed the widow to live in the East and occasionally visit family and friends in the Middle West and South. She adjusted to a quiet life. In January 1868, she went to Marietta and Belpre for five months to visit Ohio family and friends. This for a while satisfied Gage's peripatetic "longing to see the old faces and places once more."[52] When she returned to the East, Gage experienced a second stroke. One early letter to a friend summarized several doctors' diagnoses, "I could not expect to be ever much healthier."

During these years, Frances Gage was fortunate to often have her two daughters and youngest son nearby. Joseph Barker Gage, affectionately called "Joe," left home at age nineteen to serve as an infantry soldier and returned with ruined health. Joe Gage married in 1838 in Taunton, Massachusetts and worked in New York City. He was the adult son who remained nearest to his mother, a pleasure for her as she admitted to a friend on Sept. 20, 1857, "I know I am selfish, wicked, and cruel, but I cannot let him go."[52] Years after she slipped away, Joe Gage tragically died on

June 9, 1893 in the "Ford Theatre disaster" when employees from the War Department were killed by the upper floor collapse.

Her eldest son, George Whiting Gage, who traveled and worked with her and Mary on Parris Island, lived for a time in Hunterdon, New Jersey and moved back to Beaufort. Away in the West were the other brothers: Charles remained in St. Louis with his foundry; Ambrose became a merchant who moved from Milford Center, Ohio to Minneapolis, Minnesota, and later to Kansas. John and James were farming in the deep Middle West. As a mother, Gage seems to have been caring, supportive, and non-critical about the decisions each child made. She pointedly avoided criticizing her children or their choices. For instance, in the 1870s when visiting one son's family in the deep Middle West, Frances Gage overheard her daughter-in law cast aspersions at women's rights workers who, she bragged, would never be allowed under her roof. Gage did not respond except for wryly writing with amused irony about the episode to Mary Barton, her careerist friend, "Can you imagine."[53]

The National Census of July 18, 1870, lists Frances Dana Gage as an "invalid" dwelling in the home of Dr. Lucinda W. Wilcox. Her treatments included exercise, massage, nutrition, and hydropathy, cumulatively called the "water cure." Wilcox, an 1854 graduate of the Western College of Homeopathic Medicine in Cleveland, Ohio, was a progressive physician who believed the body and mind are inseparable. Gage had long encouraged women doctors, for example in 1848 "Aunt Hannah's Quilt" was written to support their endeavors and help them avoid "censure."[54]

Dr. Wilcox was one of America's leaders in Water Cure treatments and distributed an advertisement inviting "The Ladies of Vineland" to try her invigorating, shock-free "Electro-Thermal Bath." Mrs. Frances D. Gage is listed as one satisfied patron amongst a "few patients [that] can be accommodated with board." The brochure concludes: "TO INVALIDS EVERYWHERE—If you wish to avail yourselves of the benefit of one of the best climates to assist in overcoming chronic diseases, come to Vineland. There are many persons here calling themselves well, who came here 'Given up to die."[55]

The doctor's choice of Vineland, New Jersey for her nursing home was prescient. This was a planned community begun in 1861 by Charles K. Landis, a visionary who proclaimed his pursuit of beauty and sobriety. He purchased land along a railroad line that served Philadelphia and New York City. Then he invited grape grower Thomas Bramwell Welch to set up his Welch's Grape Juice business in Vineland to produce a pasteurized, non-fermenting grape beverage.

For a variety of reasons, New Jersey was popular with reformers after the Civil War; for instance, Elizabeth Cady Stanton resided in Tenafly, and Lucy Stone Blackwell lived in various communities in northern New Jersey. In 1870 a writer in the *Woman's Journal* described Vineland as industrious, wide-awake, and "the most American community in America—the most characteristic specimen of the cosmopolitan middle-class of American society." Vineland became a special haven for reforming activities, a kind of Mecca. Here women's rights activists spoke, recruited, and planned conventions. In fact, Frances Gage herself spoke there on women's rights in October 1864 and June 1866.

However, by 1870, Frances Gage could only observe politics. For a time, Dr. Wilcox's care seems to have brought her a partial recovery from paralysis because she wrote, "the use of my limbs is so far restored that I can write, move my feet, and walk with assistance." [56] In May 1871, Gage revisited Ohio which was followed by a third stroke. The perpetual optimist marveled, "my head is clearer and stronger, and I know that I gain infinitessentially every day." She remained confident reformers were making progress because, "Women's Right to suffrage is daily more and more recognized."[57]

In January of 1873, Gage described her Vineland basement apartment where weekly rent of $13 included half-hygienic board. Her life was not utopian; she wrote, "There is lots of antagonism gossip here but who cares . . . short skirts, spiritualism." She mused on Jan 31, "I fled into the wilderness of Vineland, and when I got there to my utter astonishment found myself in a kind of mental hygiene home." Gage also wrote about taking "baths controlled by magnetism and electricity."[58]

Remarkably, Gage managed to attend a few conventions in 1873, 1874, and 1875. What Frances Gage could not do at conventions, her daughter Mary for some time sustained her symbolic presence. For instance, Mary Gage attended the meeting of the American Equal Rights Association in May 1868 where she served as Corresponding Secretary. At the meetings of the Women's Rights Association's Twelfth and Thirteenth Anniversaries, Mary Gage was on the platform alongside such notables as Lucy Stone and Amelia Bloomer; she also served on the

Finance Committee with Susan B. Anthony. In 1869, Mary Gage was Secretary of the Suffrage Association of New York and briefly addressed the convention. After this date, her involvement lessened.

Mary was always attentive to her mother. When Frances Gage left New York City in 1870, her loyal daughter accompanied her to Vineland and eased the transition by temporarily moving into the third floor of Dr. Wilcox's boarding house. Once Frances Gage was truly settled in, Mary returned to her own accommodations in the city; by 1877 she was operating a Ladies Brokers Office on Wall Street in the Horton Insurance Building, fourth floor, on 5th Avenue.

Before Frances Gage moved to Vineland, she was not disposed to spend much time with her husband's Gage family in New York State or the Chicago area. The notable exceptions were their 1848 excursion with her father-in-law to New England to visit relatives, and her brother-in-law, John Gage's, kind invitation in February 1859 to join his group traveling to the West Indies. Their third interaction came from their support for James Gage's family after 1857. They provided a breath of fresh air at a terrible time for Frances Gage. The West Indies trip in 1857 built trust and buoyed up Frances Gage when her husband was failing. He died four years later, and the steady Gage clan nursed and then buried him in Illinois. Frances Gage's sense of indebtedness to them grew, and when she was paralyzed in 1867, one of the attractions of Vineland was that John and Portia had settled there toward the close of the Civil War.

John Gage's family's 1836 odyssey west from New York State to Chicago led to the burial of five children. Their 1864 move east to Vineland was motivated by the search for a healthier environment. Two of their surviving sons, John and Asaheland, accompanied them. Two of their sons served the Union in the Civil War. Henry fought with Illinois Ninety-Fifth Regiment and was an aide to General Stanley, so he fared well. On the other hand, Jared, their first-born son, who was 3 years old in 1836 when they left Litchfield, New York in a covered wagon, did not. He had been living in Wilmette and signed up with Illinois Fifteenth Regiment. Jared first fought in the Battle of Pittsburgh Landing where he was wounded. After healing, he fought at Vicksburg. Then the Illinois Ninety-Fifth Regiment attacked Atlanta where he had the misfortune of being taken as a Confederate prisoner. The young soldier was thrown into what his father justifiably called "that rebel death pen, Andersonville." At war's end, Jared Gage was a skeletal casualty. Brought "home" to Vineland, Jared languished until January 12, 1867.

This was when Aunt Frances was recuperating from a carriage accident. Her four sons were veterans who had mercifully escaped Jared's fate, which made her feel guiltily blessed. Aunt Fanny's preoccupation with the welfare of wounded soldiers grew from a Christian idea to a bloody reality in the Sea Islands. She nursed and comforted as many injured soldiers as her own health allowed. When Pierce's Experiment was being dismantled in South Carolina, she continued earning money for injured soldiers' care. When in Oct. 1864, Clara Barton asked for help, she arrived at Barton's Washington office in January 1865 to help lobby the Thirty-Ninth Congress. Aunt Fanny contacted people and wrote a Congressional appeal. On January 25 1866, Gage published "Relics of Andersonville" in the *The Independent*. This publicity pressured the Congressmen to support the nurse's efforts and reminded the public about the work of Clara Barton's Washington office.[59] President Lincoln formalized her appointment to lead the project. The bill funded Clara Barton's Civil War project, the recovery of the lost dead from the war. The work took four arduous years. Barton's report was issued in 1869 and was based on retrieved dead soldiers' items that aided their identification. This led to proper marking for 7,000 graves.

The extended Gage family was grateful, too, but after Jared Gage's death in 1867 the dynamics of the family were changed. John and Portia Gage's son Henry left Vineland for Chicago to see his brother, Augustus. When Frances Gage was paralyzed in 1870 she moved to Vineland for access to her doctor and these kind relatives. Her strength waxed and waned for the rest of her life. Through illness and political tempests, she tried to be cheerful and peripetic. In June 1874, she visited her son Charles' family at 1114 Madison Street, St. Louis, Missouri. At another son's farm home in Iowa, she tried to be "useful" by washing up and making dresses, then spent two weeks with her eldest sister in Iowa. In December 1874, she traveled by train through Nashville, Chattanooga, and Kennesaw to see her son George and his Quaker wife in Beaufort, South Carolina. At this time, Gage worried about daughter Mary losing her home and described her a death, the first she had observed in her "years wife and mother."

Early in February of 1875, another stroke disabled Gage's left hand. She wrote of the usefulness of her right hand, though worried about its being crippled by rheumatism. The next July, she traveled to Dansville, New York where she enjoyed its sanitarium and spent time with Clara Barton. Returning to Vineland, she stopped to visit Mary in New York City.

There were no guidebooks for old age, but Frances Gage was unusual in her attempts to anticipate its eventuality. As far back as 1858, she began preparing for "old age" when she composed an essay called "The Indian Summer of Life."[60] It described her learning "the true philosophy of life" from elderly women in Marietta; her Belpre Grandmother Dana kept active, another, "almost my mother," still spoiled her, and a third produced quilts, "mementos of the cheerfulness, industry, and taste." This was the sort of busy old age Gage anticipated, not the "repining of sighs and groans." She completed her volume *Poems* in 1866 and incorporated a biographical structure that integrated the topic of women's aging. At age 40, the poet admits, "I have given my strength to the boys" and states that only the decline of loved ones could bring depression. A decade later, she recalls being a child and observing how her Barker grandmother could no longer take part in activities like "nutting bees," "slides on the pond," or playing games at school like "Lost My Glove" and "Mind the Rule." Now older than her grandmother was, Frances Gage's hair is silver, hearing and sight are imperfect, and her steps are slow, though she still finds consolations in being loved and doing her duty. Most telling is her poem, "My Fiftieth Birthday," where old age is depicted through the image of a shattered violin that the author insists could be "mended and in skillful hands [and] make sweeter music than before." It was a cruel reality that such a self-conscious writer's perspective would be shattered like the poem's violin that could not be mended.

On October 23, 1879, Gage again sent a message of support to the American Women Suffrage Association Convention meeting in Ohio. In the beginning of her last decade, the 1880 Federal Census records show that Frances Gage traveled with Mary to Macoupin County, Illinois where they boarded with a family in Bunker Hill. This was the area where Gage had happily lectured during her Carbondale sojourn in 1857, and a reformer friend, Mrs. Lily Henry, still lived in the area.

Old friends and colleagues occasionally visited Gage. When Elizabeth Cady Stanton saw her in the early 1870's, she described

Gage to feminists as being able to move about her room, write, and carry on a pleasant conversation. Another old friend who visited Frances Gage early in the 1880's told Amelia Bloomer that, "her dear voice is almost silent now, still she lingers as if to catch some faint glimpse of hope." With acquaintances drifting away, family members scattered, and travel increasingly difficult, the last decade of Frances Gage's life was occupied by her reading as much as possible. She fussed over her diminished capacity, saying "I cannot read books unless very small ones," but still enjoyed such publications as Lucy Stone's *Woman's Journal*, the *New York Tribune*, and the *Atlantic Monthly*.[61] Of course, as years of disability and suffering took their toll, whatever happiness Frances Gage found came mostly from living in her mind.

    Clara Barton had not forgotten her friend during her European travels, and, perhaps, her most touching tribute was made in 1871 when she wrote Frances Gage's name in charcoal on the roof of Milan's Cathedral.[62] Gage wanted Barton to write her about churches, manners, lordly estates, and old castles, and when she returned to America in 1873 was saddened to see the degree of Gage's invalidism. Nonetheless, the Ohioan continued to provide emotional support for Clara Barton who appreciated her loyalty. Aunt Fanny or "Mother," as she signed communications to her friend, reassured Barton in the poetically effusive language of the day, writing lines like: "how truly I love you dear, always/Be sure,' mid the cares, & the toils of the day."[63]

    The younger woman continued her work for public reform and founding the Red Cross. This took decades, and Clara Barton did not die until 1912. Remembering the busy Red Cross organizer's presence buoyed Gage's spirit, and she bragged about her friend's spreading fame. Indeed, Barton became America's most decorated woman.[64] When they did meet, conversation did not lag, for, having shared the 1863 Sea Islands experience, they had much to reminisce about. For Barton, too, the period of South Carolina enchantment retained its potency. The visit from Clara Barton that seems to have most brightened Frances Gage's later years occurred in mid-summer 1878. Gage celebrated it in a thank you note from "Mother" to "daughter" Clara: "all my life long, I shall live it (the July visit) over & over again—and how I long to see you succeed [sic] in that Humanitarian effort which I know is engrossing your mind & energies."[65]

Despite Gage's brave plans for sweetness and light, bitterness eventually surfaced. Barton's loyal visits to the older woman's bedside became painful as she listened to the invalid citing petty irritations. For instance, Aunt Fanny complained about daughter Sara going to Chicago to visit her "father's numerous relatives" who she hadn't seen in 20 years. More importantly, "Mother" complained about Barton's move to Shelburne, Vermont from Dansville, rather than coming closer to Gage's domicile in Greenwich, Connecticut. Historically speaking, Gage's most interesting remarks in the late 1870s were complaints expressed to Mary Barton about reform colleagues who now ignored her. "Aunt Fanny" was "disposed to feel neglected and useless," Barton wrote in 1878. In 1882, Gage sadly complained in the *Woman's Journal,* "I have been almost isolated from all social enjoyments." Elizabeth Pryor observes that Frances Gage at this late point was "shrunken, frail, and embittered [about] being imprisoned in the house."[66] Frances Gage was living in a snug domicile in Greenwich, Connecticut with a care giver when she died on November 9, 1884.

Clara Barton staunchly aided Gage and her children whenever she could. Barton's letters helped George Gage obtain the job of Beaufort Customs Collector in 1868, though he lost the job a dozen years later when he "missed two amounts." She also certified the medical work George did in Port Royal after the Battle of Morris Island that qualified him for a Civil War pension. The nurse similarly assisted Mary Gage. It was late in 1884 when Clara Barton last visited Frances Gage. She recognized that "precious Aunt Fanny [was] now near death." When Barton learned that her old friend had died, the seasoned "Angel of the Battlefield," who had seen so much mayhem, was able to neither "speak nor write of it for nearly six months."[67]

The body of Frances Gage was buried in the cemetery of the Second Congregational Church, Greenwich, Connecticut. Her death was recorded in the *Worcester Daily Spy*, Nov. 1884, and *The New York Tribune*'s "Obituary" appeared on Nov. 13, 1884. Ohio's Hannah M. T. Cutler's eulogy appeared in the December 13, 1884 *Woman' Journal.*

From one point of view, the dilemma of Frances Gage's daughters could be called an unintentional consequence of their mother's activism. The daughters finally benefitted from Clara Barton's assistance with war benefits in their old age, but during their adult years they remained family focused and tended to their mother. Why couldn't they, too, successfully juggle private and public roles?

Neither had the drive of their mother nor found a satisfying career. Their mother as "Aunt Fanny" never addressed issues of family member dependency. In fact, the Civil War had complicated life for America's unmarried women who were sometimes labeled the "maiden sisterhood" or "Cult of Single Blessedness." Since wives were legally chattel and parallel to slave women, a wish for female autonomy grew, but the war did not free women or allow the vote. Their tethers were apparent when neither father nor brother supported them. In the era's language, women needed to gain a "competency," or self-sustaining economic resource. For instance, Clara Barton, and Susan B. Anthony detached themselves from utter reliance on family bonds. Each established vocational identities that were unconventional. But the majority of women found paid work that reflected the domestic sphere and produced little income, such as cleaning, cooking, or nursing. It was true after the Civil War that gender prescriptions loosened as historical circumstances changed. Mary Gage was enterprising. For example, in 1879, she remarkably opened a brokerage firm on Fifth Avenue, New York City, but she was not backed by Cyrus Vanderbilt, and the world was not ready for women in high finance.

Frances Dana Gage once summarized her values in a "Letter from the West." It stated her idealist's dilemma. She hated intemperance, which was the bane of women's life, as well as war, slavery, and licentiousness. But what can I do, the writer asked rhetorically, if first I do not "free myself from the fetters of conventionalism, pride, and custom?"[68] Promoting this freedom occupied the reformer's lifetime. She left behind a few memorable achievements, such as being a Western speaker and author with high visibility in major reform causes. Frances Gage's generation tried to extend woman's sphere and create a "community receptive to female influence." Yet, this "folksy wife and mother of eight" in many ways was an anomaly who was sharply critical of the patriarchal family. Nel Irvin Painter credits Frances Dana Gage with focusing "woman's rights rhetoric on strong, working-class women" and being valuable as a "radical for her time." [69]

NOTES

Chapter One

1. Joseph Barker, *Recollections of the First Settlement of Ohio*, ed. George Jordan Blazier. (Marietta College, Marietta, Ohio, 1958), iii. Originally given to Samuel Prescott Hildreth and used as a source for part of his *Pioneer History of the Ohio Valley* (Cincinnati: H. W. Derby and Co., 1848). Also a resource for Martin R. Andrews, *History of Marietta and Washington County* (Chicago, Illinois: Biographical Publishing Company, 1902).
2. Ibid.
3. John Mack Faragher. *Sugar Creek. Life on the Prairies* (New Haven, Yale University Press 1988), 15, 32. 4. W. D. Gallagher, "A Brief History," *The Hesperian*, 3, no. 4 (1833), 268..
5. Ibid. 269.
6. Julia L. Dumont, *Tecumseh" and Other Stories of the Ohio River Valley,"* ed. Sandra Parker (Bowling Green, Ohio: Bowing Green Popular Press, 2000).
7. Martin Andrews, "Reminiscences by Col. Joseph Barker," *History of Marietta:* 480.
8. Wilson Waters, *History of St. Luke's Episcopal Church* (Marietta, Ohio, 1884), 13.
9. Rodney Hood, "Genealogy and Biography of Joseph Barker," Introduction to Barker, *Recollections*, 132. In 1802 Blennerhasset hired Barker to build boats for him in his Muskingum shipyard. Barker was a "senior builder and architect" in Marietta, including his own. Several of his brick Federal style homes still exist. Several sourced place Barker among the builders of Blennerhasset's mansion.
10. Michael Burke, "A Chronicle of the Life of Harmon Blennerhasset," *West Virginia Society Quarterly,* 13, no. 1 (Jan. 1999), 1.
11. Ray Swick, "An Island Called Eden," (Parkersburg: Parkersburg Printing Co., 1999): 42.

12. Janney Family Papers, "Collection Ms. no. 142, Box 4/5 (Columbus: Ohio Historical Society), 3.

13. Celia Burleigh, "People Worth Knowing," *National Anti-Slavery Standard*, 24, no. 18 (Aug. 24, 1867): 2.

14. Frances Gage, "A*utobiography*, 1876," Scouten Collection.

15. _____, "Speech, May 10, 1867," *History of Woman's Suffrage, 1881-1902,* eds. Elizabeth Cady Stanton, Susan B. Anthony, Matilda Joslyn Gage, II (New York: Schocken Books, 1971): 224.

16. Gage, "Looking Back," *The Woman's* Advocate, 1 (Jan. 1869): 2.

17 Gage, "Woman's Sphere and Duty," *The Ohio Farmer* 17, no. 35 (Aug. 29, 1868): 55.

18. Gage, "Looking Back."

19. "Letter from Aunt Fanny," *Pittsburgh Saturday Visiter* (Nov. 16, 1850): 174.

20. Janney, 4.

21. William Turner Coggeshall, *The Poets and Poetry of the West, "Frances Gage,"* (New York: Arno Press, 1975): 393.

22. John Gage, "Vineland Letter, Autobiographical Notes," (Vineland, New Jersey: Vineland Historical Society Archives.)

23. Land Records, Document #1024, Serial #OH540_034.

24. Anya Jabour, *Marriage in the Early Republic*, (Baltimore, Maryland: Johns Hopkins University Press): 35.

25. James Gaylord and Charles Robertson, *Historical Reminiscences of Morgan* County. (Morgan County Historical Society: McConnelsville, Ohio, 1932).

26. *Daily Ohio Statesman*. (Feb 16, 1850).

27. *Daily Ohio Statesman*. (June 12, 1851).

28. Nettie H. Dougan, *McConnelsville, Ohio, 1817-1867 Sesquicentennial* (McConnelsville: Morgan Count Historical Society: 18.

29. L. P. Brockett and Mary C. Vaughan, *Woman's Work in the Civil War* (Boston: R. H. Curran, 1867): 683.

30. Frances Gage, "Letter," *The Lily* 5, no. 5 (Jan. 28, 1853): 174.

31. Henry Ward Beecher, "Letter to the Editor, (*New York Tribune*, Feb. 1860), *History* 1: 678.

32. Jane Swisshelm, "Bloomers and the Woman's Rights Conventions," *Half a Century* (New York: Sourcebook, 1970).

33. Virginia Chambers-Schiller, Lee, *Liberty, A Better Husband*, (New Haven: Yale University Press: 1984):21.

34. Jeffrey E. Smith," Frances Dana Gage: Turning the World Upside Down," *Feminist Frontiers, Women Who Shaped the Midwest*, ed. Yvonne Jonson (Kirksville, Missouri, Truman State University, 2010): 8.

35. James Lamson Gage, "American Iron for Railroads," *Missouri Republican* (Sept. 3, 1854):1

36 *Annual Review of Commerce of St. Louis for the Year 1854.* (St. Louis, Missouri, 1855): 33.

37. "Iron Mountain Region," *Western Journal and Civilian* 14, no. 2 (July 1855): 124.

38 Frances Gage, "Visit to Antioch College," *Ohio Farmer* 6, no. 2 (Jan. 10, 1857): 6,

39. Catharine Barker, "Written by Hand," Autobiography Ms. B. 57, vols. 1-3. Dawes Library Special Collections, Marietta College, Ohio.

40 Frances Gage, "Letter," *Ohio Cultivator*, 9 (November 1, 1853): 31.

41. _____, "Letter," *Ohio Cultivator, 10* (December, 1853): 11.

42. _____, "*Poems*, "Impromptu," (Philadelphia: J. B. Lippincott, 1867).

43. _____, "Letter to Catharine Barker (Collection of Jerry Devol, Devola, Ohio).

44. _____, "Aunt Fanny's Husband, "*Ohio Cultivator*, 9 no. 5 (March 1, 1853): 74.

45. James Gage, "A Letter from Illinois," *National Anti-Slavery Standard,* 23 (March 13, 1863).

46. Frances Gage, "Letter from Mrs. Frances D. Gage to Dr. Jackson," *Water Cure Journal* 14, no. 3 (Sept. 1852): 54, 57.

47. _____, "The Doctor that was Not a Humbug," *Water Cure Journal* 19, no. 6 (June 1855): 130.

48. *Barnyard Rhymes*, (New York: G. and C. Carvill and Company, 1838): 128.

49. Frances Gage, "Letter from Mrs. Frances D. Gage, the Swedish Movement Cure," *Ohio Farmer* 17, no. 1 (Jan 4 Jan 4, 1868): 10.

50. _____. "Letter 1867," Barton Correspondence.

51. _____, "Letter from Mrs. Frances D. Gage to Dr. Jackson," Wat*er-Cure Journal*, (September 1852): 54-57.

52. _____,"Letter from Mrs. Frances D. Gage, "The Doctor that was not a Humbug," *Water Cure Journal* 19, no. 6 (June 1855): 130.

53. Letter, Barton Correspondence.

54 Frances Gage, "Aunt Hannah's Quilt," *The Herald of Truth* 3 (Feb. 1, 1848): 141.

55. Lucinda S. Wilcox, "The Ladies of Vineland," Bentley Historical Library, University of Michigan: Ann Arbor Michigan Correspondence

56. Frances Gage, "Letter, How to Treat the Sick," *Herald of Health,* 15, no. 2 Feb. 1870:86-88.

57. Ibid.

58. Ibid., 59.

59. _____, "Relics of Andersonville," *Independent* 18, vo. 895 (Jan. 25, 1866): 1.

60. _____, "The Indian Summer of Life," *Ohio Cultivator*, 14, no. 18 (Sept. 15, 1858): 286.

61. _____, "The Autobiography of Frances Dana Gage," W*oman's Journal* (March 31, 1883): 1.

62. Elizabeth Brown Pryor, *Clara Baryon, Professional Angel.* Philadelphia: University of Pennsylvania Press, 1987: 172.

63. Frances Gage to Clara Barton, Correspondence.

64. Stephen N. Oates, *A Woman of Valor: Clara Barton and the Civil* War (New York: Free Press, 1994): 191.

65. Gage to Clara Barton, Correspondence.
66. Pryor, 194.
67. ____, 242.
68. Frances Gage, "Letter from the West," *Water Cure Journal,* 17, no. 2 (Feb. 1854): 15.
69. Nell Irvin Painter, *Sojourner Truth, a Life, a Symbol.* New York: W. W. Norton and Company, 1966: 175.

Chapter Two

"Go It Darkey," Gage the Abolitionist

A Cleveland abolition newspaper in 1850 published Frances Gage's "Reminiscence" about an 1815 experience of watching a childhood friend being kidnapped on the banks of the Ohio River. Nearly five decades later in 1869, Gage elaborated her story in the essay, "Looking Back." The journalistic style of each version slightly changed the tale. The facts did not alter. She observed Fanny, her seven-year-old playmate, being torn from the arms of her mother, Minta, and tossed headlong into a flatboat. It was en route to Louisiana where she would be sold to a sugar plantation owner. Gage claimed that she still heard Fanny's screams.[1]

The first essay is carefully crafted and tells the remembered trauma as if it were a child's story about ogres who intrude into paradise. It opens, "Once upon a time, long, long ago, I had a little playmate whose name was Fanny." Gage describes her bright-eyes, cheerful nature, and prettiness—white teeth, round face—and sweet temperament; she did not have tantrums or damage France's playhouse. Emphasis is on innocent children's interactions, such as picking berries or walking the meadow path. France was enchanted with Fanny's ability to charm chickens and tell "strange tales." Then ogres plunge into their innocent idyll. "Two stout men" handcuff and abduct the terrified black child. The Barker girl's hysteria is worsened by Yankee adults who fail to intervene. One Aunt justifies the kidnapping, "Fanny was a nigger. Fanny was a slave. They all have to be sold." The hysterical child merges into the outraged adult abolitionist who realizes this was a major loss of innocence. It was no fairy tale and in retrospect made Frances Barker "an Abolitionist for life."[2]

During her girlhood visits to Belpre and the extended Dana family, France Barker's other experience with slavery came from watching the women in the family covertly assist slaves who were escaping across the Ohio River from Parkersburg, Virginia. Such fugitives needed healing, rest, food, and protection. Individuals in the 1830's and 1840's did what they could. Later the

Underground Railroad evolved, and Abolitionists in the area became more effectively organized. For instance, Marietta's David Putnam, Jr. was famous, or infamous, since his Washington Street home was a station on the Underground Railroad. Laws conflicted because the Northwest Territory was not supposed to tolerate slavery, but America's 1793 Fugitive Slave Law opened the door to slavers. The price the Barker girl paid for her slave sympathies was not legal, but personal since her peers mocked her idealism. Standing up against children's jeers must have hurt France Barker, though she never doubted her instincts and was proud to be was part of a just minority. Her germinal experiences on Ohio's southern boundary provided the roots that supported her growing empathy with slaves' hurts "as though they were her own."[3]

Female friendship bonds were in a sense to blossom under the banner of abolition. Attending the 1840 World Anti-Slavery Convention in London were newlywed Elizabeth Cady Stanton and Henry Brewster Stanton. He was hired as an agent for the American Anti-Slavery Association and was beginning a speaking tour in Europe. The Convention accepted his credentials but not his wife's or those of any American woman. This discrimination was protested by Lucretia Mott who was defended by Wendell Phillips. British reporters from the *Dublin Weekly Herald* called Lucretia Mott the "Lioness of the Convention."[4] When her friend William Lloyd Garrison arrived late and learned the women were not credentialed, he added his support by sitting in the women's gallery and refusing to take part in the meeting. American journalist Theodore Tilton reported developments during their six week stay at a London hotel; Lucretia Mott skillfully argued her case over dinners, and clerical opponents "acknowledged" Mott's intellectual victory. Most importantly, Elizabeth Cady Stanton's was dazzled by the mind of Quaker Lucretia Mott. Years later she claimed that in London they began discussions about organizing to support American women's rights. However, Mott's diary corrects the record by placing such discussion years later.[5]

Mott was a Quaker and seasoned Underground Railroad activist. Her abolitionism was pragmatic about equality—even for women. In 1831, nine years before the London meeting, she resigned from William Lloyd Garrison's New England Anti-Slavery Society because it did not admit women. The next year she formed the Philadelphia Female Anti-Slavery Society. As a consequence, William Lloyd Garrison helped organize the American Anti-Slavery

Society which admitted women. He even put three women on its Executive Committee, including Lucretia Mott and Lydia Maria Child. Soon his *Liberator* was famous for advocating abolition and women's suffrage.

Abolitionist women began organizing for their rights because male abolition groups denied their membership. Many reformers were also temperance advocates, like Amelia and Dexter Bloomer. The Bloomers lived in sleepy Seneca Falls, New York and in 1845 invited the Stantons to move there from New York City where Henry Stanton was practicing law. Elizabeth Cady Stanton appreciated the change and fresh comradeship. She was studying and setting the stage for calling a reform meeting in 1848. Stanton was the most radical person there, and she insisted women deserved the "elective franchise" or vote. It took five years before Lucretia Mott endorsed the idea and proposed the formal adoption of Stanton's 1848 Declaration of Sentiments at Cleveland's first National Woman's Rights Convention.

Another Quaker idealist was Susan B. Anthony.[6] Her family moved from New England to Rochester, New York in 1846, and her earliest reform commitment was for temperance. In 1851, Elizabeth Cady Stanton met Anthony and later wrote, "Miss Anthony's life and mine became nearly one."[6] Bearing seven children restricted the high-spirited Stanton, a writer who enjoyed addressing state legislators. Anthony was her opposite in many ways, by nature a public personality. They stimulated each other's aggressiveness, as Theodore Tilton wittily phrased it, and were "diligent forgers of all manner of projectiles from fireworks to thunderbolts."[7] Susan B. Anthony's lifelong contributions to the women's rights cause included speaking at conventions, gathering petitions for married women's rights, and being arrested for voting in 1872.

It was an Englishwoman named Harriet Martineau who in 1837 foresaw American turmoil when she equated the status of American slaves and women. Both groups were legal ciphers with few rights—no vote, no right to political office, nor legal equality with white men. Women who married gave up rights to their property and earnings, could not sue for divorce, keep their children, or testify against a husband. In order to seek justice, women could try to persuade male leaders to change the rules, infiltrate the system of masculine reformers, or create their own organization. This explains why reform-minded women organized, wrote petitions, and learned how to speak in public.

Early in the nineteenth century, abolition was America's most significant reform movement. After Jan. 1, 1831 William Lloyd Garrison's *Liberator* promoted change. He was President of the American Anti-Slavery Society for forty years and America's most celebrated Anti-slavery leader. He listened to the complaints of Lucretia Mott and became a strong supporter of women's rights. He also admired reformer and author Lydia Maria Child whose abolitionist family's home was a station on the Underground Railroad.

In 1833, Child wrote *An Appeal in Favor of that Class of Americans Called African*; this was America's first anti-slavery work printed in book form, and it was said to have converted to abolitionism Wendell Phillips, Thomas Wentworth Higginson, and Charles Sumner.[8] Two years later Lydia Maria Child's *History and the Condition of Women* provided the first global overview of women's roles. Its section on the United States defended witches and African slaves. She assisted Garrison with Boston's *Liberator* during the 1830s, and also wrote for the American Anti-Slavery Society, for example its Tract No. 9, "The Duty of Disobedience to the Fugitive Slave Act."[8]

Then on June 11, 1840 she and her husband David Lee Child began publishing a second abolition publication, the *National Anti-Slavery Standard that* was based in New York City. During her editorial tenure, the *Standard* institutionalized such innovations as inclusion of novels; for instance, in 1842, it serialized Charles Dickens' *American Notes*. The Childs' editorial policies widened the abolition paper's scope. It emphasized factual reporting, excluded religious bias, sensational police reports, and derogatory references to women. The *National Anti-Slavery Standard* also carried Lydia Marie Child's, "Letters from New York," highly intellectual, yet personal essays that connected her to urban readers; this format appealed to Frances Gage.[9]

In fact, The *National Anti-Slavery Standard* was household reading for James and Frances Gage. In this newspaper, they followed features, like the writing of Englishwoman Harriet Martineau who was its "European Correspondent" between 1859 and 1862. From the beginning, this publication traced the vicissitudes of Ohio's anti-slavery movement. The *Standard* in the spring of 1863 printed James Gage's missive accusing President Lincoln of mismanaging the war. When the war broke out, it informed the Gages about the "contraband" issue in the mid-Atlantic region. On April 16, 1870 after thirty years, the newspaper closed.

In 1847, a third significant anti-slavery journal, the *National Era,* began appearing in America's capital. Its editor was Gamaliel Bailey who between 1836 and 1846 lived in Cincinnati, served as Secretary of Ohio's Anti-Slavery Society, and published the *Philanthropist.* Bailey's paper was called America's first anti-slavery publication in the West. The *Philanthropist* survived several rampaging pro-slavery mobs in 1836 that finally destroy his press. His move to Washington led to an affiliation with the American and Foreign Anti-Slavery Society which had broken away from the American Anti-Slavery Society. One of their differences was a refusal to support the women's rights movement. Bailey's *National Era* focused purely on anti-slavery sentiment. For example, it concentrated on such events as Clay's Compromise of 1850 and John Brown's 1859 Raid. The *National Era* affected a refined tone and published poets, such as Ohioan Alice Cary and New England's John Greenleaf Whittier, who had been an associate of William Lloyd Garrison. Whittier took over the job of editing the *National Era* between 1847 and the outbreak of the war. Bailey died in 1860, so the newspaper ceased. Its most noteworthy contribution was the inclusion of extended fiction after Bailey asked Cincinnati acquaintance Harriet Beecher Stowe to write a slave narrative for serial publication. Her *Uncle Tom's Cabin* ran from July 1851 for 44 weeks. Then in 1852 it appeared in novel form, and this brilliantly successful abolition narrative spearheaded slavery discussions for many years.

A fourth reform-focused periodical, the *Independent,* began in 1848 in New York City. Its owner was Henry Chandler Bowen, a Congregationalist who advocated abolition and temperance. His newspaper was editorially independent and critical of Washington's leaders. Its editorial writing was often done by Harriet Beecher Stowe's brother, Henry Ward Beecher and his associate Theodore Tilton. He was a successful *Tribune* reporter who worked with such reform leaders as William Lloyd Garrison, Lucy Mott, Elizabeth Cady Stanton, and Susan B. Anthony. In 1855, Rev. H. W. Beecher presided at Tilton's wedding. The following year, Beecher became the *Independent's* editor; in 1861 he asked Tilton to serve as Assistant Editor and Beecher stepped down two years later. Tilton edited the *Independent* until 1870 and expanded the newspaper's range and circulation by the inclusion of coverage of American culture, society, and politics.

The lifespan of these abolition newspapers was determined by the passion and health of their editors. The *National Era* changed hands and merged with another publication in 1859 when Gamaliel Bailey died; after the Civil War, William Lloyd Garrison's *Liberator* ceased in 1865, and *National Anti-Slavery Standard* closed its doors in 1870. This left Greeley's *New York Tribune* advocating reform issues. The *Independent* continued but was discredited by scandal when its presiding spirit, Rev. Henry Ward Beecher, was accused of serial lechery. The *Independent* continued for many years as a liberal newspaper, but was much less forceful without the idealism of Rev. Beecher and the intellectual vigor of Theodore Tilton.

These were the reform-minded newspapers that published Frances Gage's writing about slavery and abolition before, during, and after the Civil War. She earned the respect of liberal journalists like Bailey, Garrison, Child, Beecher, and Tilton, each of whom largely shared her political values. After Stanton and Anthony discovered late in the 1840s that Gage could think, write, speak eloquently, and rise above fatigue, she was much in demand. They sought help canvassing for women's rights in New York State. The Ohioan assisted them on this project and spoke on many Eastern platforms. She assisted their work and brought a warm vision of the heartlands that energized listeners and strengthened the rights reformers' base.

In the 1850s, Gage's Ohio was still the gateway to the West—hewn in 1787 from the slavery-prohibited Northwest Territory and largely populated by principled New Englanders. In terms of abolition, the state was strategically positioned to assist escaping slaves. Lake Erie lapped both the shores of Ontario, Canada, which welcomed escaping slaves after 1793, and Ohio's northern shore. The southern boundary of the state was also bordered by water. The Ohio River separated it from Virginia and Kentucky, which were government mandated pro-slave states. Inevitably, Ohio was an avenue taken by countless African-American fugitives heading toward Canadian freedom. It was also the battleground where many were recaptured.

Trying to anticipate and prevent the problem its geography posed, Ohio politicians in 1807 passed so-called "Black Laws" to deter fugitive slaves. Their wording was stronger than America's 1793 Fugitive Slave Law, but neither was enforceable. The state unwittingly became the proving ground for much litigation. The

Queen City, Cincinnati, had racial riots when escaped slaves and freedmen feared that the "Black Laws" might be enforced. Many fled to peaceful Wilberforce or Ontario, Canada. Such disturbances contributed to heated anti-slavery debates. After having "overrun the "Western Reserve," in the state's northeast and carried "the gospel of freedom to every hamlet," William Lloyd Garrison expanded the Anti-Slavery Society's work in Ohio to other areas of the state. Anti-slavery meetings proliferated, and Ohio's abolitionists were wrought up to a high pitch of enthusiasm. One writer in the *National Anti-Slavery Standard* stated that Ohio's reformers were more democratic than those in Eastern states. [10]

Abolition reformers saw Ohio as a prize. However, its women, like the Danas, Barkers, and Gages, were unwelcome in the state's male organizations. Ohio's first Anti-Slavery Society began in Zanesville on April 1835, founded through affiliation with Oberlin College; it adapted Garrison's Anti-Slavery Society format. Male members of this Ohio group pledged to fight for the abolition of slavery and the passage of laws to protect freed African Americans. For promotion of their cause, the Society employed lecturers. It also in 1846 sponsored Gamaliel Bailey's *The Philanthropist*.

The philosophical schism between Ohio's pro-slavery and anti-slavery adherents was exacerbated by Congressional passage of the Fugitive Slave Law in 1850. The new law amended America's original 1793 Fugitive Slave Law. Essentially, it took the responsibility for catching escaped slaves away from the state where they resided and placed it on the states to which fugitives traveled. Sanctions included a $1,000 fine and six months imprisonment for any person who failed to return alleged runaways. The law's terms were harsh: no warrant or evidence was needed to arrest an African American. There was no option of appeal or jury trial, and slavers had national immunity from prosecution. In practice, this nullified the "no slavery provision" of the Northwest Territory's inception. One journal article titled the issue, "The Ordinance of '87, No Slavery in the North West." For all of these reasons, before the Civil War the 1850 Fugitive Slave Law became the North's primary grievance against the pro-slavery South.

Cincinnati lawyer Salmon P. Chase led the repeal of Ohio's Black Laws in 1849 and was one of only three Congressmen who voted against the 1850 Fugitive Slave Law. America's literary protests ranged from famous regional voices like that of Transcendentalist Henry David Thoreau to local leaders such as Frances

Dana Gage. His "Civil Disobedience," describes the circumstances under which one should disobey an unjust law. Members of the reform-minded Beecher family also lobbied against the law. The most famous protest was Harriet Beecher Stowe's 1851 *Uncle Tom's Cabin*, which provided a rallying point for slavery's opposition. Its setting was near Ripley and outside Cincinnati, Ohio. Elizabeth Cady Stanton praised the dramatic tale because it quickened the "pulsations of every woman's heart in the nation." [11]

No propaganda was needed to persuade Frances Gage of slavery's viciousness. She had seen it on the Ohio River. The child who helped nurse fugitive slaves grew into a focused adult who wrote to convince others in regional publications. One example was the following, "Lines on the Passage of the Fugitive Slave Bill": "Oh Northmen! oh, Northmen! beware of the hour/ When you sell yourselves out to the slaveholding power,/When you barter your souls for a five-dollar fee,/ To fetter the spirit that dares to be free."[12] Another Gage anti-slavery poem, "Impromptu," scolded her native state for enforcing the Fugitive Slave Law, "'Shame on Ohio?' Yes, 'tis shame." This reform writing first appeared in regional newspapers, such as Jane Gray Swisshelm's *Pittsburgh Saturday Visiter*. It published Gage's "Letter from Aunt Fanny" that declared "war upon all opposers of progress."[13] This epistle urged men to be gentle, honorable, just, and true, then vented Gage's rage over the Fugitive Slave Law, concluding with her threat, "I should feel like abjuring my country and going to Canada with the rest of the Fugitives."

It was good that Frances Gage didn't immigrate to Canada as an antislavery protest because the following year she was asked to chair Ohio's Second Woman's Rights Convention at Akron's Stone Church. Gage prepared herself, knowing the likelihood of there being men in the audience who opposed women, like herself, speaking in public. Some opposed women's rights as a political or religious issue, while others rejected women's participation in abolition work. Frances Gage had read Sojourner Truth's autobiography, and the morning of the Akron Convention, she met Truth at her temperance hotel. On the second day of the rights' meeting, Gage gave the floor to the freed slave who made a compelling speech. One enthusiastic abolitionist in the audience called out, "Go it Darkey." It seemed odd that the official *Proceedings of the Woman's Rights Convention* omitted mention of Truth's speech. However, it was recorded by Marius Robinson, a journalist who was President of the Western Anti-Slavery Society and served as its Secretary for the Akron meeting.

A few years earlier, the fearless Robinson was tarred and feathered in Berlin Center and abandoned in a cornfield near Canfield, Ohio, resulting in life-long injuries that limited his activities. He became Truth's friend and recorded her address in Salem's *Anti-Slavery Bugle*. Here Robinson described her as a tall freed woman, one of several womanly, self-possessed, competent, and experienced anti-slavery feminists at the meeting. Following is an excerpt from his June 1851 rendition of her speech: ""I have as much muscle as any man . . . . I have heard much about the sexes being equal . . . As for intellect, all I can say is, if a woman have a pint and a man a quart—why cant she have her little pint full? . . . . I have heard the bible and have learned that Eve caused man to sin . . . . give her a chance to set it right side up again."[14] He records no dialect. After the Akron meeting, Robinson remained with Truth for two years as a co-laborer in Ohio, attending conventions and holding their own abolition meetings.

Truth had met William Lloyd Garrison and his star protégé, ex-slave Frederick Douglass, who were known as America's leading abolitionists. Douglass was born a slave named Frederick Washington Bailey. He escaped to New York City, changed his name, and spoke out against slavery; his was a heroic story of an individual fighting for freedom. Garrison met him in 1841 and hired Douglass to be an agent and lecturer for the American Anti-Slavery Society. In 1845, Garrison helped Douglass publish his autobiography, the *Narrative of the Life of Frederick Douglass*. Later the two men learned Sojourner Truth's story—born around 1787 as a slave called Isabella Van Wagenen, she fled a New York "owner" who reneged on freeing her as demanded by the state's 1827 emancipation law. They urged Sojourner Truth to tell her story, which was dictated and published in 1850 as the *Narrative of Sojourner Truth, a Northern Slave*. This included Garrison's introduction and an endorsement from Harriet Beecher Stowe, the lionized author of *Uncle Tom's Cabin*.; this "blurb" was a big asset for Sojourner Truth's *Narrative*. The ex-slave felt grateful and indebted for the assistance in selling her 25-cent book. Its income brought the freedwoman economic security and occasions to speak out as she did in Akron, Ohio. In fact, 1856, five years later, Truth moved to Battle Creek, Michigan where she bought a home with the proceeds from her autobiography.

The story behind the publication of her speech began twelve years after the Akron Convention. Sojourner Truth's Ohio performance became fodder for the national imagination through an essay written by Harriet Beecher Stowe, "Sojourner Truth, The Libyan Sibyl." It appeared in the April 1863 *Atlantic Monthly* and included a description of the Akron Rights meeting that Stowe did not attend. Two years earlier in 1850, Calvin Ellis Stowe had moved the family from Ohio to Brunswick, Maine. In order to prepare for writing her 1863 essay, Stowe reread Sojourner Truth's book and Robinson's newspaper coverage. Her ostensible goal was cultivating sympathy for African Americans in the North who were scarred by slavery. Unfortunately, Stowe had never met Truth and added her idea of Southern slave dialect. Because Sojourner Truth grew up in New York State her first language was Dutch, then English. Truth never lived in the South or had a Southern dialect.

Modern Historian Patricia R. Hill believes that Stowe composed the essay in order to "consolidate her own stature as political authority and cultural arbiter."[16] Nell Irvin Painter accuses Stowe of patronizing Sojourner Truth as an African and "primitive object d'art."[17]. Indeed, Harriet Beecher Stowe's essay stirred up interest in Sojourner Truth's symbolic significance. The essay inspired Sculptor William Westmore Story to depict Sojourner Truth in the form of a marble statue for display at the London World Exhibition. His "Libyan Sibyl" today stands in the Smithsonian Museum of American Art in Washington; D. C.

But when Frances Gage, who had chaired the Akron Convention, read The New Englander's essay, she resented Stowe's treatment of an event that she remembered differently. Certainly, Truth had no Southern dialect, and Gage believed it was presumptuous for Stowe to pretend she was there. The native Ohioan seemed to feel preempted and, perhaps, resented the New Englander's artistic slant as well. What is certain is that on the 23rd of the same month, April 1863, New York's *Independent* published Frances Gage's version of the 1852 Akron meeting. Gage drew upon her memories of the Women's Rights Convention and cast a flattering spotlight on her role defending Truth's right to take the floor. The essay presented the remarkable African-American woman," a "weird, wonderful creature, who was at once a marvel and a mystery." An excerpt of Gage's essay follows with its rendition of Truth's speech: "Nobody eber helps me into carriages. . . And ar'n't

I a woman? . . . I have plowed and planted . . . and ar'n't I a woman
. . . Whar did your Christ come from?"[18]

Like Stowe, Gage employs inaccurate language, and this literary device was wholly intentional; she used the language of the slaves she lived with on the Atlantic coastline. This was an African-English patois known as "Gullah."[20] Most importantly, Gage's oratorical skills embellish Truth's performance, creating "the ring" of authenticity that readers have since celebrated. Among Gage's contributions are four repetitions of the phrase "Ar'n't I a woman?" She also lengthens Robinson's narrative account and turns Truth into a more symbolic figure. In these ways, Frances Gage drew upon her experience as a public speaker to strengthen "Reminiscences of Sojourner Truth." Many have called "Truth's Speech at Ohio's Woman's Rights Convention," a memorably written masterpiece. Truth herself included Frances Gage's version of the speech in her 1867 edition of *Narrative of Sojourner Truth*, as did Stanton in the 1881 *History of Women's Suffrage*. Nell Irvin Painter, Truth's biographer, sees the speech as the "positive word portrait of a powerful black woman" that placed "Gage . . . as usual in the vanguard."[19]

The *Independent* in 1866 also printed Frances Gage's "Reminiscences of Sojourner Truth," an essay about their postbellum Washington reunion.[20] Truth came to the capital in 1865, worked in the Freedman's Hospital, and rode the capital's streetcars in order to undercut the city's segregation. The 80-year-old described to Frances Gage her morning's conversation with Abraham Lincoln and satisfaction with his emancipation of the slaves. Truth sought contributions of clothing for freed women and children. She told her interviewer about "scolding" freedmen to keep clean, mend clothes, share their food, and continue working. The remarkable abolitionist is presented as walking with a "springy step, as erect as when a slave, she carried a washtub on her head. . . [and] Her memory of past events is like a book."

Gage was sometimes called "Truth's feminist comrade,"[21] and she reiterated the story of the 1852 Akron convention where the tall, gaunt black woman [who wore] a gray dress and white turban, surmounted with an uncouth sun-bonnet," walking with the "air of a queen up the aisle. . . . Gage added, "This almost Amazon form, which stood nearly six feet high, head erect, and eyes piercing the upper air like one in a dream" spoke to the assemblage. Thus, the seasoned author again embellished the image of America's "glorious old mother."[21]

As time passed, Frances Gage's reputation as a writer spread. In early days, several journals had rebuffed and censored her reformist political views; for example, Worthington's *Ohio State Journal*, a Whig daily newspaper, in the late 1840's called Gage an "excellent friend and correspondent" and printed her weekly column, Aunt Fanny's "Letters from the Kitchen." But when she protested against the 1850 Fugitive Slave Law, the *Journal*'s conservative editors warned readers that they disagreed with her politics. Gage was then told that her sentiments struck at the "foundations of all law, order, and governments," so she would be removed from its pages. Gage replied, "I cheerfully retire from your columns."[22]

This scenario reoccurred a few years later when Gage lived in conservative Missouri. She submitted her writing to first one and then the second of its two leading journals, the *Missouri Democrat* and *Missouri Republican*. One editor protected her for a time, but after his death, she was blackballed. Soon both publications sent her packing. In part, editors objected to Gage's eastern activities, such as speaking on the platform of the Boston Anti-Slavery Society. In 1855, she complained to her Ohio friend, Rebecca Janney that Missouri locals responded to her, "as if I were a wild beast."[23] It was not surprising after such continued vilification from the states' pro-slavers that the family decamped for friendlier environs in anti-slavery Illinois.

A pleasant interlude occurred for her in February 1859 when her brother-in-law asked Frances Gage to join his friends for a four-month trip to the West Indies. James Gage urged his still energetic spouse to go. Her goal was learning how African slaves overcame servitude in the Caribbean islands because this could provide a model for American emancipation. She wanted to research material for a lecture series that would benefit northern freedmen since its subject matter would be slavery's peaceful growth into freedom on the islands of St. Thomas, St. Croix, and St. John.

The colonial history of these islands is a dark chapter in the history of the Americas. The islands' troubled economies were based on slavery and sugar production. Frances Gage wished to counter the beliefs of American slave holders that revolution and riot would follow abolition. She wrote that her goal was comparing the effects of slavery to the effects of emancipation. Their itinerary took them to what is currently called the Virgin Islands, St. Thomas, St. Croix, and St. John. They also went to Haiti and Cuba. The first three islands had dominantly been controlled by the Dutch West India Company with slavery abolished eleven years earlier in 1848. The question land owners asked of freed slaves was whether a salary would motivate them; as a result how would the island's economy fare? In fact, there was a resultant rise in labor costs and lessening of production.

Slavery continued in Haiti, a dominantly French colony that was the first to gain independence from European powers in 1804. Its President Jean-Pierre Boyer was overthrown in 1843, and many rulers followed; Haiti kept enforced labor and sex trafficking. Before the Civil War, the U. S. government refused to recognize Haiti.

Historian Edward Bartlett Rugemer's *The Problem of Emancipation, The Caribbean Roots of the American Civil War* emphasizes the significance of these islands for abolitionists in the hemisphere. Britain's "Mighty Experiment" outlawing slavery in 1834 did not remove the threat of rebellions. Rugemer explains how American newspapers treated the West Indian slave insurrections. For instance, in 1831 there was a slave rebellion in Jamaica. The American Consul in Jamaica between 1831 and 1858 repeatedly sent dispatches to America that promoted a climate of fear.[24]

The Caribbean was unlike the United States in many ways, but legitimate economic and cultural similarities frightened many Southerners. In 1833 England passed its Slavery Abolition Act that heartened Abolitionists. The consequences of such legal changes in the West Indies were watched for further developments. When the Gage party headed toward these islands for four months in 1859, the relevance of abolition's peaceful success was very much in the news. It made a complicated context for the Gage party's visit to these tropical isles.

In *Field Notes,* Gage explained that travel would enable her to bolster Abolitionists' ideas about how to help "freedmen" thrive.[25] *The Ohio Cultivator* readers learned of her adventure on Feb. 23, 1859. On March 4, Aunt Fanny wrote to the "Cultivator Girls" from New Orleans and told them not to think her crazy "because she has gone away to the 'Isles of the Sea,' nor that she has turned traitor to her native land . . . . Husband said go, and children said go."[26] In New Orleans, Frances Gage sent a lively description of the French Market's grog shops where "wharf rats" have their "morning dram" that "borders on iniquity." Her letter mostly raved about the city's fruit and vegetable market with its excellent produce. She was also fascinated by the mélange of races (using her verbs) talking, screaming, mimicking, twittering, snapping, barking, crying, swearing, and scolding.

In mid-March, "F. D. Gage" published a more serious letter in the *Liberator* that criticized Missouri's pro-slavery culture. She ignored New Orleans' market's flowers and wrote about racism. Gage complained that in Louisiana surfaces may be misleading because, though its slaves may laugh and appear "well treated," underneath New Orleans' glamour lurks slavery's evil. Her words referred to *Uncle Tom's Cabin*, "The Lagrees do not obtrude themselves." It concluded, "friend Garrison," there is much improvement needed in New Orleans."[27]

The missives she sent from the West Indies to different publications were artfully crafted to suit their readers. Her April 1, 1859 letter to "Mr. Garrison" in *The Liberator* covered emancipation's effect on islanders in Santa Cruz, aka St. Croix, and Santo Domingo on Hispaniola. Cuba shared the island of Hispaniola with the Dominican Republic. Gage perceived the residents as being happy, cheerful, and glad to be free of even "good masters" who had not allowed leisure. Her last sentence summarizes, "Everything I see and hear denies the assertion that Emancipation has brought injury to the slave—or to the white." [28]

Her "Letter" to *The Ohio Cultivator* from Santa Cruz complained about an island, Cuba, where slavery still reigned. In fact, its slavery did not formally end until 1886 when slaves revolted, which was two years after her death. Frances Gage woefully compared Havana's and New Orleans' markets, observing, "The people themselves half dressed, slip-shod, old, wrinkled, filthy, and ragged. . . . Every man and half the women were puffing cigars." Gage softened this grim picture for her Ohio woman readers by describing the food at her Norwegian boarding house. She was an uncomplaining traveler who accepted such things as a Spartan lack of carpets and window glass. "What care I," she wrote, "if they put onions in their peas, and tomatoes and garlic with their fish, and wine in their mutton roasts?" This letter ended good-naturedly with a description of island women carrying produce trays on their heads and an encomium, "the Island is beautiful." [29]

Another serious "Letter" titled the "Results of Emancipation in Santa Cruz" was sent to the *National Anti-Slavery Standard* and reprinted in the *Friends' Intelligencer*. It considered "the great problem of human freedom" for twenty thousand people who transitioned from being slaves. In order to effectively prove her point, Gage compared American slaves, Cuban slaves, and Santa Cruz's freedmen. The worst off were Havana's slaves who were without proper clothing or housing; they were "locked up like sheep or cattle." The positive contrast found in Santa Cruz was inspiring—the children happily attended schools; their field-hand parents exhibited "sublime self-respect," were well dressed, clean, and had comfortable houses. They worked only ten hours a day, had weekends off, and were not beaten. Men and women received equal pay, and each had land to till. Gage concluded her missive by emphasizing the fact that black children "learn quite as fast as white children." [30]

The final communiqué from her West Indies' sojourn was sent from St. Domingo City on April 7 and printed in *The Ohio Farmer* on June 18. It thoughtfully compared Caribbean history to that of Marietta, Ohio. She admired colonial architecture in the West Indies and acknowledged its superiority to rustic structures in southeast Ohio. However, Gage continued, "seventy years of industry and good government . . . in Ohio, my native state [surpasses] three hundred and fifty years of tyranny, war, oppression and misrule [that] have left this beautiful island of St. Domingo. . . a demi savage life" (sic). Readers also learned of the superb chef who owned her French boarding house and the area's tropical food and plants. The conclusion was a Spanish, "Adios." On May 6 Frances Gage left St. Domingo and on the 31st arrived back in New York City after 26 days at sea. She promptly returned to her family in St. Louis as her essay, "Mrs. Gage at Home," records in *The Ohio Cultivator* and *The Ohio Farmer*. [31]

Her valiant contribution to abolitionists' efforts to tamp down fears of the West Indies was appreciated by the American Anti-Slavery Society. Its 1861 "Annual Report" complimented Gage for her work in the islands. She set to work on lectures that compared the two cultures by looking at American and West Indies gender limitations, legal disabilities and inequalities. Lyceum courses were a sort of adult education lecture series done by many public figures, among them Susan B. Anthony, William Lloyd Garrison, and Henry Ward Beecher. Such lecture programs were remunerative. In January 1861, Frances Gage wrote in *Farm Notes* that she charged an admission fee of ten cents, while the full lyceum course earned her "stated compensation." Her series of lectures took place, for instance at Hiram College, Ohio between February and April, 1861. The program was praised on April 12 in the *Cleveland Herald* as being of "singular interest" because Gage rejected "aristocracy" and embraced the "habits and customs of the common people."32 Thus, Frances Gage, the idealist, found practical ways to support abolition, but such individuals' efforts could not avert war.

Festering racial and economic issues led Americans into a war based upon two conflicting definitions of "human rights." After Abraham Lincoln was elected to America's Presidency in the fall of 1859, unhappy events quickly transpired. South Carolina protested, seceding from the Union on Dec. 20, 1860 and was soon followed by ten other southern states. On Feb. 27, 1860, President Lincoln spoke against slavery at the Cooper Union in New York City. On April 12, 1861, the Confederated States of America was announced, and South Carolina's militia fired on Fort Sumter, a federal fortress at the entrance to Charleston's harbor.

After 34 hours of bombardment, the Federal fort was severely damaged and surrendered. Secessionists' easy acquisition of Charleston turned it into the Civil War's symbol of rebellion. There was Charleston's spectacular waterside that made it one of America's most beautiful cities. It epitomized the fruits of plantation culture that was based on kidnapped African slaves. Beyond being a meaningful symbol for both Southerners and Northerners, Charleston was a key target in the Civil War because the city was a business center for war supplies and contained weapons factories. Early anticipations of the Union's wish to recapture Charleston led Rebel military forces to strengthen its harbor defenses and establish a series of protective earthworks on nearby islands.

Certainly, everyone expected reprisals from the North. This fear was especially strong in Port Royal Sound Bay, the area north of Charleston and south of Savannah, Georgia. South Carolina's barrier islands or "Sea Islands" were occupied by wealthy cotton plantations. It was seven months before the North struck back at South Carolina, but plantation owners had fled inland for the protection of Confederate forces. They took with them portable possessions and house slaves, thus abandoning thousands of African American field workers. The federal Confiscation Act promptly declared African American slaves to be "contraband of war" and "a military resource [which] . . . should not be turned over to the enemy." These "slaves" were labeled "contrabands" or "freedmen." Previously this name was used only for persons of African descent who were granted freedom by an owner or bought it themselves. Northern government leaders were motivated by freedmen's potential "value" for two things, cotton production and military recruitment.

The Gage's acquaintance, Salmon P. Chase, had become President Lincoln's Secretary of the Treasury. He asked an associate in his Cincinnati law office, Edward L. Pierce, to go as a Special Agent to the mid-Atlantic coastal area and study the situation. This man's experience in the summer of 1861 included supervising escaped slaves at Fortress Monroe in Hampton, Virginia, which was a haven outside of Virginia's slave-owners' jurisdiction. Pierce recorded the work in his essay, "The Contrabands of Fortress Monroe" in the Nov. 1861 *Atlantic Monthly*.[34] Pierce was eager to translate his ideals to the South Carolina's Sea Islands. So, in the two weeks between Jan. 13 and 27, 1862, he visited seventeen islands, including Hilton Head and Beaufort. His report on the fortnight's work, "The Negroes at Port Royal," was turned over to Chase and President Lincoln. It was published and widely read, even by the Gages in Ohio.[33]

Edward L. Pierce summarized slavery's economic impact in the Sea Islands where 8,000 abandoned slaves expected Union protection. He proposed "The Port Royal Experiment," a revolutionary plan to reanimate the economy of cotton plantations. His argument drew upon an engaging cultural analysis of elements like slaves' church singing, clothing, and cabins. He explained that freedmen were "as industrious as any race," and would bring in the cotton crop, study literacy, and serve as colored Union soldiers. Moreover, the abolitionist argued that implementing his plan would establish a model of "beneficent reforms" which could serve as a template for the South's post-war "Reconstruction."

The immediate goal in the winter of 1862 was finding leaders to invigorate the harvesting of the upcoming season's cotton crop. This must be done within two months, March and April. On Feb. 15 Pierce returned to Boston and received permission for the Port Royal Experiment to proceed. Formal approval by President Lincoln's cabinet was withheld until July. Nonetheless, Pierce left New York's harbor on March 3, 1862 onboard a steamer with a group of 53 persons, including 12 women. This band of missionaries, teachers, and superintendents, were sometimes called "Gideonites," named after the Biblical figure whose small army conquered a large one. They headed for Beaufort, South Carolina. In April, a second group joined them from Philadelphia. All workers received Union subsistence pay as well as remuneration from abolition societies.

Frances Gage had heard Abraham Lincoln speak in Illinois and saw him as a "great and good man" who supported justice. Sitting in her Ohio parlor, Frances Gage became infected by Edward L. Pierce's enthusiasm. She knew his mentor, Salmon P. Chase, since he was the man for whom she wrote, "Dare to Stand Alone." The Ohio lawyer had served as Ohio's Governor, United States Senator, and leader of Congressional anti-slavery forces. He was also the man who strenuously persuaded President Lincoln that emancipation should be the rationale for war.

On May 26, the Gages read Ohio Governor Dennison's call for Union support; this was based on the Secretary of War's request for troops to repel the "rebellious invaders." Her ill husband supported Frances Gage's desire to receive permission to join the volunteers heading toward South Carolina's Sea Islands. She contacted everyone she thought could grant permission, including Freedmen's Associations in Boston, New York, and Philadelphia. With no immediate response, she decided to contact her old Steubenville friend in Washington, so Gage directly contacted Salmon P. Chase. He made inquiries and gave Frances Dana Gage the approval she sought. On Oct. 8, 1862, she and son, George, sailed on a steamer from New York City to Port Royal, South Carolina. During the trip, Gage chatted with Captain John Elwell of Cleveland who she was later to know as Mary Barton's special friend. Soon daughter Mary joined them, which brought the three civilian Gages into the military vortex in South Carolina's Sea Islands.

Pierce's abolitionist workers were the first to arrive at the Sea Islands, including Miss Susan Walker who kept a journal that records the earliest days of Yankee occupation. Her topics included the gentlemanly assistance of John C. Zachos, a friend of Chase who was the chief teacher and superintendent representing the Boston Abolition Society's Education Commission. She visited him on Parris Island and studied the Union warships. Walker praised the harbor and criticized the village of Beaufort because it was the seat of "family hauteur and pride" with displays of carriages, equipages, and servants in livery. The Yankee abolitionist also disapproved of Major General David Hunter who initially headed the Department of the South and tried to force freedmen to serve as unpaid laborers and gather cotton; he also was unsuccessful in attempts to recruit freedmen to join the Union army. Susan Walker's complaints were more mundane; she wrote that she was disillusioned and wearied from tasks like handing out used clothing to freedmen and doing rudimentary teaching. She declined to serve as secretary to Gideonite organizer Rev. Mansfield French from Xenia, Ohio, but was heartened on May 6 to learn that Hunter was being replaced by Rufus Saxton. This was a man she believed would properly take charge though she was uncertain about whether he "will wish me to remain and whether I wish to do so." Before learning Saxton's wishes, she soon departed.

When the Brigadier General arrived to assume leadership of the Port Royal Experiment, he, indeed, proved to be a forceful leader. For instance, Pierce's original recommendation was that each field hand receives two acres for raising his own corn and potatoes with excess being sold for personal profit. Saxton reduced that to an acre and half for able-bodied persons who produced their share of the cotton crop. He encouraged them to plant their own corn and potatoes to be used for food and sold for personal profit. The Union government also promised freedmen $3.00 for clothing and additional support for a year. Freedmen, in turn, were expected to repay the Union by producing its cotton crop and cultivating food supplies for Federal forces. During the first growing season in 1861, the freedmen met Pierce's goal, harvesting 220 acres of cotton, 300 acres of corn, 46 acres of sweet potatoes, and another 20 acres of rice and garden products.[35]

Frances Gage was supposed to replace Parris Island's first Superintendent, John Zachos', but her initial assignment was nursing a yellow fever victim, General Mitchell. Hence a medical doctor, W. P. Strickland wrote the first reference to her presence in an October 30 "Letter from Beaufort." A day later, she wrote to the *Independent* and attributed Mitchell's death to the Low Country's unhealthy climate.[36] The Ohioan made herself useful; in January 1863 her formal appointment began with her serving as "General Superintendent of the Fourth Division, Parris Island Plantation."

She replaced John Zachos who was an original "Gideonite." A native of Greece and graduate of Kenyon College, he studied medicine at Miami University in Ohio. Zachos had worked as a school principal in Dayton, and been an administrator at Antioch College. In November, Zachos decided to leave Parris Island in order to serve the Union Army as an Assistant Surgeon because he knew President Lincoln was urgently calling for able-bodied medical personnel. Zachos was highly successful in the Sea Islands where he was responsible for 6 plantations and 350 to 500 inhabitants on Parris Island. Before leaving, he submitted a valuable report to General Rufus Saxton about his achievements. This allowed a smooth transition to Frances Gage's leadership.

John C. Zachos remained in Port Royal to participate in General Saxton's January 1863 New Year's Day Independence Celebration. He contributed an "Ode" as Charlotte Forten records. Years later in 1871, he and Gage became reacquainted when Zachos was Curator of New York City's Cooper Union where adult education was free, and reformers were always welcome. Frances Gage supported this liberal institution, lectured there, and even used this building as a symbolic setting in her 1867 novella, *Gertie's Sacrifice*.

In the months after Pierce submitted his initial report on the Sea Islands' economy, everyone expected a regional outbreak of hostilities between Confederates and Union forces. Nothing happened until November 7, 1861 when Commodore Samuel F. Du Pont commenced Union military retaliation against South Carolina's coastline. He commanded the Union Navy and began shelling several Confederate forts at the entrance to Port Royal Sound. A Union eyewitness account of this battle called it a: "magnificent sight: "houses . . . crowded with anxious spectators," rebel gunboats, the attack of the Hilton Head battery. " There was "terrific noise" from the ships' "splendid broadsides" and soon the Stars and Stripes floated "over South Carolina soil and a deserted rebel battery."[37] Commodore Du Pont easily captured Ft. Walker on Hilton Head. This gave the Union control over Port Royal Sound. The bludgeoning from his ships essentially did not cease until war's end in 1865 when Charleston was pulverized. Its immediate effect, however, was to drive Confederates inland. Port Royal Sound's towns and barrier islands, such as Port Royal, Beaufort, Parris Island, and Hilton Head, were vacated. Their buildings were converted into a base for the Union's South Atlantic Blockading Squadron. The Village of Beaufort became headquarters for the Federal Army's Department of the South and provided Union offices, housing, and hospitals.

This Union occupation of the mid-Atlantic coastal region was a significant loss to the South for two reasons. First, the Union now controlled valuable coastal land that produced Sea Island cotton for a British market which was a highly profitable enterprise. Even more obviously, President Lincoln's Federal government attained a land base for retaking Charleston, the South's commercial and cultural center.

Frances Gage's assignment, Parris Island, was located near the villages of Beaufort and Port Royal. It consisted of some 20 square miles, though half was salt marshes.[38] For thirteen months, Gage her son, George, daughter, Mary, and another white person each received standard "men's "wages. They resided in part of a damaged mansion at Parris Island's southwestern tip. The Broad River separated the island on its west side from an opposing shoreline held by Confederate forces. Detachments of Federal pickets patrolled on Parris Island and occasionally shot at intrusive Confederates. From the island, residents could gaze south toward Hilton Head and watch the South Atlantic Blockading Squadron's ships unceasing coastal bombardments of Port Royal Bay. Residents on Parris Island rarely heard birds singing.

These northern workers were proud to be practically and symbolically in the eye of the storm circling the nearby prize of contention, Charleston. However, even the challenges from the environment were vast, such as South Carolina's humidity, heat, insect infestations, and sickness. Here ignorance was dangerous, and the outsiders as well needed to master Gullah culture.[39] Freedmen spoke "Gullah," a combination of African words and English sentence structure. Gage quickly learned the local patois and developed an interest in its culture, including its cuisine, music, and religion. She was delighted with this culture and would have appreciated the fact that more than a century later in 1974, the Sea Islands were designated a National Historic Landmark District; Penn School, the first school in the South for former slaves, became an international model for rural education and continues as a center for the study of Gullah culture.

Gage had no assistance learning the area's history and economics. English colonists in the seventeenth century sought the islands for potential cultivation of cash crops, trying rice, cattle, and indigo for which its sandy soil and saline water supply were unsuitable. By the beginning of the nineteenth century, a new export crop arose, "long staple" Sea Island cotton thrived here, but was year round labor intensive. The process took over a year—cotton was picked between August and January; preparation for market took four months, so planting, hoeing, picking, sorting, ginning, and packing—all required unpleasant manual labor. The best Sea Island acreage could produce up to 2,000 pounds of cotton in the seed. The final product was 350-pound bales worth about 60 cents a pound. They were transported to Beaufort by flatboat, thence to Charleston, and shipped to Lancashire, England.[40]

Records showed that in 1715, Col. Alexander Parris, treasurer of the South Carolina colony, bought Parris Island. Ownership shifted among several interrelated families, particularly those of Nathaniel Barnwell and Robert Means whose kin had lengthy occupation of the site. The plantation's slave population was imported from West Africa, Angola and the Congo during the first half of the nineteenth-century when cotton production thrived. This led the Means family to unprecedented wealth. One of them, Robert Means, was the Parris Island planter, Charleston businessman, and Beaufort civic leader, who circa 1800 built a substantial mansion on 1297 Bay Street in Beaufort, the region's county seat. This beautiful building served as a Union hospital during the Civil War and is still extant. From the 1840's until the outbreak of the war, Dr. Thomas Means occupied Parris Island's planter's house with its gardens and slave row near the Broad River. Its African-American slaves left behind artifacts like pottery chards, pipe stems and beads, as well as cemeteries. In the late twentieth century, the Means' plantation was excavated for such artifacts as well as architectural detritus, like machine-made nails.[41]

Edward L. Pierce revisited the Sea Islands a year after his initial report and wrote a second essay, "The Freedmen at Port Royal," that was released in September 1863. This essay updated readers on events in South Carolina's Sea Island's economy and covered the Port Royal Experiment's progress over year and a half. It included Parris Island's cotton production under both Zachos and Gage. During the "Experiment's" second year, 1863, Frances Gage reported increased cotton production. Her Parris Island freedmen were hard workers who honored their word, and a few saved a considerable amount of money from privately selling produce. She reported that nearly every laborer on Parris Island accepted General Saxton's term and was approaching self-sufficiency. Despite Pierce underplaying his role initiating the Port Royal Experiment, what an a*nnus mirabilis* he described for the Union—even though the 1861 agricultural plantings began six weeks late, freedmen produced an abundant crop of food and some 65,000 lbs. of cotton.

Frances Gage continued this agricultural work, and Brig. Gen. Saxton was pleased with Parris Island's management. He wished all volunteers from the Boston and Philadelphia groups were as competent as Gage. She also recruited many of the island's mature and healthy men to become soldiers in South Carolina's First Regiment. Parris Island slaves served in at least three of its units, the 21st and 33rd and 34th U.S. Colored Infantry. Overall, between 1862 and 1865, six infantry regiments and an artillery battery were raised, primarily from the freedmen in the Department of the South. It also meant Gage's population on the island was dominated by elderly women and children who could be motivated to work the fields but had specific needs that drew upon Gage's talents as a teacher and homemaker. Her freedmen particularly sought literacy which was highly prized since plantation owners had outlawed reading.

In her role as Superintendent, Frances Dana Gage occasionally rubbed shoulders with visiting luminaries from abolition and military circles. On May 28, 1863, for instance, the steamer Flora anchored nearby, and a party of distinguished guests were rowed ashore. This included John Hay, President Lincoln's personal secretary, Brigadier General Rufus Saxton, the head the Department of the South and his wife. Accompanying the group was Mrs. Jean Davenport Lander, who was the widow of Brigadier General Frederick W. Lander. He had died on March 3, 1862. She and her mother came to Port Royal to volunteer as nurses. John Hay recorded in his diary that she had been an actress and was much admired. In 1863, Mrs. Lander became supervisor of nurses in Beaufort's Union Army hospitals. Hay had been sent to the South Carolina shoreline to report on the use of ironclad vessels which were supposed to help recapture Charleston harbor. [42]

The sightseeing party included a *New York Tribune* reporter who recorded Hay's speech to assembled freedmen on Parris Island. They were told President Lincoln appreciated their work with the cotton crop and were led in giving three cheers for President Lincoln and Gen. Saxton, plus another one for the ladies. The reporter's story ended with praise for Mrs. Gage and other workers who were transforming the Sea Islands' population. A second article publicizing the visit appeared in the *National Anti-Slavery Standard*. It emphasized the picturesque setting, "the mansion . . . commands a magnificent view of the shipping at Hilton Head," and "Mrs. Gage" grouped the blacks under an oak tree with plantation slaves and field-hands in the background and "little picaninies" in the front.

This was public relations work for the Union, which Frances Dana Gage was happy to provide, but after finishing her daily Superintendent's tasks, she began what she considered her real work—being a war correspondent. Sometimes, her missives were front-page news. She continued personal journalism to her rural, Midwestern readership in the *Ohio Cultivator* and *The Ohio Farmer*, while simultaneously sending more weighty articles to Eastern papers like New York's *Independent*. Gage's war journalism described slavery's horrors, made vivid the military setting, and exhorted readers to assist abandoned Gullah freedmen. As when she was in the West Indies, Gage's most serious-minded essays were sent to the nation's two leading anti-slavery newspapers, William Lloyd Garrison's *Liberator* and the *National Anti-Slavery Standard*. Other reform papers freely borrowed from these flag bearers, for instance Pennsylvania's Quaker journal, *Friends' Intelligencer*. Her closest personal affiliation through the end of the war was with New York City's *National Anti-Slavery Standard*.

During her time at "home" on Parris Island, Gage enjoyed tending the Means house's abandoned, yet luxuriant garden. It provided her with a sense of continuity to her abiding love of the land. She often wrote from gardens, a lifelong practice, but here the beauty and sordidness provided a double incentive. Among her war related themes were recruitment needs for more New England and Western "girls" to work as teachers; Gage also called for gentle, even-tempered women to serve in Union hospitals. Another topic that emerged in the winter of 1862 was the three Gages' recognition of neighbors from "back home" in McConnelsville who had grown into battle-hardened soldiers.

Ohio's 62nd Infantry Regiment arrived at the Sea Islands on Jan. 25, 1863—a decade after the family left McConnelsville in the spring of 1853. The unit included friends of the Gage sons from school and militia. They were recruited for the Union military between September 17 and December 14, 1861, gathered at Camp Goddard near Zanesville, and went into the field in January 1862. The 62nd Regiment was part of Ohio's so-called "Putnam Brigade" which consisted of four army regiments, two from Ohio, the 62nd and 67th, plus one from New York and another from New Hampshire. When the brigade arrived at the Sea Islands, its men were already seasoned by a year's service. The Ohio regiment bivouacked on nearby Folly Island, and Frances Gage was touched by their proximity. She optimistically mused for Garrison's *Liberator,* "Maybe we failed at Charleston," but "the regiments of brave fellows from the wild hills of Southern Ohio" await orders, and when the order comes, "'Forward to Charleston'," they will say, 'Down with the accursed institution' and because 'we have nothing to do with slavery.'"[43]

They all worked under the military leadership of Brigadier General Rufus Saxton who received his charge on April 15, arrived in Port Royal on April 29, and was formally appointed to the Port Royal domain on July 1, 1862. Saxton was an 1849 West Point graduate who became noteworthy for defending Harper's Ferry's arsenal and capturing John Brown in May and June of 1859. During his years in Beaufort, Rufus Saxton's full title was Brigadier General of United States Volunteers, and he was the overseer of the Port Royal Experiment. Additionally, Saxton headed the Department of the South, a jurisdiction that went beyond "possession of all plantations" to the Atlantic coastline, including Fernandina and St. Augustine, Florida.

On Aug. 25 the War Department authorized him to recruit up to 5,000 African American soldiers for five black regiments. They were to be light infantry, composed of ten companies of about 86 men each who would be armed with muskets and officered by white men. By Nov. 7 he reached the quota for the first regiment which was mustered as the First South Carolina Volunteer Regiment. Between Nov. 3 and 10, Saxton's black recruits were sent on board a steamer to raid along the coast of Georgia and Florida.

On Nov. 5, 1862, Saxton contacted Thomas Wentworth Higginson, a Harvard graduate and Captain with the 51st Massachusetts' Regiment. He asked him to come to Port Royal and head America's First South Carolina Regiment. Higginson agreed and on Nov. 25 arrived at Port Royal. At this point, Saxton had recruited 499 freedmen; by Jan. 19, 1863, when Col. Higginson formally took over the regiment, the figure had risen to 849. In this way, the Union's freedmen regiment grew with the addition of newly escaped slaves and Sea Islands freedmen who were persuaded to enlist. Col. Higginson trained his men at the Smith Plantation south of Beaufort which was renamed Camp Saxton.

Higginson had a reputation for liberal competence, zeal and loyalty. He was a Unitarian minister who was rumored to have been part of the "Secret Six," men who funded John Brown's failed 1859 raid on the federal armory at Harpers Ferry. Rufus Saxton ignored such hearsay and sought Higginson for his leadership credentials. Higginson's wife described his reasons for accepting the Sea Islands posting. "It was a vast experiment of indirect philanthropy, one on which the war and the destiny of the Negro race might rest." Col. T. W. Higginson was assigned by Saxton to lead the second freedmen's regiment.

Higginson was involved for years in abolition initiatives and was friends with America's leading reformers. For instance, in 1853 he was among the group that escorted Antoinette Brown, Frances Gage, and other women reformers to New York City's World Temperance Convention where they were expelled for challenging the "men only" rule. Higginson urged feminists to research gender injustice and create digests of state laws' biases, educational inequalities, and women's economic disadvantages.[43] He was the iconoclast who performed Lucy Stone's and Henry Blackwell's untraditional marriage ceremony. Years later, Higginson assisted them in forming the American Woman Suffrage Association and producing its *Woman's Journal*.

During the Civil War Higginson proved the value of being a man of letters; he preserved the South Carolina's freedmen in his "Leaves from an Officer's Journal," essays printed between Nov. 1864 and 1865 in the *Atlantic Monthly*. They were published in 1870 as *Army Life in a Black Regiment*, which has never gone out of print. Thomas Wentworth Higginson recorded invaluable first-hand information about freedmen's character and traits, including their affection, wit, merriment, simplicity, docility, and restraint. The activities he described cover their ecstatic dancing and storytelling; he even preserved the freedmen's songs.

Among Higginson's Sea Island responsibilities was educating teachers and Superintendents on topics like the contrabands' sense of justice. He believed military organization had an advantage over that of civilian volunteers in the area since it could enforce discipline. After Higginson visited Port Royal's nearby plantation houses to socialize and eat wonderful meals, he spent time with workers like Mary, George, and Frances Gage who assisted him with military recruitment. Gage's admiration for Higginson was self-evident. In a March 1863 article she sent to

Garrison's *Liberator,* Higginson was called the "great champion of Liberty" who was generating the First South Carolina Regiment.[45]

On May 22, 1863, the Union government's General Order No. 143 created the U. S. Colored Troops and established a Bureau for their administration. One was the 54th Volunteer Regiment from Massachusetts which consisted of northern freedmen recruited by the state's Governor, John A. Andrew, and Frederick Douglass. The state's 54th Volunteer Regiment of freedmen were recruited from a broad area; they received $3.00 less than white troops. This regiment included two of Douglass's sons, Frederick and Lewis. Under pressure from Secretary of War, Edwin W. Stanton, Lincoln's cabinet repealed America's 1792 law barring "persons of color from serving in the militia." With the Union under duress, it was hoped that black volunteers would publicize freedmen's value, and the 54th would aid further recruitment of African American soldiers.

Gov. Andrew appointed a Harvard graduate, Col. Robert Gould Shaw, to head the regiment. He had been serving the Union as Captain of the Second Massachusetts Infantry Regiment. President Lincoln's mid-Atlantic strategy was to have Shaw's black regiment's triumph over Confederates at Morris Island and lead the conquest of Charleston. In the spring of 1863, the handsome and charismatic Shaw initially visited the Sea Islands and met Col. Higginson, head of South Carolina's first regiment. Residents like Frances Gage compared the two men and heard rumors about the handsome Shaw's military prowess and confidence that he would lead his men to victory. Little did Gage know that her "brave fellows from the wild hills of Southern Ohio" would have their fate intertwined with that of Shaw's black soldiers.

On the whole, Port Royal military officials did not relish having visitors and civilians under foot. Yet, both groups attended social gatherings, and the most popular civilian was the famous nurse, Clara Barton. She arrived in the spring of 1863 with her brother who was assigned to the Quartermaster's Office on Hilton Head Island. The nurse's reputation preceded her from distinguished battlefield service at Antietam and Fredericksburg. She came as many did because of the current belief that a decisive confrontation was eminent between Confederates and the Union forces in the Port Royal vicinity. Clara Barton was a writer who assiduously took comprehensive notes about everything going on around her.[46] For example, she recorded a gathering where Higginson and others were comparing his regiment to that of Robert

Gould Shaw, which hadn't yet arrived. Higginson confidently assert that his contraband soldiers would prove at least as worthy as Shaw's northern recruits.

On New Years Day 1863, the freedmen of Higginson's First South Carolina Regiment officially entered Union military service at a ceremony staged by Brigadier General Rufus Saxton. This was his Port Royal celebration of the Emancipation Proclamation. The historic event was preserved by a number of commentators, among observers was the black northern schoolteacher, Charlotte Forten, and two participants, the scholarly Col. H.W. Higginson, and Parris Island's Superintendent, Frances Dana Gage, who was on the speakers' platform to address "the women" in the audience. Each of these persons wrote essays about the New Years Day event. Forten's and Higginson's accounts appeared in the *Atlantic Monthly*, while Gage covered the event for the *National Anti-Slavery Standard,* which was then reprinted in the *Liberator* and *Independent*. Part of it read: "The black soldiers were marshaled before the headquarters of Gen. Saxton—a stalwart band—proudly shouldering their guns . . . . [Saxton] then administered the oath . . . . [saying] 'God never made a man to a slave.' . . . They were free: Government had acknowledged their manhood."[46]

Sometime later, Gage composed a long poem, "Ballad of Port Royal, South Carolina," that lauded the day's historic significance, and she placed it at the conclusion of her 1866 anthology, *Poems*. This "Ballad" culminated her verse written to support anti-slavery milestones. Garrison's *Liberator* intoned her words, "three hundred thousand, of volunteer freemen, to be drilled in the camp, while the foe gathers power."

The other woman who recorded the Port Royal ceremony was Charlotte L. Forten, who was an African American descendant of slaves. Her father was an educator and prominent abolitionist who helped William H Garrison organize the American Anti-Slavery Society. She was born in Philadelphia and raised by a prominent Black abolition family in Salem, Massachusetts. She was the only African American attending the Higginson Grammar School for Girls and Salem Normal School. Then Forten became the first black teacher of white students at Salem's Epes Grammar School. Her poetry appeared in *The Liberator*. When in the winter of 1862 she read Pierce's report and learned of his concern for freedmen, Forten, like Gage, promptly signed up. She joined the

Philadelphia contingent of Gideonite teachers that arrived at St. Helena Island on October 28. Forten was assigned to Oaklands, an abandoned plantation on St. Helena Island that was across the Beaufort River from Parris Island. Here for two years she ably taught 140 freed children.

    Forten's *Journal,* "Notes from Life on the Sea Islands," was first published in the May and June 1864 *Atlantic Monthly.* Her engaging prose recreated the area's local color, including the village of Beaufort and St. Helena's slave quarters. She presented fearful northern teachers who dreaded Confederate intrusion. Forten also revealed her intelligent and humble view of key players in the Sea Island's drama, centering on Union officers Saxton, Higginson, and Shaw. Having heard Higginson lecture in Worcester, she was predisposed to see him as a hero. She admired the Brigadier as "one's ideal of an officer." But Charlotte Forten virtually swooned over Robert Gould Shaw, the man of "rare and singular charm" who she met when he visited the Sea Islands on June 3, 1863. He had great potential for heroism and was just itching to fight and reclaim Charleston.

    Forten's rendition of Saxton's patriotic New Year's Day activities highlights Col. Higginson's recruitment lecture to contrabands in the vast audience. Similarly, she twice described Frances Gage's work promoting freedmen's enlistments, which took a different tack. The Midwestern matron told her wards about Santa Cruz in the West Indies where slaves shed blood in order to gain independence. Gage urged the South Carolina freedmen to seize their god-sent opportunity to join Col. Higginson's regiment and help end the Civil War. Forten was impressed by Frances Dana Gage's calm competence and reputation as a writer which made her a role model for anti-slavery activism.

    Another abolitionist who came to the Sea Islands was Harriet Tubman. Secretary of War Stanton sent her to work with Pierce's Gideonites and freedmen. She was a veteran "conductor" of the Underground Railway and in South Carolina assisted in any way possible, whether serving in Camp Saxton as a cook, nurse, or scout. She asked Boston friends to send her an Amelia Bloomer dress in order for her to more easily cross enemy lines. Truth could scout the interior and locate rebel locations and even their mines in the water of the Combahee River. Her biographer, Christopher Looby," calls her "the first woman to plan and execute an armed expedition during the Civil War."[47] In June, Tubman led a raid up the Combahee River that raided Confederate outposts, destroyed stockpiles of weapons, and liberated 700 slaves; she retrieved two pigs for federal troops to eat. Higginson was fortunate to have her advice assist his men.

The Sea Islands in 1863 were rife with the sounds and scent of war hanging heavy in the spring air, and this certainly seemed an inauspicious time for socializing. Yet, ironically, it was when Frances Gage encountered the most meaningful female friendship of her life. Nurse Clara Barton was at Hilton Head Island with her quartermaster brother and met Mary Gage at a social gathering held by Barton's friend from Cleveland, Colonel John J. Elwell, Chief Quartermaster for the Department of the South. Barton's diaries record a pleasant chat with the teacher and promise that she would soon visit the Gages on Parris Island. The visit was delayed until April 28 because Barton was tending John Elwell's illness. She left Hilton Head accompanied by Captain Samuel T. Lamb, the son of her family doctor. Meeting "Aunt Fanny" in the unlikely setting of Parris Island's ruined plantation gardens was a life-changing experience for both women. Clara Barton was enchanted by the Gages' "little paradise of flowers" and stayed for three magical days.

Both women were noteworthy when they met, Barton for military nursing and Gage for her career as a reformer and author. The basis for their congenial friendship was shared experiences and aspirations. Each woman's life began with a similar girlhood—a retired soldier-turned farmer father, Universalism, and love of literature, poetry, and nature. Each was close to her family, admired the values of kinship, but also had a commitment to women's independence. As well, they shared a "burning sense of fairness in the moral right of democratic justice." They even commiserated about personal sufferings and career obstructions. Stark contrasts existed, too. Frances Gage was fifty-four, 13 years older than Barton, and the married mother of eight children. The war hero Barton remained unmarried, her career began with teaching, and she was childless at forty-two. Yet, the two women complemented each other's temperaments.

The Gage women soon returned Clara Barton's visit by going to see her Hilton Head rooms in the Quartermaster's headquarters. The famous nurse preferred to address Frances Gage by her Ohio pen name, "Aunt Fanny," a regional moniker that carried familial associations, and a Dana family designation turned literary pseudonym. It emphasized Gage's domestic side, so the two women's relationship began as titular aunt and niece but soon deepened into that of mother and daughter. For Gage, it was as if the war had brought her a grown-up ninth child. Biographer Stephen Oates describes the growing relationship with Barton addressing Gage as my "dear adoptive mother," and "dear womanly friend," while Gage was calling Barton, "my dear darling daughter" and titling herself, "your loving mother."

Barton offered Gage desk space in her Quartermaster's rooms. Accepting this kindness gave the older woman a much-appreciated respite from Parris Island's pressures since she only infrequently left the island by steamer or canoe. During the seven months they shared in the Sea Islands, as well as for the remainder of her life, Gage often wrote to Barton. Their acquaintance blossomed into a mutually sustaining friendship that continued through the remaining 21 years of Frances Gage's life.

Gage was touched by Clara Barton's loneliness and depression. She wished to assuage the younger woman's stress. Barton's sources of anxiety were both personal and professional. The nurse had a hopeless "crush" on a married man and a prickly relationship with military authorities. Barton appreciated the mother and daughter's warmth; she valued young Mary Gage as my "best young female friend." Their bond was deepened by sharing the crucible of a month's nursing duties in Morris Island's hospital tents. Near the end of Mary Gage's life, Clara Barton's appreciative letter of recommendation guaranteed her accommodation in a nursing home for "war veterans." This again underlined her gratitude to the Gages.

The diaries and letters Clara Barton wrote from Hilton Head Island complement those of the observant Charlotte Forten and add a broad and splendid record of Parris Island and Port Royal's social life. The nurse described Frances Gage as being thin with stately bearing and sharp eyes that rarely misjudged people or situations. Initially, the two women differed on reform issues. Gage thought the intelligent Barton's social views were too narrow and saw the potential of Barton's becoming a valued colleague and ally. The nurse observed the Ohioan's mentoring her on reform issues and obligingly expanded her views on abolition and women's rights. As examples, historian Elizabeth Brown Pryor discusses Gage's dedication to helping "colored boys" and instructing Barton that "all women needed more rights and had to work for them." Such interactions altered the tenor of Barton's life; as Pryor writes,

"Not until she met Frances D. Gage in 1863 did Barton know a woman who challenged her as men did."[47]

The relative peace during the spring of 1863 was interrupted in June by personal tragedy that forced Frances Gage to paddle to Hilton Head in a dugout canoe during a nor'easter. This was a perilous voyage across some half dozen nautical miles where treacherous currents and tidal differences of as much as 11 feet occurred. She was drenched and determined to leave by the next steamer because she had just learned that her husband, James, was dying in the Midwest. This turned out to be a sadly belated warning since he had died on June 18, nine days earlier at the home of his brother, John, in Lake County, Illinois and was buried in Woodland Cemetery, McHenry County. Frances Gage planned to quickly return to South Carolina, but was delayed by grieving, tying up family affairs, and lecturing for freedmen's support. Because of gaps in communication, she did not know the Union had commenced the Morris Island siege or the danger of Barton's and Mary Gage's involvement.

Left behind on Parris Island, everyone braced themselves for an impending conflict. In July, the Union was encouraged by several developments, like the Battle of Gettysburg. On July 1, General Robert E. Lee was forced to withdraw into Virginia; on July 4, Confederate forces surrendered to Union forces in Vicksburg, Mississippi. The next step was supposed be the Charleston campaign that would end the war. This conflict began on July 7 when Ohio's 62nd Infantry Regiment captured fourteen Confederate siege guns, garrison equipage, and prisoners.

In preparation for the bigger Morris Island battle, medical support was sent from Port Royal harbor on the Flagship Fulton. It brought Nurse Clara Barton and her friend, Chief Quartermaster Col. John J. Elwell, who provided her with a saddle horse and ambulance.50 Hospital areas were established at the safer end of the island. Soon another steamship, the Philadelphia, carried Mary Gage and other visitors to visit Barton, and they invited her aboard for supper. Afterwards, Mary Gage volunteered to join Clara Barton and assist nursing wounded Union soldiers. Sadly, nothing else about the Battle of Morris Island went well.

Historian Steven Wise describes the stages of the upcoming battle.[49] The biggest obstacle that Union forces needed to overcome was Morris Island itself, 840 acres of uninhabited sand dunes that were unattractive battle sites. It was accessible only by boat.

Confederates had prepared two earthen roofed "forts," Fort Wagner and Battery Greg. The fort was circled by a ten-foot moat with a sluice gate for seawater. Rebel fortifications included land mines, sharpened palmetto takes, and an earthen wall. Confederate sharpshooters were camouflaged and quiet. The island was shrewdly designed for Rebel sharpshooters to be impervious to incoming shells, and they were positioned to shower a deadly crossfire into enemy lines.

The Union did no reconnaissance or training of its troops. General Quincy A. Gillmore, the Union leader in charge, used no guides, nor requested softening skirmishes. He asserted that 280 days of bombardment, the new science of gunnery tactics, must be adequate to have flattened enemy defenses. Moreover, the unit intended to head the attack was led by the glamorous Col. Robert Gould Shaw. Nonetheless, on July 18 Gillmore commanded the Massachusetts 54th Volunteer Regiment of black troops to take Fort Wagner. They were unprepared and entered a well-baited trap. Wily Rebel defenders waited until Shaw and his men reached the fort's parapet. Then the heroic black soldiers were mowed down, and their white leader died beside them. All were hastily buried on Morris Island, including Frederick Douglass' 22-year-old son. His brother, Lewis, survived. General Gilmore never explained about the delay sending reinforcements; when the more experienced Ohio 62nd Regiment soldiers arrived, Confederate snipers also pinned them down.

The ferocious Morris Island assault claimed 40% casualties of the 62nd, killing 500 Ohio men. That first day, July 18, the regiment lost 150 men, including all commissioned officers. Years later, a veteran of the McConnelsville regiment described "Rebs" calling Morris Island a "slaughter pen." "E" explained the problem was the Confederate's proximity to Shaw's and Putnam's men. He described survivors' discomforts as they huddled in trenches; these included sand flies, mosquitoes, and the fierce southern sun. The soldiers were thirsty, hungry, and deafened by the constant roar of bombardments and infantry.[51] Union leaders changed the name of Morris Island's Battery Gregg to Fort Putnam as a tribute to the Ohio "boys" grit from "Putnam's Brigade."

Originally, Col. Higginson's First South Carolina Regiment had been assigned to be the third unit that would follow Ohio's 62nd and 67th Regiments. Gilmore changed his orders after the initial onslaught decimated Shaw's Massachusetts 54th Volunteer

Regiment and badly chewed up the Ohio soldiers; he told Higginson's men to pull back and support the siege. They did so for 58-days, stopping only after Confederate soldiers stealthily evacuated the island by sea on Sept. 7. The Rebels won the battle, leaving behind 1,115 Union dead and 1,689 casualties. The Union's control of Morris Island never led to its being used as a launching point for an attack on Charleston.

Thus Col. T. W. Higginson's First South Carolina Regiment escaped the worse consequences of Gilmore's misjudgments. One factor in Higginson's freedmen' survival in the siege was that they alone had effective training. Starting in the spring of 1863, Higginson introduced his men to military action by taking them on several small military expeditions to Florida and Georgia. They were led by Harriet Tubman who came to Port Royal with Pierce's workers and operated under orders from Secretary Stanton. She assisted in various ways from nursing, to cooking, or spying. Tubman, it was said, cooked and fed Col. Robert Gould Shaw what turned out to be his last meal.

Between Jan. 23 and Feb. 1, 1863, she, the veteran "conductor" of the Underground Railway, scouted rivers and marshes for Col. Higginson's Regiment, infiltrated Confederate lines, and took his men up the St. Mary's River to rescue slaves from behind Confederate lines.[50] During one of these exploratory raids on the South Edisto River near Wiltown Bluff, South Carolina on May 1863, Higginson was injured while leading the regiment. A letter he sent to his mother described the mishap as receiving a "knock in his side from Confederate artillery."[52] This injury lamed him before the Morris Island battle, so he was sidelined, and Lt. Col. Trobridge led his soldiers in the Morris Island siege and the rest of the war. In August, Col. H. W. Higginson was sent him home for further recuperation, and in October he was discharged from the United States Army. Later he acknowledged the "other" black regiment's notoriety and mentioned regret that his regiment was not placed within immediate reach of Fort Wagner.

The dead Col. Robert Shaw and his black soldiers were called heroes. Their celebrity status with Union leaders and the public promoted freedmen's recruitment. Federal propaganda used the martyrdom of these men as proof of freedmen's innate nobility and loyalty to the Union. They orchestrated a patriotic melodrama about abolition and the gratification of men's sacrifice. The 54th Regiment's fame was spread by pro-military art. For instance,

Ohio-bred Alice Cary penned a poem, "Hero of Fort Wagner,"[53] that celebrated the Morris island battle. Louisa May Alcott, who nursed soldiers in Washington, D. C. and authored *Hospital Sketches*, composed a wiser treatment of the Fort Wagner mayhem in a story published in the *Atlantic Monthly* in 1867 called "My Contraband; or, the Brothers." This story presents two half-brothers, one in Shaw's 54th Regiment, the other a Confederate sharpshooter who unwittingly kills his sibling.[54] Augustus Saint Gaudens erected a monument on Boston Commons to commemorate the 54th Massachusetts Infantry, and William James dedicated this. The episode's reverberations continued in 1890 when the Chicago firm Kurtz & Allison produced a dramatic chromolithograph called "Storming Fort Wagner." In 1964, Robert Lowell's poem "For the Union Dead" similarly celebrated Shaw's men.

On the other hand, the dark truth of the Morris Island battle can be found in Clara Barton's journals, the notes of war correspondents, and commentaries by a few surviving soldiers. One "embedded" journalist called Clara Barton, that "noble and heroic Worcester woman," and expressed awe of her remarkable physical courage. He described her walking and riding amidst the carnage while remaining unscathed. One of her selfless acts of courage was the rescue of her friend, Col. John J. Elwell. The Head Quartermaster was there to observe, but after seeing the carnage, he started back to beg Gilmore for reinforcements. However, it was not be because an Enfield cartridge ripped into his leg, throwing Elwell off his horse and into the melee. Clara Barton saw this and ran to him through raining bullets; she applied a tourniquet and sought help. Elwell recorded later, "two boys of the 62nd of Ohio found me and carried me" out of the line of fire. They put him on a horse, and he dazedly rode a mile and a half back to the Union hospital tents.[55] Of course, Clara Barton, Mary Gage, and Union medics shared the physical miseries of injured soldiers and worked around the clock in hospital tents. As well, in post battle lulls they scoured the island's sandy beaches for survivors. Then they re-walked the sands to locate bodies for quick burials in the July heat.

Mary Gage volunteered to be the only woman nurse on a hospital ship that transported wounded soldiers back to Port Royal. With her mother away in Ohio, Mary gained independence. When Frances Gage returned to Parris Island late in July, the siege was underway, her friend and daughter were still on Morris Island, and wounded soldiers were being shipped back to Beaufort. Frances

Gage pitched in to help and was glad on August 18 when Gen. Gilmore forced Clara Barton to return to Hilton Head because of her dysentery. Before long, the recovering Barton wanted to return to Morris Island, but the General declared Union regulations prevented it. He did not want Clara Barton to die there. Seven years later Frances Gage finally expressed in writing her dismay over Mary's risk. She waited because neither her daughter nor Clara Barton would accept criticism of their labors on Morris Island. "Mother" knew it would be unwise to articulate her fear. All she wrote was, "four weeks term of nursing among the wounded and dying of Morris Island!"[56]

The Gage family's acquaintances in the 62nd Ohio Infantry Regiment, unlike Col. Shaw's men, did not become famous from their role in the Morris Island battle. The civilians with the Port Royal Experiment helped nurse Union survivors, and in so far as she could, Frances Gage sought out maimed soldiers she knew from Ohio's 62nd Regiment. The matronly Gage complained to Clara Barton, for whom all soldiers were strangers, how terrible it was to grieve over "local Buckeye boys," that included "scores of young men I have known for years, dead."[57]

Survivors of Ohio's 62nd Infantry Regiment on Nov. 7 returned to Hilton Head for guard duty. In April 1864, the regiment went to Yorktown, Virginia, and in 1865, it joined Lt. General Ulysses S. Grant's Union Forces at the Battle of Appomattox Courthouse. This was the war's final engagement. When the Ohio 62nd Regiment was mustered out on Dec. 12, 1865, it had 293 survivors, which was half its original size; 150 Ohio enlisted men were dead from disease and 131 from combat.[58]

Higginson's men largely survived. Led by Lt. Col. Trobridge, the First South Carolina Regiment was sent to Folly Island to rest after the Morris Island siege. They were later at the battle of Honey Hill, captured a fort on James Island, took Jacksonville, Florida, and invaded part of Tide Water, South Carolina. In February 1865, the regiment was assigned guard duty in Charleston and marched to Savannah. On Feb. 9, 1866, surviving members of the First South Carolina Regiment were mustered out of military service on Morris Island's burial site of Shaw and his Union dead.[59]

One consequence of the mounting deaths in the Sea Islands was the call for a new national cemetery near Beaufort, and it became the resting place for more than 9,000 soldiers. This figure included

4,400 "unknown soldiers" and 1,700 African American soldiers. With bravery and dedication, 179,000 black men served as the United States Colored Troops after May 22, 1863. Their segregated units continued to be led by white officers. They received less pay and were designated "United States Colored Troops" until President Harry Truman changed the law in 1948 and integrated black soldiers.

After the summer battle in 1863, Morris Island seemed irrelevant; no attack on Charleston followed, though the sea bombardment continued. Somehow the tenor of events was changed in the Sea Islands. Frances Gage's "war correspondence" for the *Liberator, National Anti- Slavery Standard*, and *Independent* newspapers, for instance, shifted from writing about wounded soldiers to focusing upon freedmen's sufferings. For example, on August 29, 1863 she concentrated on rampaging disease, saying my "whole island seemed like a hospital, small-pox, chicken pox, fevers." Gage's missive ends with the story of an aged black "nuss" who recounted the history of black women's sexual abuse on the Means' Plantation and cited the excessive mortality rate amongst its half-breed children.[60] Gage elaborates in an October 16 missive praising the Parris Island freedmen who harvested a robust cotton crop and volunteered their own produce to feed wounded and sick soldiers. The essay's most riveting feature was an interview with an elderly slave woman whose job on the Means plantation was collecting three-week old babies from their field hand mothers and trying to feed a hundred or so babies hominy soup. Fewer than half survived. Gage added, "These human animals were to be reared for the auction block."[61]

On September 16, 1863 Frances Gage learned that President Lincoln was going to sell South Carolina's coastal land. The Union owned most of the sea Island land, including Parris Island where units were reserved to be sold to "the heads of families of the African race." Also, parts of two Parris Island plantations were designated to be School Farms of 160 acres. General Saxton issued a circular to the freedmen that authorized them to locate lands that were about to be sold by the U. S. Tax Commissioner. He urged them to buy land by submitting a description and paying a deposit for $1.25 per acre, not exceeding 20 acres per family. Government lands would be thrown open for bids at the first tax sale in the spring of 1864. The second sale took place in March Yet in the spring of 1864, the Union still owned most of the Sea Island land.[62] This meant that Superintendents and teachers of the Port Royal Experiment were becoming redundant.

Gage and her cohorts in the Port Royal Experiment realized their job was over.

The widow had no desire to stay and watch the disassembly of her Parris Island community. The charms Port Royal, Beaufort, and Hilton Head were now numbed memories. She wrote an essay, "A Few Thoughts on the War," for *The National Anti-Slavery Standard* about her widow's grief. After her resignation with Brigadier General Rufus Saxton, she departed on Dec. 19, 1863. Her fears were expressed in a Jan. 3, 1864 letter she wrote to her Ohio friend Rebecca Janney, "The lands are to be sold for taxes in February and we will tremble for the result."[64]

She sailed on a steamship to Fernandina on Florida's Amelia Island. Here Gage stretched her legs and assisted at its Union hospital. The "sunshine state" was the third to secede from the Union, but never played a significant role in the Civil War. In 1862, a flotilla of 28 Union gunboats took Amelia Island without firing a shot because General Lee had anticipated Union presence and evacuated his Confederate troops. The island's incomplete Fort Clinch never served a military purpose; it became a Union supply base and military hospital until 1869 when Union troops departed. During Frances Gage's brief stay at Fernandina, she appreciated a change of scenery, but after 13 months of dealing with military culture in the South decided her best service to the Union would be a return to the northern lecture circuit.

That year, 1864, Frances Gage was hired by the Western Sanitary Commission as a lecturer and recruiter. Stephen Mintz describes it as the major philanthropic organization that emerged from the Civil War.[65] It was modeled after an English organization that aided Crimean War veterans and coordinated relief by distributing medical supplies. This was a precursor to the American Red Cross and began its role in Sept. 1861 by promoting sanitary Union Army camps and field hospitals in lands west of the Mississippi. The Commission also operated hospital steamers on western rivers, sent medical staff to short-handed southern hospitals, and, after March 1862, assisted escaping refugees. In the summer of 1864, Gage volunteered for a medical mission down the Mississippi River into the South. She went to the cities of war-torn Memphis, Natchez, and Vicksburg to help nurse wounded soldiers. Ever fighting racism, Gage also insisted upon a work assignment in a so-called "Contraband Hospital" where she cared for black soldiers.

A highlight of her voyage presented itself when Frances Gage was invited to join an interesting daytrip as a guest of workers at the Vicksburg's Soldiers' Home. Their picnic excursion was to the unoccupied plantation of the Confederacy's President, Jefferson Davis. Frances Dana Gage's letter to the *Liberator*, called "Fourth of July at the House That Jeff Built," provides a fascinating account of his mansion and grounds. Northern readers were regaled with rich details about the contrast between slave owner's luxury and his slaves' squalor—their quarters were replete with whipping posts, manacles, and a jail.[66] This potent experience inspired Gage to include a satiric depiction of Jefferson Davis and his wife in her last novel, *Steps Upward*. Here she placed them at a pre-war social gathering in Washington, D. C. where Davis darkly schemes for the Confederacy. When her southern Commission tour was finished, Gage's June 18 "Letter" in *The National Anti-Slavery Standard* adopts humorous military vocabulary to explain her upcoming plans: "I concluded about the first of August to change my base, and by a masterly retreat, or flank movement, or something, to escape the scourging enemy of the army and the South . . . having gathered my best weapons together . . . I sallied forth . . . to make an attack upon the State of Illinois."[67] She resumed lecturing but was disappointed to learn that her western audiences often wanted to hear about Clara Barton's nursing work and missing soldiers' project, not the woes of the freedmen.

For instance, Gage's 1864 speeches focused on the plight of "her" Sea Islands' freedmen, even, for example, explaining that she was collecting goods for a Parris Island store that would teach freedmen how to handle money. All her lecture proceeds, funneled through Rufus Saxton and the Freedman's Bureau, went to ex-slaves and soldiers, except compensation for personal expenses. She worked diligently to put the name of Parris Island and its freedmen in front of the American public, believing that if Northerners could sympathize with Sea Island freedmen, they would be glad to assist. In the spring, Gage joined fellow abolitionists in Philadelphia to celebrate the third decade of the American Anti-Slavery Society. On its platform, she spoke about freedmen's "goodness, patient hope, unwavering faith in God, and intense desire for knowledge" and fondly recalled Parris Island, her "lone little isle of the Sea."

Meanwhile, her restless friend, Clara Barton, also became unhappy in Beaufort and on December 27, 1863 she left for Washington, D. C. She was blocked from battlefront nursing, "Aunt Fanny" or "Mother" was gone, her man friend, John Elwell, was increasingly distant. Also her employer, the Union Patent Office, was withholding half her salary that she had been promised for medical supplies. Even Dorothea Dix, who carried the title Superintendent of Army Nurses, was breathing down her neck. So, eight days after Frances Gage left and two days after her 42nd birthday Barton boarded the steamship Fulton and left Hilton Head. Back in Washington, she received comforting letters from Frances Gage which aimed to stave off the nurse's tendency to depression. These epistles used the period's traditional female language of support for a friend's distraught heart, as "Mother" wrote," What shall I do to save, its love/ And stop its endless boiling? . . . So tell me darling what to do/ with your dear heart; I pray you do."[68]

Barton decided to help grieving northern families and turned her prodigious energies toward documenting the fate of missing Union soldiers. What she lacked was Congressional support, so in October 1864, she contacted the American Anti-Slavery Society's *Standard*'s office in New York City to request Frances Gage's forwarding address. She wanted her friend to come to the capital and assist.[68] At the time, the older woman was in St. Louis at her son's home and could not get to Washington until January 1865. Knocking on Mary Barton' door led to a month's visit; Gage talked about her experiences lecturing for Soldier's Aid Societies in New York, Pennsylvania, Ohio, Illinois, and Mississippi and described nursing in Vicksburg. Barton talked about the inadequacy of funding for tracing lost Civil War soldiers. Together the friends collaborated on a plan to persuade the Thirty-Ninth Congress to support Barton's work. Since the pen was Gage's forte, she wrote to the *Independent* newspaper and Congressional legislators. She moralized and chided them for ignoring the dead soldiers' issue. Congress soon granted the requested funds, and President Lincoln formalized Barton's appointment to lead the program. It took four grueling years for Clara Barton to issue a final report in 1869; the nurse verified the fate of 20,000 soldiers who were reported as missing in action. Her garret in Washington, D. C. where this work was done is located in a commercial building on 7th Street, N. W. Today it is open to the public as a Women's History Site operated by the General Services Administration.

Frances Gage resumed her lecture tour in the spring and summer of 1865. She traveled from New England to Pennsylvania, New York, Illinois, Missouri, as well as Ohio. Her highly popular lectures drew upon case histories and personal anecdotes which offered the audience a window into the experiences of injured soldiers and beleaguered freedmen. Aside from newspapers, Americans had no first-hand information about war events, unless they heard a participant like Frances Gage speak. She was powerful on the public platform, as historian James Parton noted she addressed audiences less as an orator than as an extemporaneous talker, and as a result Frances Gage never failed to hold an audience.68 For instance, a typical reviewer in Nov. 20, 1863 wrote in the *Syracuse Journal* that one of her lectures filled the house with an "audience [that] listened with unabated attention . . . [about] the damage which slavery has done . . . and of the Freedmen's Relief Association ['s work]." He concluded, Mrs. Gage is a "fluent, graceful, and impressive speaker."[69]

    Then in September her speaking career ended when tragedy struck. It was after an evening's program at Dr. Edward Beecher's church in Indiana. He was an old friend who had formed the state's first anti-slavery society; of course he was a member of the famous Beecher family whose name was identified with clerical abolitionism. Following her address, Frances Gage was injured in an upturned carriage accident that damaged her spine, ribs, and shoulder. Through that fall and into the winter of 1866, she painfully convalesced at her son's home in St. Louis. In March, she was well enough to take her daughters to a rental house in New Jersey where she could continue recuperating.

    Her immediate preoccupation as the war wound down was her soldier sons who signed up for military duty in the Union army. At least she could supervise the son and daughter who served with her at Parris Island and Beaufort. Two of her sons enlisted when the war commenced. In the fall of 1862, Ambrose Gage joined the 125th Regiment of the Ohio Infantry with the rank of first sergeant and was mustered out with the same rank. His unit went by train and steamboat to Louisville, Nashville, and Chattanooga. In January 1863, General Woods christened it "The Tiger Regiment of Ohio." and described its being "conspicuous for bravery." After Atlanta fell, the 125th Regiment returned to protect Nashville, and then was sent to Louisiana and Texas.

    Their youngest son, Joseph Gage, enlisted as a private and completed his service as first lieutenant with the 19th Independent Battery, Ohio Light Artillery. This unit was organized at Xenia on Jan. 9, 1862, mustered at Camp Dennison, and was sent to St. Louis, Missouri. It did picket and scouting duty in West Virginia, marched through many states, served at Vicksburg and beyond, until she wrote its "men were worn out with sickness and service." Another son, Charles Gage, was mustered into service on May 9, 1864; he joined the 154th Regiment, Ohio Infantry, which was the state's National Guard; his unit formed in Columbus. It went to West Virginia to perform guard, picket, and escort duty until the war's end. Charles entered as a sergeant and held the same rank at war's end.[71]. She especially fretted over her youngest son, Joseph, who was an exhausted foot soldier marching with Sherman's armies through South Carolina, and Gage was sick at heart over her nephew, Jared Gage, who was languishing in Georgia's infamous prison camp, Andersonville

    Finally, Charleston's Confederate forces under General Beauregard evacuated the flattened Charleston on Feb. 15, 1865, and the Union Navy resumed its peaceful cruising in Charleston's harbor. Three days later, Union troops entered. In distant lands, the fall of Charleston brought international jubilation. For example, the *New York Times* on March 22, 1865 quoted the *London Times*' coverage describing Liverpool's abundant placards reading, "Babylon the Great is fallen," a quote borrowed from the 18th Chapter of *Revelations*.

    Gage had waited more than two years for this resolution yet felt little glee when it occurred. The ugliness of the Sea Islands confrontation ended what began at Fort Sumter. There were abolitionists who muttered that it was a pitiful and anticlimactic for the exhausted nation. Gage was distressed about the destruction the Union had wrought and appalled at the cost in terms of humanity and property, as exemplified by the flattened city of Charleston that was once America's "most beautiful city." Back in 1863, Frances Gage had yearned for the "men from the southern hills of Ohio" to overrun Charleston. What she sought was an ideological triumph, the ending of the rebellion and Charleston's secessionist symbolism, not the city's devastation. As the granddaughter and daughter of men who designed and built magnificent homes, she appreciated architecture and saw that buildings had aesthetic, historic, sentimental, and symbolic value. She had seen ruins on Blennerhasset Island, in the West Indies, and the Sea Islands' moldering plantation houses. Gage experienced arson at her home in St. Louis, and lived amidst ruins on Parris Island while being deafened by the roar of bombardments. The dubious protection of a few Union pickets never made the Gages feel inviolate.

The war's physical consequences are described in her poem "Coming Home" published in July 1865; it tells of her sons surviving "picket, march, and raid, and many a bloody battle-field." They are placed on a map: one in "Texas, one in Tennessee, and one marching with Sherman to the sea." Through sheer luck James and Frances Gages' children survived, though each was changed by war. The worst was Joseph who suffered in a Union hospital and never recovered fully from chronic health issues caused, she believed, by encampments' vile sanitary conditions. After mustering out, Joe lived near his mother and slowly recuperated. Frances Gage watched his lingering health problems and in 1882, near her own death, complained to Clara Barton about how the war damaged her baby, saying, Joe departed from me at the age of 19, "left all his life's interests to serve his country and was released to me only when the war closed—a broken down man—not injured by bullets but by disease, the dysentery in the camp . . . made him unfit."[70]

Inevitably, some of the war's dead were known to Aunt Fanny, like the son of her fellow Ohio reformer, Hannah Tracy Cutler. A number of the Gage boys' friends from McConnelsville were also unfortunate. Frances Gage described her deep pity, for instance, for the tragedy of a McConnelsville neighbor, Mrs. Morris whose son joined Ohio's 62nd Infantry and served as part of the Putnam Brigade. He was among the dead at the "fight of Wagner" in July 1863.

Frances Gage followed the newspaper stories about the end of the conflict. The Civil War saga that began with South Carolina's secession on Dec. 17, 1860 and concluded on April 9, 1865, with General Robert E. Lee's surrender. On April 14, five days later, President Abraham Lincoln was assassinated. This vicious act transferred leadership to a Southerner, Andrew Johnson, who became 17th President of the United States. She deplored his being a slave-owning U. S. Senator from Tennessee whose reactionary spirit could drastically alter post-war history. Johnson's reactionary agenda was revealed on May 29 when he pardoned war crimes and gave amnesty to Southern landowners. He restored planters' property and limited freedmen's right to buy confiscated land that was condemned and sold by decree.

Many freedmen had already received leases for a small number of acres and were told to evacuate their homes. Those who refused were forcibly removed by Union soldiers, some of whom destroyed their land "certificates." Nonetheless, on Parris Island between April 17, 1865 and Nov. 27, 1869 many former soldiers and community residents Gage had supervised were issued Head of Family Certificates; these went to 208 black men and women who wished to remain on Parris Island and preserve their large freedmen's community. Of course, the wealthy Confederate Means family quickly "redeemed" much of Parris Island's useful acreage. [71]

The key abolitionists in the Sea Islands region drifted away. It was as if the drama of the transformative process begun in 1862 and 1863 was silently reversed in 1864. Pierce ceased visiting the Sea Islands and remained in Massachusetts where he became famous as a writer, biographer, and philanthropist. Most Gideonites and anti-slavery reformers went home. For example, H. W. Higginson returned to scholarly pursuits in New England; Charlotte Forten left St. Helena's classrooms in late fall 1863 and returned to New England where she married into the abolitionist Grimke family. A century later, these fellow writers, Higginson and Forten, were celebrated by the cultural critic Edmund Wilson in his study *Patriotic Gore*. He commented that their Sea Islands' interval must have been "a strange new experience, both idyllic and exacting."[72]

Brigadier General Rufus Saxton, the supervisor of the Sea Islands, in 1865 was named Assistant Commissioner of the Freedmen's Bureau for South Carolina. Saxton was a committed and honorable man who continued to fight for African Americans having the "highest right to a soil they have cultivated." His enemies were resentful Southern plantation owners who accused Saxton of being too liberal with supplies for the Sea Islands' freed slaves and "too much the advocate of his wards," who trusted and loved him.[73] In January 1866, Rufus Saxton was returned to his pre-war grade of Major in the Quartermaster Department of the Army. Thirty years later, in 1893, he was awarded America's Medal of Honor for his work at Harper's Ferry, rather than his unique and valuable work in the Sea Islands. Aside from abolitionists who appreciated his conscientiousness, like Forten and Gage, Saxton received little contemporary credit for his stewardship of freedmen.

An important exception came from retired Union officer Carl Schurz who in the fall of 1865 was assigned to assess conditions in the post-war South. He was tasked with producing a Congressional Report by December that would describe Saxton's management of the cotton harvests of 1863 and 1864.[74] Schurz was impressed by the successful management of the Freedmen's Bureau that fed, clothed, protected, and medically assisted countless needy freedmen. Overall, the records show that Saxton's Bureau spent $17,000, established

4,000 schools, 100 hospitals, and provided food and homes for countless former slaves. Carl Schurz defined its most lasting achievement as being the groundbreaking establishment of schools—educational institutions that grew into South Carolina's state public school system.[75] He was accompanied and assisted by Ulysses S. Grant. However, President Johnson ignored their report.

This President enjoyed power for only one term during which he obstructed Reconstruction—he vetoed Constitutional Amendments that would empower black men, as well as Freedman's Bureau funding Bills, Civil Rights Bills, and Reconstruction Acts. Each veto was overridden by a Republican Congress. He was ironically saved from impeachment in March 1868 by Salmon P. Chase who was now a Supreme Court Justice and voted against it. The unabashed Johnson continued to veto extensions of the Freedman's Bureau. Racist attacks such as one in *The Nation* on July 19, 1866.[76] had the effect of rendering the Bureau impotent. Ulysses S. Grant became President in 1866; his Republican-controlled Congress terminated the Freedmen's Bureau in 1870, except for its work in education. Two years later, President Grant and Congress ended that too. Contemporaries like Gage, Pierce, Chase, and Schurz watched these developments. A twentieth-century scholar summarized, "The story of the government's mismanagement of the problem of the abandoned lands in South Carolina is a sad one."[79]

Though Port Royal Experiment's promise for the Sea Islands was never fulfilled, an observer could see some changes were afoot. A few freedmen blossomed like Robert Smalls who was born into slavery and descended from slaves stolen from Guinea. His father was a white Beaufort merchant who used the boy as a house slave. Robert Smalls stole a Confederate transport steamer that was loaded with armaments and gained fame during the Civil War. Celebrated as a "hero," Smalls met President Abraham Lincoln and was lionized by Greeley's *New York Tribune*. He aided recruitment of black troops, was the United States Navy's first black captain of a vessel, and purchased the Beaufort house where he was once a slave. He served as a State Senator and Reconstruction Congressman for nearly 20 years. For five decades, Smalls was called the most important black person in South Carolina.[78] In 1909, Robert Smalls persuaded Congress to establish a naval station on Parris Island. This was after Frances Gage's death, but it meant that finally the Means family had to leave Parris Island. Its freedmen were reimbursed for their land and relocated.

The once contentious location became useful for the Marine Corps. The Gullah culture Frances Dana Gage tried to nourish on Parris Island in 1863 was to be fostered elsewhere.

Other consequences of the war fell into place. The former Confederacy President, Jefferson Davis, was incarcerated at Virginia's Fortress Monroe where in 1861 Edward L. Pierce had supervised a freedmen's retreat. The *Liberator* ceased on Dec. 29, 1865 because William Lloyd Garrison stated in his "Valedictory" that: "extermination of chattel slavery," was gloriously consummated. His Anti-Slavery Society dissolved in 1867, though its other organ, the *National Anti-Slavery Standard,* continued until the Fifteenth Amendment passed in 1870. Such optimism was, in one sense, naive and premature since "peace" and "victory" in practice meant that most ex-slaves in the South had to shift for themselves. A Reconstruction historian, James Brewer Stewart, writes "In theory, for a time in practice, emancipated slaves came to enjoy full legal protection and civil rights . . . But in the end . . . [it] led to sharecropping, segregation, and the terrors of white vigilantism."[79]

Between Frances Gage's recuperation from the carriage accident in 1865 and the summer of 1867 when she was paralyzed, the Ohio-born reformer was recognized as a bright light amongst abolitionists. Her newest concern was that black women deserved to be included in pending suffrage legislation. Frances Dana Gage lectured, for instance, at the Twenty Ninth Annual Meeting of Pennsylvania's Anti-Slavery Society where one of her auditors was the *Independent*'s editor Theodore Tilton. He admired Gage and at the Dec. 27, 1866 Eleventh National Woman's Rights Convention, quoted her speech; he proposed a new organization to be called the American Equal Rights Association or AERA. It would combine justice issues for both race and sex. He suggested that the *National Anti-Slavery Standard* could be its organ, though some women's advocates bristled. Garrison declined involvement, but Frederick Douglass, joined the AERA.

The American Equal Rights Association began in the spring of 1866 as a coalition of experienced reformers. On March 31, Frances Gage attended its Women's Rights Committee meeting about strategy. The AERA hired Gage to work as a writer and speaker. At its first meeting, Elizabeth Cady Stanton was the keynote speaker, followed by Frances D. Gage, who emphasized freedwomen's need for the vote. Next on the podium was Gage's

Sea Islands employer, Major Rufus Saxton. The coalition's second meeting on May 9, 1867 was presided over by the Quaker Abolitionist Lucretia Mott; its program included the octogenarian Sojourner Truth. Then Henry Ward Beecher, a supporter of the AERA's demand for universal suffrage, surprised the audience by proposing that only African American men should receive suffrage. He wanted the AERA to push for women's inclusion at a later time. There was an uproar.

Paralyzed by her first stroke in July 26, 1867, Frances Dana Gage could no longer work for the organization. At the third meeting of AERA on May 14, 1868 at the Cooper Institute in New York City letters were read from John Stuart Mill and Frances D. Gage; her daughter Mary E. Gage served as Corresponding Secretary. At its fourth meeting in 1869, competing tensions publicly surfaced when Elizabeth Cady Stanton called African Americans "Sambo." Frederick Douglass challenged her saying that he would no longer tolerate racism. This event forced the disbanding of the AERA.

The public saw conflict. Elizabeth Cady Stanton's views were complex. The opposition faction was led by Lucy Stone who insisted the reformers remain committed to both race and sex equity. After the withdrawal of Stanton and her followers, Stone's faction took the name American Suffrage Association or AWSA, and Frances Gage supported them. Race however, received little attention after passage of three Constitutional Amendments. Frances Gage celebrated the passage of America's Thirteenth Amendment on Dec. 6, 1865 that abolished slavery, as well as the Fourteenth Amendment that passed on July 9, 1868; it redefined "citizenship" to include ex-slaves. Then on Feb. 3, 1870 the Fifteenth Amendment passed promising no citizen could be denied the right to vote based on "race, color, or previous condition of servitude." Gage wrote from Vineland on May 10, 1870 that these three anti-slavery Constitutional Amendments crowned "my labors of twenty-five years."[80] However, she remained distressed over black and white women not having the franchise.

Gage believed the worst justifications for slavery were abolished. Her body had once been threatened by lameness and typhoid fever had "impaired her memory and health for a number of years." But her noteworthy stamina never returned after the 1865 carriage crash and 1867 stroke. Frances Gage surveyed her situation. Lacking health, financial resources, wealthy relatives, home, or husband, she wrote "Aunt Fanny in the Garden," for her Ohio readers on Aug. 6, 1865. This essay was, of course, published in a farm journal and shows Gage reassessing her role as reformer, war correspondent, and freedmen's advocate.[81] The countless lectures and military experiences had emptied her emotional reserves. So, before additional strokes rendered her impotent, Gage decided she must support herself through writing.

Convalescence was occupied by publishing a volume of poetry and three novels. The first and most impressive was *Elsie Magoon; or the Old Still-House in the Hollow*; it and *Poems* were published in 1867. Then two more works of fiction followed, each of which dealt with slavery. In 1869 *Gertie's Sacrifice* appeared, a moralistic novella that deals with racism, war separated families, and hardships for wives. Her final narrative was published in 1870; *Steps Upward* includes a freed slave who is content being a domestic but grieves over her stolen children.

Like John C. Zachos, who after the war produced a phonetic reader for the freedmen, Gage did not abandon her Sea Islands flock. She never forgot the impressive months spent in South Carolina and when health permitted visited the Low Country in South Carolina where her son, George, put down roots and raised a family. Also his married daughter, her niece, lived on Dumfuski Island under the married name Scouten.

At the same time, her friend, Clara Barton, was exhausted by her missing soldiers work and left America for Europe. While there, she became fascinated by different approaches to disaster clean up. Barton did not return until September 1873, went briefly to Washington, moved to Dansville, New York, and later retired to New England. The two old friends remained in contact, and the frail matron endeavored to express her unflagging admiration and support for Clara Barton's travails founding the Red Cross.

When they talked, Aunt Fanny admitted that the Civil War's tolls were the price the Gage family paid for being reform minded. Her husband died without the care of his children or wife. Their sons and daughters lived with a mother who was often away—Joseph Gage was a semi invalid; George Gage needed Barton's help for a military pension; Sarah Gage went to the Woman's Relief Corps Home at Madison Ohio, and noble Mary Gage—sold her home to pay for admittance to the Chapin Home in New York City—needed Clara Barton's imprimatur to remain. This was her reward for assisting Barton at the Battle of Fort Wagner on Morris Island.

Of course, anti-slavery reformers like Frances Gage believed such sacrifices were worthwhile because the Civil War ended America's slavery. She was proud to have contributed to the demise of this worst nineteenth-century injustice. Then, too, she never stopped wondering what happened to her black girlhood friend, Fanny.

Chapter Two

Notes

1. Frances Gage, "Reminiscences of Childhood" *Daily True Democrat,* September 19, 1850, 2.
2. Gage, "Looking Back" *The Woman's Advocate,* January 1869, 3.
3. Ibid.
4. L. P. Brockett and Mary C. Vaughan, *Woman's Work in the Civil War* (Philadelphia: Zeigler, McCurdy and Co., 1867), 683.
5. Frederick B. Tolles, ed., Lucretia Mott, "Slavery and the Woman Question, Lucretia Mott's Diary of her Visit to Great Britain," Supplement #23, *Journal of Friends Historical Society*, 1952.
6. James Parton, Horace and Greeley, eds., "The Woman's Rights Movement and Its Champions in the United States," in *Eminent Women of the Age* (Hartford: S. M. Betts & Co., 1871), 314.
7. Theodore Tilton, "*Mrs. Elizabeth Cady Stanton,*" in Parton et al. *Eminent*, 344.
8. Lydia Maria Child, "The Duty of Disobedience to the Fugitive Slave Act," Anti- Slavery Tract No. 9 (Boston: American Anti-Slaver Society, 1850).
9. Elizabeth Cady Stanton and Matilda Joslyn Gage, eds., *History of Woman Suffrage. 1881-1902,* 1 (New York: Schocken Books, 1971), 101.
10. E. D. Hudson, "Report from Mt. Pleasant," *The National Anti-Slavery Standard*, June 17, 18, June 17, 1840, no. 13: 6.
11. Stanton, *Eighty Years and More, Reminiscences, 1817-1897,* (New York: Schocken Books, 1971), 102.
12. Gage, *Poems (*Philadelphia: J. B. Lippincott, 1867), 212.
13. Ibid., 214.

14. Marius Robinson, "Akron Woman's Right Convention," *Salem Anti-Slavery Bugle,* June 21, 1851, 1.

15. Patricia R. Hill, "Writing Out the War: Harriet Beecher Stowe's Averted Gaze," in Ed. Catharine Clinton and Nina Silber *Divided Houses, Gender and the Civil War* (New York: Oxford University Press, 261.

16. Nell Irvin Painter, *Sojourner Truth, A Life, A Symbol,* (New York, W. W. Norton and Co., 1996), 154.

17. Gage, Sojourner Truth, "Aren't I a Woman?" *Independent, April 23, 1863; History,* 2, 541.

18. Painter, *Sojourner Truth,* 175.

19. "Reminiscences of Sojourner Truth," *Independent, 1866;* History, vol. 2, 541

20. Mari Jo Buhle and Paul Buhle, Eds. *The Concise History of Woman Suffrage (*Urbana: University of Illinois Press, 1978), 103.

21. Gage, "Reminiscences," 543.

22. Gage in Brockett, *Woman's Work*, 685.

23. Gage in Janney Family Papers. Collection Ms. No. 142, JBNox 4/5. Ohio Historical Society, Columbus, Ohio.

24. Edward Bartlett Rugemer, *The Problem of Emancipation, The Caribbean Roots of the American Civil War,* (New Haven, Yale University Press, 1988).

25. Gage, "Greetings," *Field Notes,* 1 January 3 (1861), 4.

26. ____,"Letter from F. D. Gage," *The Liberator,* March 1859, 41.

27 ____," Letter," *Liberator*, 29, no. 11, 1864.

28. ____, "Letter," *The Ohio Cultivator*, April 5, 1859, 142.

29. ____, "The Results of Emancipation in Santa Cruz," *National Anti-Slavery Standard*, June 11, 1859, 204.

30. ____, "Letter from Mrs. Gage," *Ohio Farmer*, June 18, 1859, 198.

31. ____, "Mrs. Gage at Home," *Ohio Farmer* vol. 8, no. 26 June 25, 1859: 208.

32. *Cleveland Herald*, April 12, 1861, 58.

33. Edward L. Pierce, "The Contrabands of Fortress Monroe," *Atlantic Monthly*, November 1861, 626-640.

34. _____, "The Negroes at Port Royal," *Atlantic Monthly*, September 1863; reprinted in *Rebellion Record*.

35. Brockett, 689.

36. Gage, "Last Moments of General Mitchell," *National Anti-Slavery Standard,* November 15, 1862, 3.

37. *Life of Luther C. Lad,* Concord, New Hampshire, P. B. Coggeswell Printer, 1862.

38. Robert Mills, *Statistics of South Carolina*, Spartanburg: The Reprint Company, 154.

39. Catharine Lee Shumpert, "The Eighteenth and Nineteenth Century Plantation Components on Parris Island, South Carolina," (M. A. Thesis: University of South Carolina, 2001) 79.

40. Michael Burlingame and John R. T. Ettlinger, eds. *Complete War Diary of John Jay* (Carbondale: Southern Illinois University Press, 1999), 57-58

41. Gage, Letter from Frances D. Gage," *Liberator*, March 2, 1863.

42. ____, "Letter from Mrs. Gage," *Liberator*, March 16, 1863.

43. Elizabeth Brown Pryor, *Clara Barton, Professional Angel,* (Philadelphia: University of Pennsylvania Press, 1997), 120.

44. Thomas Wentworth Higginson, "Letter to Mother," in *T. W. Higginson: the Story of his Life,* ed. Mary Thatcher Higginson (Boston: Houghton Mifflin, 1914), 230.

45. Pryor, 112.

46. Ibid., 145.

47. Steven R. Wise, *Gate of Hell, Campaign for Charleston Harbor, 1863,* Columbia, University of South Carolina Press, 1994, 38.

48. Oates, 115.

49. Higginson, "Letter," 148.

50. "E," Some Entertaining Reminiscences of the Siege of Morris Island," *National Tribune* (June 28, 1888), Philadelphia: Grand Army of the Republic Museum." 176.

51. Higginson, "Letter."

52. Alice Cary, "Hero of Fort Wagner, *The Poetical Works of Alice and Phoebe Cary*, (Cambridge: Riverside Press, 1880), 401.

53. Louisa May Alcott, "My Contraband; or, the Brothers," *Atlantic Monthly,* August 1863, 584-595.

54. Oates, 173.

55. Gage, Barton Correspondence.

56. Reid Whitlaw, *Ohio in the War,* vol. 1 (Cincinnati: Wilstach, Baldwin & Co., 1871) 368-372.

57. Larry Stevens, "The 62nd Ohio Infantry," <http://www. ohiocivilwar.comcw62.html>

58. ____, "Letter from Mrs. Gage," *The New York Tribune,"* Aug. 29, 1863.

59. ____, "Letter from Mrs. Gage," *The New York Tribune,"* Oct. 16, 1863.

60. Willie Lee Rose, *Rehearsal for Reconstruction: The Port Royal Experiment* (New York: Vintage Books, Random House, 1964), 296.

61. Gage, "A Few Thoughts on the War," *The National Anti-Slavery Standard*, 32, no. 51 (Dec. 19, 1863)),3.

62. ____," Letter," January 3, 1864 in Janney Correspondence.

63. Steven Mintz, *Moralists and Modernizers, America's Pre-Civil War Reformers,* (Baltimore: Johns Hopkins University Press, 1995).

64. Gage, "Fourth of July at the House that Jeff Built," *Liberator,* July 29, 1864, 1.

65. ____, "Letter from Mrs. Gage," *The National Anti-Slavery Standard* October 22, 1864, 3.

66. ____, Barton Correspondence.

67. Oates, 350.

68. James Parton, "Frances D. Gage," *Eminent Women of the Age* Hartford: S. M. Betts & Co., 1868, 383.

69. "West Indies," *Syracuse Journa*l, November 20, 1863.

70. Whitlaw, *Ohio*.

71. Gage, "Barton Correspondence."

72. Willie E. Rose, *Rehearsal for Reconstruction: The Port Royal Experiment.* (New York: Vintage Books, Random House, 1964), 296.

73. Edmund Wilson, *Patriotic Gore*, (New York: W. W. Norton and Company, 1994).

74. W. E. Burghardt Dubois, "The Freedmen's Bureau, *Atlantic Monthly*, vol., 87, 1901, 354-365.

75. Laura Josephine Webster, "The Operation of the Freedmen's Bureau in South Carolina,"" *Smith College Studies in History, January 1916,* vol. l, no. 2, *103.*

76. Carl Schurz and Ulysses S. Grant, "Report of the Joint Committee on Reconstruction," Executive Document no. 2, 39th Congress, 1st Session, Part 2, 233; Part 3, 35.

77. *The Nation,* July 19, 1866, 65.

78. W. E. Burghardt DuBois, he Freedmen's Bureau," *Atlantic Monthly*, 1901, 354-365.

79. <www.robertsmalls.org/about.htm>

80. James Brewer Stuart, *Holy Warriors*, (New York: Hill & Wang, 1966). 182.

81. Gage, "Letter, May 10, 1870," *History,* vol. 2, 789.

82. ____, "Aunt Fanny in the Garden," *Ohio Farmer* 14, no. 31 (Aug. 5, 1865), 241.

Chapter Three

"A Moveable Feast"

Frances Barker never forgot the humiliation caused by her father's gender rules. Her common sense insisted that gender prescriptions on the frontier were wrong headed. Despite the fact that she was only a child in the 1820s and 1830s, she resisted conformity, yet was anguished over criticism. When the Barker girl objected to masculine injustice, she was called "strange." This led France to cultivate a series of jokes about widening or breaking women's sphere. Her preoccupation with gender justice was uncharacteristic for a country lass whose only claims to just authority came in print. Some books, however, made things worse, most notably William Blackstone's *Commentaries on the Laws of England*. It defined the British legal code that justified unequal gender laws. Common law's rule of "coverture" most repelled the American girl since it argued that wives relinquish legal existence.

She saw in the village of Marietta the price some women paid for men's cruel injustice. There were vicious husbands who inflicted pain on their families, and no one intervened. One man whipped his wife and threw her and their children out of the house; another stole the money his wife earned from weaving so that he could continue a "binge." Such actions were legal. The girl's empathy for these victims led her to sympathize and complain about the problems with Blackstone. Joseph Barker was initially speechless and certainly was impressed by his young daughter's intellect. But instead of agreeing, he both flattered and hurt her by saying that she should have attended college and been "a lawyer. I wish you were a boy"[1]

The only sympathy France found came from her mother's less conventional Dana relatives in Belpre who preserved New England's liberal tradition of reform. For the rest of her life, she thanked them by signing much of her reform writing "Frances 'Dana' Gage." She wished to emulate them and serve as a role model for justice. Contacts with this liberal extended family set up a contrast to her patriarch's rigidity, and then she transitioned to a congenial husband who offered genuine moral support. Her move from the Barker homestead to James Gage's egalitarian home was fortuitous in every way. As she set up housekeeping in the village of McConnelsville, the bride found doors were opening for her. Both literally and metaphorically, the young woman stepped into public life, which eventually led to her identity as a noteworthy "woman's rights" leader.[2]

Frances Gage expanded her reading and knowledge beyond her father's small library. She was introduced to modern European viewpoints, like those of Alexis de Tocqueville and Harriet Martineau, each of whom reinforced her sense that American women's secondary legal status was unjust. The prescient Frenchman's 1835 *Democracy in America* asked why the new republic failed to extend liberty, equality, and "sorority" to women. de Tocqueville observed, "In no country has such constant care been taken . . . to trace two clearly distinct lines of action for the two sexes."[3] Two years later, Harriet Martineau's *Society in America* included an insightful chapter called "The Political Non-existence of Women." She compared American women's status to that of female plantation slaves. This so impressed the abolitionist Frances Gage in Ohio that she wrote an appreciative letter to Martineau.

Gage retained new knowledge that supported her beliefs, such as the fact that during America's Revolutionary War women raised money to pay Continental Army soldiers. Also, between 1790 and 1807, New Jersey women voted, participating in the ideal of self-government until men revoked their privilege. If foreigners were perplexed by masculine Americans' denial of legal status and citizenship privileges to women, so were the perceptive half of the culture that was hurt by this double standard. Countless female pioneers like the Danas did subsistence farming alongside men and defended their children against Indian attacks. Yet, like slaves, their roles were proscribed by males who pretended they were merely domestic. The anomaly that was not lost on Frances Dana Gage who, despite motherhood and household duties, developed strategies to assert herself and speak up for her fellow women. She "scribbled," submitting poems and articles to regional newspapers and periodicals, such as New York State's *Cauga Chief, Pittsburgh Saturday Evening Visitor,* and the *Ohio State Journal.* Years later in her 1883 autobiography she explained her rationale, "I shall write for women and children and men who will never hear one thing of my ideas in a Ladies Book."

Her reform interest was gratified in the summer of 1848 when the young matron was traveling in the Northeast with her husband and father-in-law. They read a newspaper account of Elizabeth Cady Stanton's Seneca Falls Women's Rights Convention. Gage was disappointed to note that Lucy Mott's husband, James, had presided. Her interest piqued, she studied Stanton's "Declaration of Sentiments." It was modeled after the nation's Declaration of Independence and included a call for regional women's rights conventions. Most radical of all, it argued women should receive the franchise.

Post-pioneer Ohio was already experiencing what Elizabeth Cady Stanton called for in 1848—local women's gatherings that could grow into regional women's rights conventions. Frances Gage had been inviting women into her home to talk about her three commitments, temperance, abolition, and women's rights. Initially she feared her "notoriety as an Abolitionist" might scare other women off, making it "difficult for me to reach people at home."[4] Frances Gage believed the Seneca Falls meeting as an implicit endorsement of her own ideas. News of the Eastern women's movement lit up erstwhile Ohio reformers. It was April 1850 when Ohio's first Woman's Rights Convention met in Salem. Gage couldn't attend because of domestic obligations, but its Minutes include her letter of support that expressed a desire to, "Remodel public opinion. . . The laws of public opinion are now more oppressive, if possible, than the written laws of the land."[5]

Thus, Ohio was an early leader in American reform for women, and at the state's second women's rights meeting, Gage made a point Stanton had missed. The Ohio gathering was not chaired by a man as it specifically "excluded men's participation," and was officered entirely by women.[6]

The breath taking evolution of women's rights in Ohio was traced by Paulina Wright Davis, a contemporary historian. When Salem's April gathering called for petitions to be taken to Ohio's upcoming Constitutional Convention, Gage had a head start. She had accumulated 70 McConnelsville signatures and called a meeting in Chesterfield. Gage also led two 1850 meetings in Akron and Massillon; each added names to petitions demanding, "Equal rights regardless of color or sex." In the spring of 1851, legislators at Ohio's Constitutional Convention received woman's rights' colleagues who were armed with petitions demanding redress of gender based legal and political wrongs. While attending Columbus

Senate hearings, Frances Gage submitted two original documents. One requested the removal of the words "white" and "male" from Ohio's pending Constitution; the second summarized a list of "the unequal laws on our statute books with regard to women."[7]

These lobbyists were well received. An observer at the Ohio 1851 Constitution Revision meetings recorded: " Columbus has seldom seen so refined and intelligent an audience as . . . those women, mothers, and two of them grandmothers, received congratulations and assurances that their noble and earnest arguments had fully prevailed."[8] It was a heady time. Nonetheless, the Ohio women's voices failed to influence their male legislators. For the rest of her life, Frances Gage was proud to say that she was the most radical person at these Constitutional Revision meetings, since even among her Ohio peers she alone sought the ballot for women. Gage never stopped praising this group of Ohio women who created America's "first petitions that ever were presented . . . for the Equality of Women and Negroes." She thought of this as her second coup, as they superseded Stanton's work by making Ohio the first state in America to connect "race and gender discrimination."[9]

The most famous of Gage's regional gatherings occurred in November 1852 in Mount Gilead, a hamlet north of Columbus in Morrow County. She received a letter requesting her attendance and traveled two days by steamboat and rail to meet its organizer who turned out to be a boy of nineteen. He led her to an empty barn and feared no audience would come. So Frances Gage took charge and publicized their meeting. "I called some boys . . . . 'Go to every house in this town and tell everybody that "Aunt Fanny" will speak here at 11 A.M. and if you get me fifty to come and hear, I will give you each ten cents . . .' and [I] was ready for my audience."

So many people appeared that there were three crowded sessions. Gage spoke to an estimated 300-400 Quakers and abolitionists. The meeting lasted two days, moving into the Presbyterian Church and then into the larger Methodist Church. At its close, a Quaker Preacher said to her, "Frances, thee had great Freedom. The ox-cart inspired thee." Nor did it hurt that Frances Dana Gage, also known as the writer and poet, "Aunt Fanny," inspired farmers' wives to bring "huge boxes and pans of provisions," making it "a delightful day." [10]

Her organizing and oratical skills were firmly in place at this early date. The other leadership role she undertook was exercising her argumentation skills and expository prose through writing. One of Gage's early goals was getting published in Pennsylvania at Jane Gray Swisshelm's weekly *Pittsburgh Saturday Visiter* (sic). Swisshelm was famous. She had authored an influential article for the *Pennsylvania Commercial Journal* that swayed public opinion; her argument was supported by two publicized legal cases, and Swisshelm's lobbying came into play. As a result, Pennsylvania's legislators in 1848 passed a law protecting married women's property rights. This was a real coup, since it took Ohio another thirteen years before similarly giving married women limited property rights.

Swisshelm was proud her state's married woman's reform. On Dec. 20, 1847, she began her periodical under the masthead, "A Family Newspaper Intended to Promote Moral Reform." One of her publication's goals was educating the public about the need to pass laws to curb men's intemperance. Sometimes called a "radical abolition newspaper," it had a circulation of 6,000 at the height of its success. When she accepted submissions from Frances Gage, the Middle Westerner's image was cultivated by the publication; for instance, in 1851 Swisshelm printed seven of Gage's articles.

All of this helps to explain the strange story of what happened in the spring of 1851 when Jane Gray Swisshelm came to Akron Ohio's Stone Church for the Women's Rights Convention. It was crowded with Buckeyes, and she was forced to sit on the steps of the pulpit. No one paid attention to her, but Frances Dana Gage, the popular and charismatic Ohio reformer who she knew from her *Visiter* correspondence was elected to chair the meeting. Being overlooked may have hurt Swisshelm's feelings. Later she criticized the abolition gathering and stopped accepting Gage's submissions to the *Visiter*.

Then three years later, on Jan. 28, 1854, Swisshelm ceased publishing the *Pittsburg Saturday Visiter*. She continued on her idealistic and solitary reformer's path. In 1857, Swisshelm left her husband, moved out of Pittsburg, and went to the West. In Minnesota, she started two reform papers, one of which conservatives destroyed. Her reputation for stubborn excellence continued; Horace Greeley admired her journalism and paid Swisshelm $5 a week to write a *New York Tribune* column. Later, he asked her to be its Washington correspondent. During the Civil War, Swisshelm nursed soldiers; afterwards, she obtained a position in the capital and started a newspaper called *Reconstructionist*. In it, she criticized President Johnson. This caused the loss of her job and the destruction of her printing press. One constant was Amelia Bloomer's friendship, and she staunchly defended Swisshelm for her "daredevil" achievements.11

Meanwhile, Frances Gage continued with her plan to write others of like mind. This included Amelia Bloomer, the publisher of *The Lily* in New York State, who appreciatively responded. Their friendship thrived for many years. Bloomer, like Swisshelm, entered public discourse as a temperance advocate. Amelia and Dexter Bloomer were postmaster and deputy postmaster in Seneca Falls, New York. In 1849, they were enthused after hearing visiting speakers known as Washingtonians speak for temperance. Men in Seneca Falls formed a sex exclusive temperance organization. Amelia Bloomer at first assisted them and then became disgusted. She decided to produce a temperance newspaper for women called *The Lily* and invited contributors. Bloomer remained a steady temperance advocate, and in 1853, chaired a committee for the state's legislature to study the prohibition of liquor.

The first thing that *The Lily* included from Frances Gage was a reprinted "Letter" from the *Pittsburgh Saturday Visiter*. Encouraged by its reception, Gage composed a poem about the publication's symbol, "The Lily," and from that time her "Letters" appeared regularly until *The Lily* ceased publication in 1856. These ruminative "Letters" turned out to be an apt form of self-expression for Frances Gage. Recent commentator Susan Phinney Conrad points out that Gage was amongst those who found their "own voice in talking about themselves."[12]

Frances Gage's reform career escalated after the May 1851 Second Woman's Rights Convention. This was her first experience leading a large meeting and what historian Eleanor Flexnor called her "baptism by fire" and "maiden speech."[13] That day, the McConnelsville matron opened by apologizing for her inexperience, and then proceeded to demonstrate her leadership skills. Gage's keynote speech was recorded by abolition journalist Marius Robinson and featured on the front page of his *Anti-Slavery Bugle*. Gage compared America's founding forefathers to women's rights advocates. She celebrated the enterprising patriarchs who, like her father, had "mountains of established law and custom to overcome; a wilderness of prejudice to be subdued; a powerful foe of selfishness and self-interest to overthrow." Then she questioned the basis for masculine injustice—asking what gives men authority over the other half of humanity? Her answer was physiology, often referred to as, "the power of the strong over the weak." The keynoter added that women need not fear men as enemies, but neither should they expect men to initiate women's equality. Gage concluded, "Woman must act for herself" because her own actions "could create a revolution without armies."[14]

Frances Gage clarified this point eighteen years later when she wrote that women remain vulnerable—even when benevolent men are present because conservative men retained the potential to reverse fair gender laws. She wrote, "Drunkards are voters," so it was imperative that women have the franchise in order to protect themselves.[15] The background to these developments was "men only" abolition meetings, most famously the 1840 anti-slavery meeting in London. Eight years later Elizabeth Cady Stanton called woman's rights to gather at her house in Seneca Falls. She claimed her inspiration came from Quaker Lucretia Mott who "opened to me a new world of thought."[16] Participants at Stanton's meeting received her document, a "Declaration of Sentiments." This was clever and progressive since it called for women's education, professional opportunities, property rights, access to divorce, child custody, and, most revolutionary of all, the franchise. At first, even Lucretia Mott thought this was too radical. Frances Dana Gage did not live to see women vote. But years later, she saw in the West Indies that positive social change happens when women's legal status rose above that of slaves. In other words, both race and gender statuses were, indeed, mutable and responsive to economics.

Frances Gage read about Eastern gatherings and was eager to meet its luminaries. Amelia Bloomer introduced her to the sweet natured James and Lucretia Mott in 1852. They warmly encouraged her to join their broad coalition of reformers. The Motts sought equality on many fronts. The initial fight might be temperance or abolition, but then one pursuit of justice evolved into other issues, like whether or not to "support the ballot for women."[17]

In this sense, the public career of Frances Dana Gage demonstrates a not atypical path taken by nineteenth-century reformers. On March 22, 1852, Susan B. Anthony asked Gage to write "words of counsel" for her women's New York State temperance organization. Anthony discovered that, not only did the Ohioan write delightful prose, but in her home state she had already been gathering petitions for married women's rights. So, Frances Gage was invited to accompany Anthony on a petition campaign in

New York State during the winter of 1853. This was Frances Gage's entrance into Eastern activism. The Middle Westerner debuted on the platform as a lecturer standing alongside Susan B. Anthony, Elizabeth Cady Stanton, and Antoinette Brown. She gained valuable experience from lecturing in New York State with these reform leaders. *History* notes, this foursome spearheaded the passage of bills relating to women's rights to property, earnings, and guardianship of children.[18]

A bright light among them was Antoinette Brown, a young reformer Frances Gage came to admire. She grew up in Henrietta, New York with a supportive Congregationalist family that helped their gifted daughter save for college tuition in order to become a teacher. This led to an Ohio connection for Gage because in 1846 Brown enrolled at Oberlin College. By the following year, Brown completed its two year prescribed course for women in English Literature. After receiving a B. A., she applied for admission to Oberlin's theology program and was informed that a woman could take courses but would receive no formal recognition. Nonetheless, the far sighted woman proceeded with her religious studies. In August 1849, she received a letter from a new college friend, Lucy Stone, warning her that Oberlin might try to dampen her "free spirit."[19] Antoinette Brown was not dampened and published an essay in the *Oberlin Quarterly Review* on the Apostle Paul's famous lines "let your women keep silence in the churches." She argued that the book's historical context made it meaningful at the time, but simultaneously disproved its nineteenth century validity. In the spring of 1850, Brown completed Oberlin College's three-year theology program but was not awarded its degree for many years. She was not embittered.

Lucy Stone was Brown's best friend at Oberlin and another "charter feminist" Francis Gage met at this time. Stone was a native of West Brookfield, Massachusetts and was inured to hardship. Like Joseph Barker, her father refused to support his girl's passion for education. Lucy Stone was inspired by Sarah Grimke's 1837 *Letters on the Equality of the Sexes and the Condition of Women* and left the family's farm. In 1839, Stone enrolled at Mount Holyoke Female Seminary for four years and then traveled by canal boat and stagecoach to Oberlin, Ohio. The village was a hotbed of abolition and a stop on the Underground Railroad. Its college opened in 1833, and women were only admitted to its college preparatory program. Four years later, women were formally enrolled, allowing Oberlin to call itself America's first co-educational college. At the college, Lucy Stone rolled up her sleeves to work for paying her expenses. This included tutoring escaped slaves who were surprised to learn a woman could teach.

Stone had reservations about Oberlin College's gender inequities. One example that loomed large for her was the fact that women students were denied public speaking privileges in debating societies. In 1846, the infuriated Lucy Stone led women students into the woods where they convened their own debating society. When Oberlin's graduation ceremony approached in 1847, Stone was asked to write a commencement speech but was told she could not read it in public. She refused.

Lucy Stone returned to Massachusetts where she spoke at her brother's Congregational Church and worked as an agent for William Lloyd Garrison's American Anti-Slavery Society. She split her time. Weekends were used to promote abolition, while during the week she spoke on women's rights, for which admission was charged. Then Stone resigned from anti-slavery society work in order to devote herself primarily to women's rights. Biographer and daughter Alice Stone Blackwell explained her reason, "I was a woman before I was an abolitionist."[20]

Lucy Stone and Paulina Wright Davis in 1850 organized America's first National Woman's Rights Convention in Worcester, Massachusetts. The timing was right. More than three hundred attended and joined the Woman's Rights Association, including such famous men as Ralph Waldo Emerson, Henry Ward Beecher, and Horace Mann. The opening address was given by Paulina Wright Davis, followed by Lucretia Mott. Her keynote speech was so powerful that it was sent to England where some believed it inspired Harriet Taylor and John Stuart Mill who in July 1851 to publish "The Enfranchisement of Women" in the *Westminster Review*. If this is so, these American woman's rights reformers influenced international sentiments.

At the Worcester meeting, the friends Lucy Stone and Antoinette Brown were on the program. Brown's speech created a stir since it argued that gender pronouncements in the Bible were often inapplicable to the modern world. She was alight with passion for public advocacy and was a strong abolitionist who was also writing for Frederick Douglass' newspaper, *The North Star*. Brown undertook many speaking tours on rights issues, but her religious convictions led her down another path. In 1853, she was ordained by a Methodist minister and became pastor of South Butler, New York's Congregational Church. However, because Brown was uncomfortable with Congregational doctrines and not supported by some parishioners, she resigned after ten months in the parish.

While serving as minister of that church, she attended two significant New York City Conventions for woman's rights and temperance. She then returned to speaking engagements, social work, and writing, but suspended this work in Jan. 21, 1856 to marry Samuel Blackwell. This companionate marriage led to seven births and five living daughters. She did not return to even limited public life until late in the 1860's because she saw marriage as an absolute commitment. After the children were raised, Antoinette Brown Blackwell helped found New Jersey's Woman's Suffrage Association. In 1869, she supported Lucy Stone's leadership at American Woman Suffrage Association meetings. This energetic woman was the last surviving participant from the 1850 first Woman's Rights Convention to make use of the Nineteenth Amendment in 1920 and vote.

Her friend Lucy Stone in 1855 married Antoinette's brother-in-law, Henry Blackwell. He was an English born abolitionist and woman's rights supporter who resided in Cincinnati. This egalitarian couple designed their wedding ceremony so that the bride retained her birth name, and the word "obey" was removed from their vows. The presiding minister was their friend, Rev. Thomas Wentworth Higginson, who a decade later was famous for serving in the Civil War. Many disapproved of Lucy Stone's retention of her birth name. Their Quaker friend Lucretia Mott supported her decision, as well as the more conventional choice Antoinette Brown made to take her husband's name. The two families for many years congenially lived near each other in New Jersey.

Such friendships were essential to the woman's movement, and reformers sustained their colleagueship at National Women's Rights Conventions that annually rotated between four states: New York, Pennsylvania, Massachusetts, and Ohio. The meetings resembled the women's 1850 Worcester gathering that, in turn, reflected the pattern of earlier temperance conventions. For a Middle Westerner like Frances Dana Gage, this resource provided what has been called "a moveable feast—a college and a long conversation."[21] The agenda typically included letters from non-attendees, recent resolutions, proceedings, and regional reports on states' political and legal status. Thus participants learned about troubling American policies. Gage made more acquaintances; among them was New Englander Paulina Wright Davis, convention organizer and writer, who similarly shared her faith that "their own intellectual journey offered unquestionable poof of their representative womanhood."[22]

As family obligations allowed, Frances Gage eagerly attended many national reform conventions. These often led to further opportunities. Just as Swisshelm's *Pittsburg Saturday Visiter* led to Amelia Bloomer's *The Lily*, and both helped to create an audience interested in following Gage's experiences and thoughts, her growing contacts helped her to bridge Middle Western and Eastern viewpoints. She was quite self-conscious about this plan to bring Ohio's nascent civil rights groundswell into closer contact with the national arena. The process quickly evolved, for example, at Ohio's 1853 National Woman's Rights Convention she saw Amelia Bloomer who expressed pleasure that "Mrs. F. D. Gage, our dear Aunt Fanny, is President."[23] That year the two women nearly became neighbors. Amelia and Dexter Chamberlain Bloomer left Seneca Falls, New York for a new home in Mount Vernon, Ohio. Here Amelia Bloomer continued publishing *The Lily* and assisted her husband with a new family paper, called the *Western Home Visitor*. Then in April 1853 Frances Gage departed from McConnelsville when James Gage precipitously moved his family west to St. Louis, Missouri.

Nor did the Bloomers stay long in Ohio; two years later in July 1855, Dexter Bloomer sold his paper and purchased land in Council Bluffs, Iowa where he relocated the family. Amelia Bloomer realized it would be unrealistic to continue serving as Corresponding Secretary for Ohio's Woman's State Temperance Society, headquartered in Columbus and resigned in January 1854. She sold *The Lily* to Mary Birdsall from Richmond, Indiana and continued submitting material to the journal until it ceased publication in 1856.

On the way to Iowa, Amelia Bloomer visited the Gage family in St. Louis where the two women led a large woman's suffrage meeting. After that, Bloomer accepted fewer invitations to speak because, she wrote, Iowa stagecoaches were uncomfortable. The two women still crossed paths at conventions. After the Civil War at a Western Sanitary Commission Fair in Chicago, Amelia Bloomer expressed her admiration for Gage's work with freedmen and injured soldiers in South Carolina's Sea Islands. Her husband, D. C.

Bloomer, summed up their relationship by saying that between Frances Gage and "Mrs. Bloomer there existed for many years and until Mrs. Gage's decease the warmest friendship."[24]

On the other hand, Frances Gage's introduction to Elizabeth Cady Stanton was not so placid. Stanton sought recruits to support her self-proclaimed leadership of America's woman's rights movement, and she saw Gage as a potential foot soldier. The two women's endowments were similar, but circumstances took them along different paths. Each was precocious and had a demanding father who wished she were a boy. Each daughter responded as a boy might—by rebelling against gender conventions. Local contexts shaped each girl's character—Elizabeth Cady's field of action was rich since she lived on America's Brahmin East Coast. She was tutored in Greek, Latin, and mathematics, attended a local academy with boys, and then Mrs. Willard's Seminary in Troy, New York. Cady heard about abolition and met an escaping slave girl, but came to the cause through the enthusiasm of her cousin, Gerrit Smith, who was part of the Underground Railroad. Smith introduced her to his friend, Henry B. Stanton, and she seemed to support their abolition reform efforts. Elizabeth Cady married him in 1840, and on his maiden abolition lecture series to Europe, the naive bride was angered by being relegated to a balcony at London's World Temperance Convention. Her admiration for Lucretia Mott's response to this incivility propelled Elizabeth Cady Stanton into her life's mission—fighting America's denial of woman's rights.

Frances Dana's commitment to women's rights was more visceral and emerged from misadventures in childhood. If there is such a thing as an instinctive reformer, it would explain France Dana's nature. In reformers' company, she was a fast learner who gained sophistication from new friends and their reform experiences. Gage felt "at home" amongst Easterners from whom she was separated by only one generation. Her talent for making reform friendships extended to men, such as anti-slavery advocates William Lloyd Garrison and ex-slave Frederick Douglass. They helped her gain valuable experience on abolition platforms. She served these colleagues well, being by nature peripatetic and invigorated by travel, whether by train, stagecoach, wagon, or horseback. Of course, with maturity she, like Bloomer, preferred rail and water.

The April 1853 move of the family away from Ohio and to slave holding Missouri pushed Frances Gage further into what was still America's West. During the next half dozen years, she was forced her to reassess the scope of her writing and travels. Many consequences of life in Missouri seem retrospectively to have been inevitable. Frances Gage was vigorously discriminated against by Missouri's defiant anti-abolitionists. Despite this, she addressed Missouri's House of Representatives on women's rights.[25] She endeavored to write for its two major regional publications and was rejected. Receiving the "cold shoulder" meant that such efforts were unsuccessful, but nothing stopped her from continuing to write for Middle Western and Eastern publications or continuing with her advocacy work.

    The most obvious challenge was distance that imposed limitations and required choices. For example, she declined to chair Ravenna, Ohio's 1853 Women's Rights Convention. By September, she sharpened her priorities and attended New York City's Woman's Rights Convention where she was a featured speaker and presented a clever innovation—a last will and testament that substituted the name of the wife in place of the husband. Her wit and humor amused the audience as she ironically inverted traditional masculine viewpoints. Gage switched nouns and pronouns to show how wills are absurdly gender restrictive. With tongue in cheek, the matron suggested that America should deny men the right to bequeath property. It was one of her best performances and a polemical masterpiece.

    The next month Gage presided over America's Fourth National Woman's Rights Convention in Cleveland. Her friend, Lucretia Mott, called the meeting to order, Frances Gage was elected chair, and she asked her old friend Rev. Antoinette Brown to offer a prayer. After the meeting, she traveled to Richmond, Indiana to attend its Woman's Rights Convention where Gage spoke and did so annually for the next half a dozen years.

    The following year, 1854, found her frequently away from Missouri because she was in New York State assisting Susan B. Anthony to canvass for married women's rights. Two years later in Jan. 4, 1856, Anthony again requested Frances Gage to rejoin her for a second speaking tour through New York State. She obliged though inclement weather interfered. As historian Ida Husted Harper describes, "There was a hard siege ahead of them." The diary says: 'January 8: Terribly cold and windy; only a dozen people in the hall. . . January 9: Mercury 12 degrees below zero but we took sleigh for Nunda. Trains all blocked by snow and no mail for several days, yet we had a full house."[26]

Her contributions ended when Gage was called home by family illness. Between being exhausted by such reform travels and caring for ill family members, Frances Gage in November felt she had to miss New York City's Seventh National Woman's Rights Convention which saddened her. She expressed her regrets to Lucy Stone, "I should be the only representative from the west side of the great Father of Waters. . . There is much thought in the free States of the great west—much less of conservatism and rigid adherence to the old-time customs of law and theology among the masses, than in the East."

So, Frances Gage, the self-conscious standard bearer for cross-regional communication, worried that western women need more connections with their "Eastern sisters."[27] Family matters, however, did not often deter Gage from continuing her frenetic lecture circuit in the Midwest, and in 1855 and 1856 Frances Gage added speeches about women's rights at the Territorial Legislatures of Illinois and Nebraska.

In March she and her elder son undertook travel down the Mississippi into the "Deep South," on the paddle wheeler Martha Jewett. In New Orleans, Frances Dana Gage became the first and only women's rights lecturer to speak in the city.[28] She was respectfully reviewed in the *Daily Picayune*, which praised her "lecture on the social, industrial, and civil disabilities of women in our country . . . a lady of intellectual culture, writes well, speaks ably, and beyond all doubt feels sincerely and deeply."[29] Nonetheless, she disliked the city's racial oppression. New Orleans was a slave stronghold, she wrote in the *Ohio Cultivator,* where "dissipation and folly are reigning deities."[30]

In October, Gage helped organize Philadelphia's Fifth National Woman's Rights Convention where she was elected vice-president and reelected annually until the Civil War brought a hiatus. On such occasions, she was greeted by crowded houses; one reporter commented; "Mrs. Gage . . . possesses those interior springs of thought and feeling . . . . sparkling with wit and humor."[31] Yet, Frances Gage was occasionally heckled, and one patronizing reporter smirked that her success was merely due to "the novel sight of a woman on the platform."[32] After 1853 when the family lived in pro-slavery St. Louis, Frances Dana's personal stress may have been alleviated by her reform activities, but nothing mitigated the fact that Missouri's opposition to abolition frightened the married couple.

Problems grew increasingly conspicuous in Missouri. Her writing and speaking was a lightning rod that drew local controversy; also, James Gage's new wheel foundry ran into problems. It was the era of America's economic "Panic of 1857" with a subsequent recession. There were three attempted arsons at their home, financial reversals, and James became extremely ill. Suddenly the couple was impoverished and departed for the safety of nearby Illinois. Surprisingly, these reverses did not lead Frances Gage to lessen her hectic reformer's pace that included canvassing Ohio for signatures on petitions that demanded women's legal equality as "feme sole."[33]

Historian Laurence Friedman wittily described the laws these women were trying to change, "husband and wife were one flesh; but the man was the owner of that flesh."[34] Just as Pennsylvania in the 1840's granted married women property rights, so did New York State a decade later—based largely on the efforts of Anthony's team of women reformers. Buoyed by this success, the Quaker believed more laborious lecture tours in Ohio would achieve the same result. However, she did not credit the amount of work Ohio women had already expended in this quirky state.

So, when Anthony sought Ohio workers, she was disappointed that Francis Gage did not leap to assist her. The Ohioan declined an official position in Susan B. Anthony's Ohio taskforce. The timing was wrong. She was maintaining an invalided husband and keeping a schedule of written submissions and lectures. Nonetheless, she remembered her Ohio reform colleagues and gladly rejoined friends, like J. Elizabeth Jones and Hannah Tracy Cutter. They attended joint committee meetings of the 1861 Ohio Legislature. As they had done a decade earlier, these women testified before Ohio's Senators and again received glowing newspaper reports. One Columbus journalist called the women earnest, truthful, womanly,—all richly cultivated by the experiences of practical life, and he noted, "Many were mothers!"[35] This time their good character, petitions, and testimony led the male legislators to more seriously examine Ohio's laws concerning women's legal status. What a difference a decade can make. This time they won.

Victory came in April 1861 when Ohio passed its landmark Woman's Rights Bill that granted limited property rights to wives. They could their own property and wages.[36] On May 16, J. Elizabeth Jones, the Association's General Agent in Ohio, thanked Frances Gage for her active support of this legislation.[37] In a similar way, countless American lobbyists, like these Midwestern women, precipitated improvements in married women's property rights. The cumulative effect of these reformers instituted a sea change in American culture. When Civil War hostilities broke out, 14 states had enacted legislation that guaranteed property rights to married women; Ohio, Massachusetts, and New York were amongst the most liberal.

    Meanwhile, the Gage's family affairs were not sanguine. James Gage was ill, unable to work, and depressed. Some of their sons remained in the deep Midwest, and the diminished family experienced poverty. In December of 1860, they left Illinois and returned to Ohio where Frances Gage sought paid employment. A decade earlier, she began contributing to *The Ohio Cultivator*'s "Housewife's Department" or "Home Department" under the name "Aunt Fanny." Her journalism was popularly received, and she continued to write for the "Cultivator Girls" during her sojourn in Missouri and Illinois. Gage applied for a paid position in 1861 and began to serve as the journal's Associate Editor. She contributed to the *Ohio Cultivator* for 12 years. After the journal changed hands and left Columbus for Cleveland, Gage took a position with her editor's new publication called *Field Notes*.

    With the outbreak of the Civil War, woman's rights work was tacitly set aside. Conventions were postponed for the duration, although Elizabeth Cady Stanton did not want to shelve reform meetings. In 1863, she implemented a clever strategy to return women's rights to the fore. She would emphasize the war's significance by galvanizing women's support for the Union. Stanton initiated a group called The Woman's Loyal National League that was headquartered in New York City's Cooper Union. Frances Gage gladly joined a speakers' list of notables who agreed to donate their lecture fees to the League. The group supported Secretary of War Sumner's demands that Congress approve the enlistment of blacks in the Army. It also gathered 400,000 signatures to petition Congress for the Fourteenth Amendment's inclusion of women. Then the League fell silent and melted away.

    One possible reason for this setback and cessation of Stanton's leadership of the Woman's Loyal National League may be found in New York City's history at the time. Dangerous Draft

Riots were breaking out, and Elizabeth Cady Stanton wanted to protect her sons, none of whom served in the Civil War. She took her family and fled to the countryside. Henry Stanton and one son remained in the city where they worked as reporters. Whatever else was going on, no woman reformers emerged to head the League at Cooper Union.

Shortly after the Civil War's end was declared at Appottomax in 1865, President Abraham Lincoln was assassinated. Reformers' optimism wavered. In 1866 the Eleventh National Women's Rights Convention was held. Change was in the air. Feminist reform leaders included Stanton, Anthony, Stone, and the *Independent's* editor, Theodore Tilton. Frederick Douglass proposed that they form a coalition of anti-slavery advocates and woman's rights workers that would be called the American Equal Rights Association or AERA. Lucretia Mott was named its first President. Frances Gage was elected to be one of its vice-presidents. Its initial meeting on May 9, 1866 and was dedicated to securing "Equal Rights to all American citizens, especially the right of suffrage, irrespective of race, color, or sex." The first keynote speaker was Elizabeth Cady Stanton, and she was followed by Frances Dana Gage. The third keynote speaker was Gage's respected commanding officer in South Carolina's Sea Islands, Brig. General Rufus Saxton, who affirmed the need to strengthen the link between anti-slavery concerns and women's rights.

Unbeknownst to her, this event occasioned Frances Dana Gage's final speech. In it, she summarized her classic civil rights themes: the home belongs to both women and men; each sex needs power to do well; the enemy is "higgling" politicians and "grogshop emissaries"; educated women who vote will move "dram-bottles out of the home" and render obsolete "nuisance dram shops." [38] Gage emphasized her newest concern; freedwomen require the franchise in order to protect themselves and their children from drunken men who may intrude on their rights. [39] Her rationale was that freedwomen who are empowered to act independently will be empowered to avoid masculine oppression. The AERA hired Frances Gage to work as one of its lobbyists and writers, but in the summer of 1867 she was disabled by a massive stroke and subsequently only watched events unfold.

Establishing AERA support groups was called for, and thus Anthony, Stanton, and Stone began touring the Northeast. The following year, 1867, Kansas elections loomed; its new state constitution would determine the civil rights of African Americans and women. So Lucy Stone and Henry Blackwell went to Kansas to lobby for the cause—gender and race equity. When they returned, Stanton and Anthony replaced them and sought men's assistance. As it turned out, this innocent plan altered the tenor of their reform work. Stanton traveled with an ex-governor who bored her. However, Susan B. Anthony worked with a charismatic and unconventional entrepreneur named George Francis Train. His wealth came from the Credit Mobilier, a holding company for the Union Pacific Railroad. He aroused strong feelings; the two woman's rights workers were charmed, while others saw through his façade like William Lloyd Garrison who called him a "harlequin and semi lunatic."[40] Several historians have agreed with the abolitionist and label Train a "Democratic financier and Negrophobe."[41]

The autobiographical writings of Susan B. Anthony and Elizabeth Cady Stanton paint an enthusiastic picture. They saw only Train's strength as a promoter for woman's reform votes. He was a handsome and emphatic public speaker who hated African Americans and opposed the Fifteenth Amendment to the Constitution. This inevitably undercut the "justice" message of woman's rights. Anthony and Stanton, enchanted by his charisma and flattered, accepted his promise to help them to start a new reform newspaper for women. He gave them $600 in startup funds. Train promised to contribute essays on economics and politics. Since the women saw the reform movement as war, the publication was named *The Revolution*.

This moment began an unfurling of events that no one could have anticipated. Anthony and Stanton saw themselves as at odds with other liberal reformers; they defended Train against charges of racism. Many abolitionists, like Lucy Stone, believed his racist position made women's suffrage a "laughing stock." Finally, Train was insulted by Lucy Stone's supporters and the AERA's indifference. He planned to run for President and, if woman's rights reformers would not be an asset, he believed he should simply walk away. On Jan. 8 1868, Train sailed for Ireland; on arrival he was thrown in Battersea prison for 10 months because he was travelling with literature that supported Irish radicals. Anthony and Stanton feared for their *The Revolution* and by 1869 his essays and financial support ceased. When Train returned to America, he had lost interest in Anthony and Stanton's paper because he wanted to campaign for the upcoming Presidential election. But he made another misstep, expressing sympathy for Victoria Woodhull whose new periodical offended authorities. George Francis Train's defended her right to state her opinion in print, another legal offense that led to his spending four months in the Tombs, New York City's jail.

As far as the Kansas vote was concerned, neither women nor black men received the franchise. Far more importantly, the implications of Susan B. Anthony and Elizabeth Cady Stanton supporting a racist brought to light intrinsic contradictions among the priorities of woman's rights reformers. Could black men's vote be more important than white and black women's vote? Then Frederick Douglas proposed that the AERA give precedence to enfranchising black men. This crystallized the franchise issue by giving race precedence over woman's rights. The future of the AERA hung in the balance because black women's and white women's rights could be indefinitely postponed. So it came to pass.

The AERA meeting on May 15, 1869 was anticipated by many who expected public conflict. The *Brooklyn Daily,* one New York City newspaper, reported there was "a lawless scrabble" to reserve seats. Several factions struggled to prioritize their reform values, and abolitionist men were outspoken. Elizabeth Cady Stanton and Susan B. Anthony led a woman's rights faction from New York City. This subset of the AERA wanted to widen women's rights issues. A second faction was led by Lucy Stone whose New Englanders sustained their conservative sympathies for abolition. They encouraged male ministers to be part of AERA, which led Henry Ward Beecher to join. In the words of modern historian Eleanor Flexnor, there was pending a "serious quarrel between Miss Anthony and Mrs. Stanton and the Train admixture."[42]

As the May 9 meeting date dawned, Lucretia Mott was ill, so Elizabeth Cady Stanton chaired the AERA business meeting. She was questioned from the floor regarding Train's racism and opposition to the Fifteenth Amendment, as well as about Susan B. Anthony's AERA financial record keeping. The defensive Stanton snapped, declaring that the Negro is "Sambo." This was her first public admission of an elitist racial view. Frederick Douglass came to the platform to protest. Stanton proceeded to defend Anthony's bookkeeping, and eventually agreed to repudiate the misalliance with George Francis Train. However, she did not take back or deny the "Sambo" remark.

The consequences of this tempestuous meeting can hardly be overrated in feminist history. Lucy Stone's abolitionists despaired over the fractures in their alliance. The public read about the divisive tensions between the New York City and Boston feminists. Initially, Stanton and Anthony were reluctant to acknowledge what they had done. Elizabeth Cady Stanton, the neophyte Abolitionist in 1840 London, now rejected the implications of abolition. One contemporary participant called the AERA "an awful humbug" because it allowed these two women to endlessly manipulate women's issues. Modern historians recall this 1856 meeting as a break between two "camps."

The writing was on the wall, and the AERA's strained reform coalition was about to dissolve. When Lucy Stone consulted with Stanton and Anthony, they denied splitting from AERA. So, the New England contingent departed, believing the rift might be healed. However, Anthony and Stanton promptly called a meeting at the Women's Bureau where they produced *The Revolution*. This impromptu business meeting formed the National Woman Suffrage Association or NWSA, which Stanton wished to close to male membership. That exclusionary idea was voted down, and the NWSA named Henry Ward Beecher as its president. In the short run, this put Elizabeth Cady Stanton in the unusual position of fighting the word "male" in the Fourteenth Amendment Constitution while operating within an organization headed by a man.

In June 1866 the Amendment was introduced and enacted in July of 1868. The NWSA also opposed the Fifteenth Amendment because it did not include the word "gender," although it prohibited denial of suffrage based on "race, color, or servitude." It was enacted in February 1870. The NWSA's "wish list" or platform included many progressive issues beyond suffrage; for example, they sought increased married women's rights, lenient divorce laws, equal pay for equal work, and eight-hour work days.

The shrewd journalist, Theodore Tilton, attempted to reconcile Stanton and Stone, but to no avail. His colorful essay, "A Law Against Women" in the *Independent* newspaper argued that denying woman's rights after their support in the war was like "The spider-crab walking backward." Tilton urged reformers, "let us break the legs of the spider-crab." Lucy Stone's woman's rights faction steadfastly continued the AERA's philosophy of supporting abolition, though the issue was legally settled. Stone's group took the name National Woman's Suffrage Association or NWSA. At its first meeting on May 17, 1870 NWSA met in New York City and there was a call from the floor for a "popular man" to lead this organization. This would parallel HenryWard Beecher's heading AWSA. So, Theodore Tilton was named President of the NWSA. As events transpired, two years later both Beecher and Tilton were forced to resign when a scandal rocked these two men and by implication, the women's rights organizations each headed.

Lucretia Mott, who must have loved everybody, was sorry her presidency was over when the AERA dissolved after only three years. She continued to admire elements in her old friends—Anthony's zeal, Stanton's vigorous writing, and Lucy Stone's energy. She wrote," Lucy Stone is worth a dozen quiet workers. Give me *noise* on this subject; a real Boaerges."[43] Yet, Mott kept herself above the fray. She refused to be harangued into joining any post-war faction and wrote, "I am weary of everlasting complaints, and . . . I do not mean to be drawn in." Respecting Anthony's and Stanton's "devotion to their great work," she intended to cooperate "as circumstances admit."[44] However, a few months later Lucretia Mott complained that Anthony's intrusive sincerity and plain speaking were difficult to bear. Loyal as she was, Lucretia Mott attended meetings of both the New York NWSA and Boston AWSA and commented on January 22, 1870 about the irony of "each advocating the self-same measures."[45] Soon the frail and widowed Mott shifted her energies to working for international peace.

The rippling discontents amongst reformers at the close of the 1860s decade did not diminish. Susan B. Anthony and Elizabeth Cady Stanton continued to believe woman's rights agitation was equivalent to war. *The Revolution* began on Jan. 8, 1868 with Anthony publisher, manager, and co-editor with a colleague, Parker Pilsbury. The weekly paper was the official voice of the NWSA and advocated many issues, such as suffrage, freedmen's rights, equal pay, and more liberal divorce laws. It published Mary Wollstonecraft's groundbreaking essay *Vindication of the Rights of Women*. After Train's financial contributions ended in 1870, the paper struggled to locate supporters and advertising revenue. One issue was Susan B. Anthony's refusal to publish advertisements for "quack medicines" or abortifacients. Elizabeth Cady Stanton tried and failed to create a joint stock company of "ladies and gentlemen" who were worth millions and would run *The Revolution.*

Then, hoping an infusion of "new blood" might invigorate the newspaper, in 1870 sold it for $1.00 to Mrs. Laura Curtis Bullard. Her parents' wealth was accrued from Mrs. Winslow's Soothing Syrup, a morphine laden patent medicine. Bullard was experienced with editing a paper called *The Ladies Visitor and Drawing Room Companion;* she was assisted by Ohio-born Phoebe Cary, sister of the poet Alice Cary. As it happened, Bullard was also a special friend of Theodore Tilton who described her as "young, brave, brilliant, and beautiful." Things did not go as Bullard had planned; on Oct. 12, 1871, after eighteen months, her "Valedictory" essay appeared, and she departed for Europe. *The Revolution* was languishing; it remained $10,000 in debt and facing bankruptcy. *The Revolution* ceased and was absorbed into a Unitarian publication, *The Liberal Enquirer.* Susan B. Anthony assumed the debt and paid it off in seven years

Meanwhile, Lucy Stone was undertaking the challenge of creating s different woman's reform newspaper that would be classier in tone and content. She asked her husband to assist her with this new journal; they moved from New Jersey to Boston and placed their twelve-year-old daughter, Alice Stone Blackwell, in a boarding school. Stone began the spadework by contacting potential financial backers in Boston. Called the *Woman's Journal*, its first issue appeared on Jan. 8, 1870, not coincidentally the second anniversary of *The Revolution.* Its offices were on Park Street in Boston, and its advertising policy excluded tobacco, liquor, or drugs. The *Woman's Journal* was the organ of the American Woman Suffrage Association, and its original funding came from six prominent Boston businessmen who initially invested $10,000 each. Funding also came from advertising, a marketing campaign for subscriptions, and occasional bazaars in Boston which were presented as sparkling social events.

Its initial editor was Mary Livermore, though over the years, Lucy Stone and Henry Blackwell edited the publication. Its contributors included three Beechers: Catharine, Harriet, and Henry Ward, as well as such fellow reformers as H. W. Higginson who was a Contributing Editor. Humble supporters of reform like Frances Dana Gage's in-laws, John and Portia Gage, were amongst early stockholders in the *Woman's Journal* and committed themselves to including it as a bequest in their estate planning.

Frances Gage had no money to spare, but she wished to write for *The Woman's Journal* and did so when she was able. It was the most successful of all suffrage newspapers, running for 16 years until 1931.

The successful new publication could have been seen as an insult to the failed journal of Stanton and Anthony, but these two feminists had other irons in the fire. As if immune to the rancor aroused by their alliance with George Frances Train, they proceeded to a second misalliance that had even more devastating consequences. Stanton's search for money to support the NWSA drew her to meet a recently famous woman named Victoria Woodhull. She and her sister, Tennessee Claflin, in the summer of 1868 had introduced themselves to Commodore Cornelius Vanderbilt, the wealthiest man in America. They advised him on stock investments that paid off handsomely, and Vanderbilt courted Claflin. In the winter of 1869, the sisters opened Woodhull, Claflin, and Co., a woman's stockbrokerage office at 44 Broad Street. It was luxurious, and newspapers like the *New York Herald* feted the sisters with labels like "The Queens of Finance" and "The Bewitching Brokers." However, the glamorous sisters did not participate in the firm's day-to-day business which was transacted by men, and its economic viability leaned upon the acknowledged backing of Commodore Vanderbilt.

Soon Elizabeth Cady Stanton visited Woodhull, Claflin & Co. and, like the millionaire, was charmed by Victoria Woodhull. She wrote about their enterprise in *The Revolution* and invited Woodhull to join the feminist cause. These two women appeared to be wildly different but conversation led each to realize that they shared a number of concerns, one was American women's need for easier access to divorce. Each woman's motives were personal. Woodhull came from unpretentious Midwestern roots and had what in the era might be called a "checkered past," having been uncongenially wed as a teenager and divorced from Canning Woodhull. In 1866, she married a war hero, Col. James Harvey Blood; their relationship was complicated by another divorce and remarriage which in winter of 1875 produced a second and final divorce from Col. Blood.

Stanton's personal situation was less obvious. The year the two women met, Elizabeth Cady Stanton inherited a legacy from her father and bought a house in Tenafly, New Jersey. Her husband, Henry Brewster Stanton, had abandoned his early abolition career and branched out. He became a reporter in New York City and declined to move to New Jersey. He preferred to reside separately from his wife. This occurred at the same time Lucy Stone became worried that her husband was infatuated with Abby Hutchinson Patton from the singing family that entertained at women's rights conventions. Lucy Stone opposed divorce; she and sister-in-law, Dr. Emily Blackwell, pressured Henry B. Blackwell into stopping his flirtation and recommitting to his marriage. Hence, Woodhull and Stanton each sought lenient divorce laws, while Stone opposed them.

In the spring of 1870, Woodhull and Claflin drew funds from their brokerage business and began to publish a journal, *Woodhull & Claflin's Weekly*. Appearing from May 14, 1870 to June 10, 1876, it was controversial and provided an eclectic and progressive mix of its editors' interests in diverse topics, including politics, spiritualism, sex education, vegetarianism, prostitution, free love, and divorce laws. The paper on Dec. 30, 1871 published Karl Marx's *Communist Manifesto*.

At the NWSA's third convention in the capital on January 11, 1871, Victoria Woodhull invited members to hear her address called "The Memorial of Victoria Woodhull." It would be delivered to members of the combined Judiciary Committees of both houses of Congress. This was a success, a dignified presentation that argued women already had the right to vote under the terms of the Fourteenth Amendment. The event was celebrated as *Frank Leslie's Illustrated Weekly* with a full-page engraving. Anthony and Stanton enjoyed her speech, and Woodhull promised them a $10,000 donation for NWSA. However, they had not forgotten that the flamboyant actress and spiritualist had to be handled with care. Stanton wrote to Anthony on Jan. 31, 1871, we must be careful "not to have another Train affair with Mrs. Woodhull."[46]

A few years earlier in November 1866 Elizabeth Cady Stanton had petitioned Congress and declared herself a candidate for Congress from the 8th Congressional District of New York; she received 24 votes. So, she was not surprised when six years later another woman's political candidacy occurred. On May 10, 1872, Victoria Woodhull declared herself a Presidential candidate running on a People's Party ticket. She listed Frederick Douglass as her running mate, though he declined. Woodhull's intention was to run against several other candidates, including her friend, George Frances Train, as well as newspaperman, Horace Greeley, and the incumbent, Ulysses S. Grant. *Woodhull and Claflin's Weekly* began campaigning for her run for the Presidency.

Such hopes were dashed after the sisters' newspaper, the *Woodhull & Claflin Weekly*, got into hot water by publishing a special edition that inflamed its readers. Woodhull later said that her intention was the endorsement of "free love." She heard from Stanton that the famous Reverend Henry Ward Beecher had extra marital affairs. The era's readers supported the sanctity of marriage; they were titillated but offended by womanizing and hypocrisy. Public outrage boomeranged against the publisher. The two sisters were arrested under Anthony Comstock's new anti-obscenity law that had passed on March 3, 1873. This allowed federal marshals to imprison for a month in the city's Ludlow Street Victoria Woodhull, her husband, Captain Blood, and sister Tennessee Claflin. Six months later, they were acquitted on a technicality. Woodhull and Claflin thus were victims of the scandal they naively unleashed.

Harriet Beecher Stowe in "My Wife and I," a serial in the *Christian Union*, mocked Woodhull as a character named Audacia Dangyereyes. Other consequences appeared: the sisters' *Weekly* was discredited, Woodhull's Presidential candidacy ended, as did her Peoples' Party aka Equal Rights Party. The election returned Ulysses S. Grant to the White House. Yet the behavior at the heart of Beecher's affair did not come to a head until two years later. On Jan. 11, 1875 Theodore Tilton brought a civil suit against Rev. Henry Ward Beecher. The court case fascinated the media, partly because the Reverend's mistress was Theodore Tilton's wife. At the same time, Theodore Tilton was involved with Laura Curtis Bullard, *The Revolution*'s editor. For 112 days, the case continued, and was ended by a hung jury and dismissal. This officially ended the contretemps.

This sorry episode occurred after Elizabeth Cady Stanton repeated a confidence to Victoria Woodhull. In fact, Rev. Beecher was a serial seducer of married women, but the public accepted his declaration of innocence, and he left the city on a speaking tour. The supposedly "injured party," Theodore Tilton, was shamed and bankrupt. Neither journalist returned to *The Independent,* NWSA, or AWSA. Tilton lost his wife, his mistress, and his job. He became an expatriate, moving to Parris where for 24 years he resided in a room on the Ile. St. Louis. This silenced his brilliant editorial voice until in 1895 Tilton published a eulogy, "Sonnets to the Memory of Frederick Douglass." His one-time lady friend, Laura Curtis

Bullard, abandoned *The Revolution*. Woodhull and Claflin shut down their *Weekly*. With a promised inheritance from Cornelius Vanderbilt's estate, they left America for London. Woodhull learned from her mistakes. She finalized her divorce, changed her name, and married a banker.

    The disharmony spilled over and made bad press for the America's reform movement. Perhaps the angriest reformer over these events was the Quaker Susan B. Anthony. She had long distrusted Victoria Woodhull's flamboyance and felt her freethinking interfered with responsible feminism. The Quaker was so angry that she destroyed her diary pages covering June 11, 22, and July 23 to July 28, 1871, expunging the records that expressed her outrage. Although Elizabeth Cady Stanton herself had brought Woodhull into the movement and ignited the spark that lit the conflagration, she was impervious to criticism, and Anthony seems not to have long sustained anger against her "soul mate." An interesting facet of this story was that one of the Reverend Beecher's younger sisters did blame him for womanizing. Isabella Beecher Hooker and her husband shared Anthony's sense of shame, and it was John Hooker who prophetically wrote, "A reaction in the public mind will send the [woman's] struggle down to another generation and postpone its triumph for thirty years."[47]

    Indeed, most saw Woodhull's free love advocacy as a threat to the sanctity of the family, and while scandal's political implications may be immeasurable, Stanton's and Anthony's NWSA never escaped its taint. For a short while, Elizabeth Cady Stanton tried to justify Victoria Woodhull's attempt to enlarge discussion of women's freedoms—whether within or outside social institutions. Then on August 3, 1872 Stanton yielded to pressures to repudiate Victoria Woodhull. She published an article in Lucy Stone's *Woman's Journal* about NWSA withdrawing its support for Woodhull and her unorthodox methods. Of course, this belated repudiation of the Woodhull alliance did little to quiet public discontent over woman's rights. The ongoing publicity brought widespread departures from NWSA and crippled feminist recruitment for many years.

    The Woodhull affair created further divisions between the New York City and Boston suffrage factions. In Connecticut, Olympia Brown severed her state's ties with NWSA. By the end of 1871, 14 out of 15 state suffrage societies voted to become auxiliaries of AWSA. During the period when America had two suffrage organizations no significant breakthroughs occurred. In fact, there were thirty-two losses at the state level. Thus, suffrage languished during the last third of the nineteenth century because battling women reformers' tactical maneuvering often-eclipsed ethics questions.[49]

Lucretia Mott and Frances Gage were two feminists who watched all this from the sidelines, though for different reasons. Like Mott, Frances Gage expressed satisfaction about being out of the fray, an attitude imposed by her 1867 stroke. By temperament, each woman quietly disapproved of rancor amongst reformers. From her invalid's bed, Frances Gage followed the brouhaha and dryly commented in a note to Clara Barton, "I confess the Woodhull Movement doesn't commend itself to my highest perceptions."[49] Irony aside, she was appalled that Train and Woodhull had stained the movement's public image.

Consider the amazing reversals that followed the Civil War. At first, Frances Dana Gage's was celebrated as a bright star amongst American reformers because of her unique credentials. Theodore Tilton, prestigious Editor of the *Independent*, at the Twenty Ninth Meeting of Pennsylvania's Anti-Slavery Society, quoted her speech from the 1866 Eleventh National Woman's Rights Convention. He praised Frances Gage's political acumen and influence on legislative committees. Tilton emphasized the fact that Gage's writing and speaking enlarged women's legal and civil status.[50]

Her words also echoed at a Senate Congressional Hearing, "Suffrage in the District." On December 11, 1866, Democratic Senator Cowan from Pennsylvania placed Frances Dana Gage's words in the *Proceedings*. He praised her as "a lady, a lady of brain and intellect, of courage and force"; Cowan quoted parts of speech Gage had recently given; it explained why woman's problems would arise if only black men received suffrage. This included references to her Beaufort experience with two black freedwomen whose hard-earned savings needed to be protected from impecunious husbands. Frances Gage also referred to San Domingo where she observed unequal marriages in which women suffered under their husbands' tyranny. Hence, she opposed Congressional proposals that threatened to impose marriage upon freedwomen. Rep. Cowan concluded his speech by warning Congressmen, "Mrs. Elizabeth Cady Stanton, Mrs. Frances Dana Gage, Miss Susan B. Anthony, are upon your heels . . . their cry is for justice."[51]

Sadly, this prescient warning fell on deaf ears. After August 1867, Frances Gage was no longer upon anyone's heels. She remained housebound in New York City and disappointed by the schism amongst women reformers. Her sympathies continued with Lucy Stone and the New England feminists. Like them, she felt blindsided by Anthony's and Stanton's abandonment of the AERA. However, Gage supported the abolitionists' Constitutional protections for freedmen. Her philosophy was that half a loaf was better than none, and she wrote, "Could I with breath defeat the Fifteenth Amendment, I would not do it."[52] She was unable to attend Lucy Stone's organizing convention in Cleveland for the American Women's Suffrage Association or AWSA, but was listed as a supporter. The group was supported by a cadre of Gage's old friends; among them were Henry B. Blackwell, Julia Ward Howe, Antoinette Brown Blackwell, and Henry Ward Beecher who at that time was asked to head the AWSA. The organization argued that women's enfranchisement could be pursued at the state level, just as married women's rights were before the Civil War. The popular AWSA drew membership from 22 states and territories.

Through visitors and reading, Frances Gage intently followed such postbellum developments. Late in the 1860,'s she left her daughter's New York City home and moved to Vineland, New Jersey where she hoped to recuperate at a progressive residential care facility being run by Dr. Wilcox. The village was a place she knew well, having previously given rights speeches there, and it was conveniently located with train service to Philadelphia and New York City. In 1865, its population was 5,500, and the forward thinking village built Plum Street Hall to welcome lecturers. So, when Frances Dana Gage went to Vineland, she gained an address that made her accessible to reform friends, as well as placed her near Gage family relatives.

The town was characterized by encouragement of rights activity. Lucy Stone in 1858 refused to pay property taxes in Vineland because she was denied suffrage. Eight years later, she and Henry Blackstone formed the Equal Rights Association in Vineland. In Nov. 1867, Lucretia and James Mott, along with Stone and Blackwell, held a Women's Rights Convention in Vineland. That year the New Jersey Women's Suffrage Association began in Vineland, and Lucy Stone addressed the State Legislature on "Woman Suffrage in New Jersey," reminding legislators that between 1797 and 1807 their Constitution approved votes by "he or she."⁵³ In 1868, old friends Lucy Stone and Antoinette Brown Blackwell petitioned the New Jersey Legislature for improved women's property rights, which were denied. That year among the village's visiting speakers were the prominent reformers Frederick Douglas and Susan B. Anthony.

So, friends percolated through Vineland. The invalided Ohioan was also near her husband's Gage's family relatives, namely her brother-in-law, John Gage, his wife Portia, and their sons who moved to Vineland in 1864. Their son, Jared Gage, was brought home from Andersonville prison in Georgia where he nearly starved. He lingered until January 12, 1868. This pathetic Gage death spurred the family of John and Portia into political activity. That spring, the couple went to the polls and demanded that Portia Gage vote in her dead son's place. They were among those who helped found the New Jersey Suffrage Association.

John Gage agreed with his sister-in-law that it was possible to honor both race and sex equity. He called a public meeting to prepare material for "impartial suffrage irrespective of sex or color" at Trenton's upcoming suffrage convention. When Cleveland's next American Women's Rights Convention met, Lucy Stone celebrated Portia Gage's Vineland revolt. Her defiance of the political status quo was also seized upon by Stanton and Anthony who covered it in *The Revolution*. In August that year, these women built on this reform publicity, and each woman addressed Vineland suffrage gatherings. Election Day Nov. 3, 1868 became famous because 171 Vineland women challenged authorities at the polls. The *Cincinnati Daily Gazette* on Nov. 26, 1869 reprinted a dispatch about Portia Gage's assertiveness called, "Women of the Period."⁵⁴

Frances Gage watched this Vineland political activity. She was aware her brother-in-law's family members were invigorated autumnal reformers and knew the "Gage" name she had made famous might "ring a bell" and buoy up Portia Gage's reception. The invalid certainly was aware that Stanton and Anthony used her nephew's death and sister-in-law's suffrage lobbying as useful tools for woman's rights publicity. Portia Gage's activism continued in several directions, for example, she criticized Vineland churches' for their tax exemptions and corresponded with national figures like Clara Barton and Sojourner Truth to whom in 1867 she sent $20. The aged Truth traveled through New Jersey in 1870 and visited Vineland where she thanked Portia Gage who wrote, "Our house received a new baptism, through Sojourner Truth . . . a wonderful teacher." [55]

Elizabeth Cady Stanton did not maintain contact with Gage after her 1867 stroke and removal from the AERA's deconstruction; she was aware the Ohioan had sided with her old friend Lucy Stone and the "traditional reform" faction. Tension between Stanton and Gage surfaced in 1871 when Stanton published biographical essays about "champions" of the women's rights movement. Her brief entry on "Frances D. Gage" contained several factual errors that Gage considered "only a little less criminal than forgery or theft." When Frances Gage finally was visited by Stanton, she complained about this "unscrupulous handling the facts," and Stanton replied, "What need you care?" The underlying basis of this animosity is unclear. Possibly, Stanton felt pique because Frances Dana Gage supported the AWSA, or it might have been more longstanding. Or, for that matter, Stanton may just have been a lazy writer with a lack of interpersonal sensitivity. The effect of her dismissal was to further estrange the invalid Gage who felt used and abandoned. This altercation helps to explain her subsequent complaints in letters to Clara Barton. She wrote, "Stanton and Anthony have never recognized me as a worker in any way as having been a leader. They and only they have nurtured this great country." She added at another time that it was a relief to be no longer obliged to "worship at the Anthony Stanton shrine."[56]

Elizabeth Cady Stanton is a quixotic figure. She once bragged to a friend, "I usually present the exterior of a saint."[57] This was her cultivated self-image. Good fortune gave her wonderful health and a patriarch who provided financial stability. Both her Seneca Falls and New Jersey houses were paid for with his largesse, making her economically independent from her husband. Her speeches seem to be lawyerly, ironic and rambling. Her alter ego, Susan B. Anthony, was an enabler. Stanton's autobiography and editorship of the long work known as *History* offers what one biographer calls, "a narrow perch from which to declaim universal truths."[58]

Many reformers struggled over Elizabeth Cady Stanton's refusal to accept the idea that black men should be granted the franchise, while women, black and white, were denied. No war had been fought for woman's rights, but Stanton's *The Revolution* expressed the idea that it was a war and had never ceased. Needing funding for her newspaper may have clouded Stanton's judgment.

Her rapturous endorsement of George Frances Train and subsequent bid for financial support from Victoria Woodhull were precarious reeds to lean upon. These failures isolated Stanton who grew ungracious to other reformers.

There was lack of communication. Stanton drove away Rev. Beecher, Theodore Tilden, and Woodhull; she angered Lucy Stone, Francis Gage, and other reformers. The estrangement of old colleagues did not preoccupy Elizabeth Cady Stanton because she was pursuing another idea. She would cement a positive reputation for woman's rights through permanent media—written history. Another late idea was to rewrite the *Bible*.

The question differences between Stanton and Gage is, perhaps, self-evident. Meeting as successful adults in the 1850s, each calculated how the other's origins were different. One was pioneer stock and the other a Brahmin eastern product. Both women began their public lives about the same time and simultaneously raised a large family. Abolition in 1840 was an idea that taught Elizabeth Cady Stanton about hierarchical organizing to advocate social change. She transferred this idea to her personal situation and mulled over organizing for woman's rights. Then she cultivated an army of reformers to promote woman's suffrage, so that she could lead the movement.

Gage began as a "hands on" abolition worker who assisted escaped slaves. She was committed and glad to follow a leader. Whereas Stanton looked for acolytes, Gage looked for peers. Whereas Stanton saw battle, Gage saw amity. The end of the Civil War brought changes in society and in social movements for change. Frances Gage was willing to compromise on abolition and women's rights so long as she could continue to fight intemperance. Stowe was not a compromiser or a quitter, and if women could not have the franchise, she would continue fighting for new goals; if those stalled, she would preserve their work in written history.

History is, indeed, told by the survivors. Frances Dana Gage was not destined to be such a survivor. The conflict between these two women illustrates how the idealist was injured by the strategist. To be precise, Frances Gage believed in sisterhood and expected Elizabeth Cady Stanton to correct her inaccurate biographical essay. She refused. Gage waited; as an invalid, it was all she could do, but then in March 1883, a year before her death, Gage published "Autobiography" in the *Woman's Journal*. Her essay corrects Stanton's depiction of Barker-Gage family members.[59] She repudiated Stanton's calling her father, Joseph Barker, a "cooper" because he was a substantial land-owning farmer, judge, and lawmaker. She corrected his birthplace. Frances Gage thought the biggest insult from the New Yorker was the dismissal of her girlhood's mental training. Stanton wrote, "A log cabin in the woods was the seminary where Frances Barker acquired the rudiments of education." The worst thing for Gage was the assertion that her pioneer family life provided "few early advantages."[60]

There was a time in her life when Frances Gage sought to extend her reputation through new friendships, including Stanton and Anthony. The Ohio born matron eventually became independent from the New Yorkers' ideological control and came to resent their manipulative sense of superiority. Gage compared them unfavorably to Clara Barton who offered authentic friendship and "good true nature."[61]

If young Elizabeth Cady Stanton's budding friendship with abolitionist Lucretia Mott had somehow freed her to plan for woman's rights, what an odd development to later see Stanton spurn other reform friendships. It was finally as if neither abolition nor temperance seriously interested the New Yorker, but each was a useful stage for proclamations. Regionalism for Stanton sounded like a strategy, although her tolerance for diversity was thin; for instance, she proclaimed herself heroic for surviving a brief Middle Western visit that included wild pigs, insects, and clodhoppers. Accustomed to wealth, Stanton relished luxuries and in 1869 joined James Redpath's Lyceum Bureau. She worked this circuit for the next 12 years, receiving fees of one to two hundred dollars a night.

Into the 1870's, the national woman's rights movement, per se, became quiescent, but women in Frances Gage's home state were busy exercising civil disobedience. During the winter of 1874, grass roots ferment burst into the news from Hillsboro, Ohio, a tiny village located 74 miles east of Cincinnati. Ordinarily conservative Midwestern women organized marches, sit-ins, pray-ins, and sing-ins that closed saloons. National notoriety about Ohio's disruptive events highlighted the women's bravery. The "Woman's Crusade" led to a reform movement called the Women's Christian Temperance Union or WCTU that was headquartered in Cleveland.

In the spring of 1874, Ohio's Constitutional Convention met to discuss topics like women's rights and liquor regulation. Rebecca Janney, a childhood friend, led this convention and carried

Gage's letter of support to Ohio Legislators, but the feminists were rebuffed. Ohio's political climate was rancorous, and the state's voters rejected Ohio's proposed 1874 Constitution, which left questions of women's rights in limbo.

It appears that Ohio women's late century activism was a reawakening of the colleagueship that Frances Dana Gage's generation experienced at 1850's reform conventions. She rejoiced over Ohio's women's reappearance in public life. If she were well enough to have read Mark Twain's 1883 description of the Hillsboro women's activism in the WCTU's publication, *Union Signal*, Frances Gage would have been elated by the group's endorsement of woman's suffrage. This resurgence of moral rectitude was articulated by the group's historian, suffragist Mary Livermore, who wrote about the power of woman-to-woman associations.[62]

Before Frances Dana Gage passed away in 1884, a different generation was taking up the standard. One example of a younger woman who became a reform leader was Olympia Brown. In 1857, when she was studying religion at Antioch College in Yellow Springs she heard Frances Gage lecture. By 1874, Olympia Brown was a women's rights reformer in Wisconsin. This transitional rights' figure wrote in her autobiography, "Aunt Fanny Gage was really one of the ablest women we have ever had in this country. She was strong and true and original."[63]

Overall, "Aunt Fanny" aka Frances Dana Gage, was a significant personality who at the time aroused consciousness of women's desperate need for legal rights. She brought national connections to a large swath of the Middle West. Just as her parents' trekked from New England over the Appalachian Mountains, their peripatetic daughter had a goal. Gage's woman's reform activities in the Midwest included—Indiana, Missouri, Nebraska, Ohio, Iowa, and Illinois. The intrepid trailblazer introduced woman's rights activism in Iowa and Illinois; in 1864, she aided Illinois to become the first state east of the Mississippi to pass a woman suffrage law. In the South, Gage worked in South Carolina, Tennessee, Florida, Mississippi, and Louisiana where Gage was the state's first woman's rights speaker in New Orleans. In the Northeast, she lectured in Massachusetts, Vermont, Pennsylvania, and New York.

For several decades, Aunt Fanny brought sincerity and constancy to Mid-Western reformers. The Buckeye's study, contacts, and convention participation enriched her grass roots outreach to isolated farmwomen for whom she was an invaluable mentor and role model. Her reform career propelled her into the ranks of nationally prized orators, although the validation was short lived because of her 1867 collapse. Gage had been courted by Eastern women's rights advocates whose later billowing self-importance and misused authority angered her. Being told she had outlived her usefulness was unkind, unnecessary, and unjust.

History's volumes quote a variety of contemporaries who praised Frances Dana Gage, but the best measure of Gage's worth is seen in her reprinted writings. As Lillian O'Connor points out in *Pioneer Woman Orators,* many of her early speeches were not preserved.[64] The ones that are extant present the clever author, despite her "modesty of self,"[65] to a later era's readers. Among the preserved speeches are those from such historic gatherings as Akron's Second Ohio Woman's Rights Conference in Sept. 1851 and Cincinnati's first Ohio Woman's Temperance Convention. These provide a sense of a quick mind and fresh wit embodied in wonderful stories told with panache. Gage tempered her anger with humor and irony to assail those who attacked woman's rights advocates.

A typical example was her early tale about dueling with a McConnelsville judge who sneered at women's petitions to close grog shops. Law was on his side but logic was not. He wanted women to remain in the nursery and parlor and blamed mothers for their sons' failures. Gage seized the opportunity to retort, "What mother ever taught her son to drink rum, gamble, swear, smoke, and chew tobacco?" She warned the patriarch that mothers cannot impose moral standards on sons that their fathers will not follow. Her argument concluded that a son who is taught his mother is inferior will find it unmanly to obey her guidelines.[66] The judge grew silent. In this way, Frances Dana Gage's reputation for firm public stands on women's issues grew in McConnelsville.

America's woman's reform movement left Frances Gage on its sidelines in 1867. It split in two and achieved little for several decades. In fact, the bad publicity garnered by Susan B. Anthony and Elizabeth Cady Stanton from their courting of George Francis Train and Victoria Woodhull turned many Americans against the woman's rights movement. Seeing this happen disappointed Gage but did not surprise her because she believed that temperament foretold events. On the other hand, the meetings and infrastructure created in her home state during the early 1850's again brought passionate reformers together into genuine friendships. Moreover, their work educated politicians and won over supporters. They did not need Eastern reformers like Antony to speed the process. Frances Gage was justly proud of their success in 1861 with the Married Women's Rights Bill. This was a satisfying step forward. In fact, for Gage it was a matter of being shown a field that needed to be tilled and undertaking the job. That her "crop" was a product called rights for women was very gratifying.

Chapter 3

NOTES

1. Frances Gage, "Looking Back, "*The Woman's Advocate* 1 (January 1869):2.
2. Nell Irvin Painter, *Sojourner Truth, a Life, a Symbol* (New York: W.W. Norton and Company, 1966), 175.
3. Alexis De Tocqueville, *Democracy in America*, eds. Harvey Mansfield and Delba Winthrop. (Chicago: University of Chicago Press, 2000), 131.
4. Gage, "Letter to Salem Women's Rights Convention, April, 1850," *Woman on Woman Suffrage, 1881-1902)* 1 ed. Elizabeth Cad Stanton et al. (New York: Schocken Books, 1970), 117.
5. Barbara A. Terzian, "Frances D. Gage and the Northern Woman's Reform Activities in the Nineteenth Century, *Builders of Ohio* (Columbus: Ohio State University Press, 2003) 112.
6. *History* 1, 117.
7. J. Elizabeth Jones, "Report, May 16, 1861," *History* 1, 169.
8. Terzian, 113-114.
9. Gage, "Letter from Mrs. Gage,: *Ohio Cultivator* 8, no. 23 (Dec. 1, 1852), 366,
10. ____, "Woman's Rights Meeting in a Barn, May 1852," and "John's Convention, Mount Gilead, Ohio, Dec. 1, 1852," in "Letter to Matilda J. Gage," *History* 1, 118.
11. Amelia Bloomer, "Letter, July 30, 1880," *The Life and Writings of Amelia Bloomer*, ed. Dexter Bloomer (New York: Schocken Books, 1975), 41.
12. Susan Conrad Phinney, *Perish the Thought* (New York: Oxford University Press, 1976), 242.
13. Eleanor Flexnor, *Century of Struggle* ((Cambridge: Harvard University Press, 1959), 91.
14. Susan Cummins Miller, *Sweet Separate Intimacy, Women Writers of the American Frontier, 1800-1822,* (Salt Lake City: University of Utah Press, 2000), 32-34.
15. Gage, "Looking," 5.
16. Elizabeth Cady Stanton, *Eighty Years and More, Reminiscences, 1815-1897* (New York: Schocken Books, 1971), 83.

17. Janet Zollinger Giele, *Two Paths to Woman's Equality* (New York: Twayne Press, 1995), 3.

18. *History* 1, 689-99.

19. Lucy Stone, *Friends and Sisters: Letters between Lucy Stone and Antoinette Brown Blackwell, 1846-1893,* (Urbana: University of Illinois Press, 1997).

20. Alice Stone Blackwell, *Lucy Stone: Pioneer of Woman's Rights* (Boston: Brown and Little: 1930).

21. Phinney, 139.

22. Ibid., 242.

23. Bloomer, 97.

24. Ibid., 133.

25. Ida Husted Harper, ed. *The Life and Works of Susan B. Anthony* (Indianapolis: Bower-Merrill Company, 1898), 184.

26. Ibid.

27. Gage, *History* 1, 656.

28. Lillian O'Connor, *Pioneer Woman Orators* (New York: Columbia University Press, 1954), 91.

29. "The Speakers," *Daily Picayune* (March 17, 1854): 92.

30. Gage, "Letter," *History* 1, 126.

31. Clara C. Holtzman, *Frances Gage*, M. A. Thesis, (Ohio State University, 1931), 27.

32. Gage, "Letter," *Field Notes*, (April 12, 1861).

33. Laurence Friedman, *A History of the Law* (New York: Simon and Shuster, 1973), 184.

34. Ibid.

35. *History* 1, 168.

36. Elizabeth Jones, "Report," *Field Notes* (April 1861).

37. Jones, "Letter to Frances Gage," *History* 1, 174.

38. Gage, *History* 1, 168.

39. Ann Russo and Cherri Kramarae, *Radical Women's Press of the 1850's* (New York: Rutledge, 1991), 301-302.

40. William Lloyd Garrison, in Eleanor Rice Hays, *Morning Star, Biography of Lucy Stone, 1818-1891,* (New York: Octagon Books, 1961), 197.

41. Flexnor, 150.

42. Ibid.

43. Lucretia Mott, "Letter to Cousin Mary, Oct. 16, 1855," *James and Lucretia Mott's Life and Letters*, ed. Anna Davis Hallowell (Cambridge: Houghton and Mifflin, Co., 1884), 383.

44. ____, "Letter June 10, 1866," 418.

45. ___, "Letter," 454.
46. Elizabeth Cady Stanton, "Letter to Susan B. Anthony, Jan. 31, 1871," Elizabeth Cady Stanton (Washington: D. C. Collection, Library of Congress).
47. John Hooker, "Letter to Isabella Beecher Hooker, Oct. 31, 1871," Isabella Beecher Hooker Project, "Letters and Papers," (Hartford, Conn.: Harriet Beecher Stowe Center).
48. Phinney, 240.
49. Gage, "Letter, Jan 6, 178," Barton Correspondence.
50. Theodore Tilton, "Address,: *Proceedings of the Eleventh National Woman's Rights Convention, May 10, 1866."*
51. Rep. Cowan, "Suffrage in the District, Congressional Hearing, Dec. 1, 1866) *History* 2, 116.
52. Gage, "Letter," Barton Correspondence.
53. Lucy Stone, "Woman Suffrage in New Jersey," Address delivered to Legislature, March 6, 1867 (Boston: C H. Simonds & Co., Publishers).
54. *History* 6, 113-114.
55. Portia Gage in Carleton and Susan Mabee, *Sojourner Truth: Slave, Prophet, Legend* (New York: New York University Press, 1995), 181.
56. Gage, "Letter to Barton," Barton Correspondence.
57. Stanton, "Letter to Martha Coffin Wright, March 8, 1873," in *Selected Papers*, 2, ed. Ann D. Gordon (New Jersey: Rutgers University Press, 1977), 306.
58. Lori Ginzburg, *Elizabeth Cady Stanton: an American Life* (New York: Hill and Wang, 2009), 193.
59. Gage, "Autobiography."
60. Stanton, "The Woman's Rights Movement and Its Champions in the United States," eds. James Parton et al. *Women of the Age: Being Narratives of the Lives and Deeds of the Most Prominent Women of the Present Generation* Hartford: S. M Betts & Co., 1871), 382.
61. Gage, "Letter, 1872," Barton Correspondence.
62. Mary Livermore, *Union Signal* (Dec. 20, 1883): 7-9.
63. Olympia Brown, *Acquaintances Old and New Among Reformers* (Milwaukee: S. E. ate, 1911), 10.
64. O'Conner, 93.
65. Ibid.
66. Gage, "Speech for Ohio Woman's Rights Convention," *History* 1, 360.

Barker Cabin

Colonel Joseph Barker's Home

Elizabeth Cady Stanton   Susan B. Anthony

Sojourner Truth   Frederick Douglas

Lucy Stone　　　Antoinette Brown

Clara Barton

Chapter Four

"Devil's Broth," Gage and Temperance

In a sense, France Barker's earliest and most passionate "cause" was hated of drunkenness. This resentment grew from her dislike of her father's still on their farm.[1] It was a family skeleton that inspired her first novel *Elsie Magoon, or the Old Still House in the Hollow, a Tale of the Past.* This work dramatized an Ohio Valley pioneer settlement vitiated by alcoholism. The protagonist's surname, "Magoon" is Gaelic and was adopted by Frances Gage from an Aunt Fanny Dana who married Josiah Magoon in New Hampshire in 1809. He was wounded while serving in the Continental Army.

Observation of drunkenness was detestable; France Barker was horrified by the intemperance she witnessed in Marietta. Of course, her father defended his still on the Barker property. Eventually she learned that temperance had a long tradition in America's nineteenth century reform movement with contexts that included spiritual, cultural and social ferment. She was a pragmatist. Without legal ways to prevent drunkenness, alcoholics faced only the consequences of a hangover. The underlying ethical issue was other persons' welfare, usually the family. Her instinctive repugnance reflected a broader sense in the culture that Steven Mintz explains as a new moral perspective that was "acutely sensitive to cruelty, drunkenness, and physical disorder."[2]

It was not until she was a young wife in McConnelsville that Frances Gage could enter public discussions and become a temperance advocate in Ohio. In McConnelsville, Frances Gage gradually became a local leader in Ohio's temperance movement as she called meetings and began to publish her sentiments. For instance, her "Letter" to Amelia Bloomer's *The Lily* in May 6, 1851 describes an overflowing meeting in Mount Airy where the noteworthy politician John B. Gough spoke, leading many McConnelsville guests to sign temperance pledges.[3] Later her expanded activism included supporting various proposals for Ohio legislative changes that proposed restrictions on alcohol sales. These were similar to the 1851 Maine Law. They were obstructed by Ohio's economic and political forces that blocked legal impediments to alcohol production and distribution. Later in the decade, many temperance advocates, like Gage, shifted their energies toward more responsive rights issues, notably anti-slavery and women's rights. Yet, Frances Gage was loyal to the cause and never diminished her hated of intemperance because she believed men's drunkenness undermines the family and victimizes women and children. She thought widespread anti-social consequences were created by alcoholism and most "criminals of our land are the victims of intemperance."[4] In her maturity, the experiences of living in St. Louis's sodden environs and in South Carolina's Sea Islands where "our boys" were encouraged by hyper masculine military culture to regularly drink alcohol reinforced Gage's hatred of alcohol. It was the Civil War and official endorsement of alcohol rations that gave temperance workers in the early 1860s little hope for outlawing demon alcohol.

Over the years Frances Gage's opposition to alcohol is preserved in temperance essays that employed a variety of approaches. At first, she wrote what the era called "moral suasion," meaning women in general should use their influence to urge men to remain sober. Like other women, she wished to revise the Ohio Constitution. Some of her early temperance essays were outright polemical attacks on unjust laws. This approach was adapted for a certain type of moralistic fiction or short fables that resembled Lydia Sigourney's "The Wife of the Intemperate" which the *National Anti-Slavery Standard* published in July 20, 1843. More than a decade later, Frances Gage in 1854 composed two similar "Tales of Truth" for *The Lily*. Each taught the value of sobriety by illustrating women being damaged by intemperate husbands. A third narrative strategy was philosophically arguing for justice; this was a social class appeal that explained to upper class men how they could offer aid and set an example for lower class men. The corollary of this approach was an implied threat—if men refused to help victims, and then women would become engaged, gain the franchise, and vote against alcohol production and distribution.

Behind these temperance strategies, lay decades of American attempts to solve the problem of alcohol abusing others' personal liberty. As early as 1784, Dr. Benjamin Rush published an influential pamphlet, "An Inquiry into the Effects of Ardent Spirits upon the Human Body and Mind." A more prominent leader, Benjamin Franklin, also pointed out that spirits cause observable ill effects on the body. He was reinforced by a chorus of voices. The

Society of Friends in 1760, the Methodist Church in 1780, and the Universalists in 1800—all opposed spirits. About 1813, protests developed among Eastern men's organizations, including the Massachusetts' Society for the Suppression of Intemperance. In 1825 clergyman Lyman Beecher of Litchfield, Connecticut preached "Six Sermons on Intemperance" that repudiated all use of liquor, and the following year the American Temperance Society was established. It combined religious and secular forces and used writers to promote its cause, as did similar groups, like the American Temperance Legion (1836), the American Temperance Union (1838), Good Templars (1851), and the National Temperance Society and Publication House (1865).

Public debates, however, did not squelch Americans' taste for spirits. For many decades, alcoholic beverages had been a daily diet staple and a form of liquid nourishment. Alcohol was used in cooking and was often more safely consumed than water which, until the advent of municipal waterworks in the 1840's, was frequently polluted. As well, milk was sometimes unavailable, and tea and coffee were expensive. Often drinking alcohol was an element of domestic hospitality that took place in family or community-defined environments. In fact, at one time alcohol was looked on as a pharmacopoeia—"it numbed pain, eased headaches, lowered fever, cured infection, soothed troubled minds and revived low spirits."[5] Nor was there an early accepted concept of "addiction" to spirits. Occasional drunkards' behavior was tolerated. As a result, adult Americans' per capita consumption by 1830 reached nearly four gallons of absolute alcohol.[6]

During the mid-century decades, the word "temperance" shifted between three different meanings. At first, being "temperate" meant "abstention from distilled liquors and moderate consumption of beer, wine, and hard cider," which were often not considered to be alcohol.[7] Then a second meaning evolved, and "temperance" came to mean total abstinence. Later, a third meaning appeared that refined "total abstinence"— that was "teetotalism." This meant a Temperance Pledge card was usually signed with a conspicuous "T" for "Total Abstainer," and it became popular. The American Temperance Union promoted teetotalism with its Pledge. Frances Gage illustrates such meetings in her two novels, *Elsie Magoon* and *Steps Upward,* the happily converted sign temperance pledges. A typical example follows: "The use of intoxicating liquor . . .[is] hurtful to the social, civil, and religious interests of men; . . .

[we] agree, that we will not use it, or traffic in it;. . . we will discountenance the use of it throughout the community."[8]

"Dry" temperance advocates often stressed the need for punitive social controls. Many did not understand alcohol's role in masculine social culture or its economic dimension. In the first place, pioneer migration and social dislocation sent men into places outside the home, which weakened traditional community restraints on their behavior. Secondly, frontier men who engaged in hard physical labor out of doors saw drinking spirits as a voluntary and informal group activity. Taverns and saloons became male social institutions that provided homosocial environments for men to enjoy outside the family. Here men found male companionship, often including rituals like talking, wrestling, and competitive drinking of spirits. Moreover, alcohol was an indispensable painkiller that was believed to increase productivity, heighten stamina, and lengthen longevity. In fact, spirits were expected at work sites and provided as refreshment at social events. A historian records, "Alcohol lubricated work in frontier Ohio."[9] For all of these reasons, stills like that of Frances Barker's father were among the first buildings erected in a new settlement."[10]

Other aspects of spirits' role in American culture were political, legal, and economic. Questions arose over whether distillers had the unimpeded right to sell or government the right to tax alcohol. Many early government measures were designed to enforce temperance goals, such as Massachusetts' 1838 "Fifteen-Gallon Law" which prohibited the sale of small quantities of spirits, except for medical or "mechanical purposes." In Ohio, temperance reformers in the 1840s and 1850s sought to modify the State's Constitution, and many municipalities passed local statutes to this effect. Gage never focuses upon government taxation. In *Elsie Magoon*, the still burns down and life goes on. Her final novel, *Steps Upward*, presents a distillery owner who converts a vast distillery into other uses. It joins social responsibility and profit. Hence, Gage's late novels demonstrate the closing an evil still, and society improves. It is to her credit that by the end of her productive life in the postbellum era Frances Gage sought pragmatic economic alternatives to distilling alcohol's.

Temperance fiction blamed male drunkenness for absence, violence, domestic abuse, irresponsible behavior, and failure of family support—all undermining America's domestic values. It avoided the reality that pioneer settlers and frontier housewives did brewing, drank patent medicines, and used liquor for cooking. In this sense women and children, too, had long been complicit in an alcohol tolerant culture. Eventually, America's ideology of separate gender spheres matured and social disapproval grew toward women's consumption of spirits. By mid-century, native-born American women "were probably either cautious drinkers or abstainers."[11] Many novels of the period depict well-bred women who are repulsed by alcohol. Yet, Gage's second novella, *Gertie's Sacrifice,* told a dirty truth—some women sneaked drinks and defied the code of female sobriety. It was shocking to nineteenth-century women readers when an alcoholic upper-class matron falls into disrepute. "The wages of sin" is dying in prison on Governor's Island. This was not typical temperance fiction.

Another facet of America's alcohol problem was the influx of European immigrants from Germany and Ireland. Many brought "indulgent attitudes toward drink." The group that interests Francis Gage is the Irish. They fled the 1840s famine and were among America's largest pre-Civil War group of immigrants. They reputedly had an indulgent and guilt-free view of alcohol and rationalized its presence; this significantly influenced America's working-class ethics.[12] Gage was familiar with Irish immigrants, and her fiction describes the practices of several Irish topers. One woman is reformed and "dry" before the novel opens and aims to be a force for sobriety, while another is a washerwoman who repudiates alcohol only after her drunken husband drowns in a pig's mud hole.

Following the Revolutionary War, rum trade with the West Indies declined, so American production increased. By 1810, alcohol represented ten per cent of the country's total manufacturing output, making it America's third most important industrial product. The spirits industry had deep pockets and political clout. On the national level, temperance represented a line was drawn in the sand—on one side were distillers, farmers, grog shop owners, and men who protected their prerogatives. This lobbying group publicly argued that democracy must be characterized by freedom of choice.

The state of Ohio represents a useful microcosm of nineteenth-century American temperance issues. The region was granted statehood in 1803, and its first recorded temperance lecture occurred two years later when a white man preached to a group of Indians near Toledo.[13] The state often led American temperance activities and was influential "as a populous state on national political developments."[14] Between 1792 and 1851, Ohioans studied legislation that would license alcoholic establishments. In 1838 and

1839, "petitions" were submitted to abolish the licensing system, though it was not until 1847 that two "dry" bills passed, one required "scientific temperance instruction" in public schools, and the other gave local townships the option of voting to be wet or dry. The state's citizens organized its first temperance society in 1818 in Springfield; twelve years later, there were 30 such groups. Branches of the American Temperance Society arose in Ohio by 1829, and the Ohio State Temperance Society was formed the following year. The Washingtonian Society appeared in Ohio in 1840 and the Sons of Temperance in 1845.[15]

An early strategy of such reformers was education. Ohioans enjoyed reading about temperance and by the 1830s supported eleven weekly or monthly regional temperance publications. Each served a local Ohio region, for instance Columbus had its *Advocate*; Cincinnati supported the *Western Temperance Journal, Morning Star,* and *Philanthropist*; Massillon had the *Genius of Temperance*; Medina County read *The Pledge*; and in northeast Ohio Clevelanders read the *Temple of Honor*. Whether such publications changed the climate of opinion about alcohol production is unclear, but by mid-century Ohio farmers were shifting from turning corn into whisky to using it for livestock feed. This was a national trend as Americans' per capita consumption underwent a precipitous decline in 1840 from "nearly four gallons in 1830 to about two gallons." [16] By this point, a tenth of America's population belonged to temperance societies. Historians credit both the influence of temperance advocates and evolving economic realities for Ohio Valley farmers. They felt the discipline of the market and changed their perceptions of managing their farmhands.

The dynamics of production were simple. When the corn crop was converted into domestic whiskey, it allowed easy preservation and transport on rivers. Hence, many farmers supported distilleries. Historian Jack S. Blocker reports, "As settlers moved into the new lands of the Ohio Valley they found them well suited to growing grain, especially corn, but poorly situated for marketing their crops."[17] This wasn't true for Rufus Putnam's settlers who built Marietta distilleries. They had the Muskingum, Ohio, and Mississippi River system at hand. The rivers were useful for moving grain and spirits south to the New Orleans' market; also Ohio whiskey was transported across the Allegheny Mountains where it sold for less than eastern whiskey.

Frances Gage undertook challenging "corn's" economic value in her two "western" novels; each claiming to illustrate that there were more profitable uses for grain. From the beginning, Frances Gage saw a vacuum into which she could pitch her viewpoints and enter the public sphere; she enjoyed controversy and sent temperance writing and letters to those who might publish them. Perhaps her earliest success was with Amelia Bloomer in New York State. Their epistles led to friendship. After 1851 Gage was regularly publishing in *The Lily,* which became America's most notable temperance publication. Between Jan. 1, 1841 and 1854, Bloomer included a number of Gage's poems, stories, and "Letters" as valued perspectives from the Middle West. Bloomer became a temperance advocate after hearing Washingtonian lecturers, and Elizabeth Cady Stanton convinced her to expand her publication into "Emancipation of Woman from Intemperance, Injustice, Prejudice, and Bigotry." Stanton contributed high-minded woman's rights essays. As *The Lily's* influence grew, its circulation went from 300 issues a month to 6,000.

Amelia Bloomer is ironically remembered today as an advocate of women's clothing reform. It was seen as notorious in some quarters but progressive in others. She promoted "the bloomer costume"—a medium length skirt over slacks. This style was worn, at least temporarily, by such brave souls as Bloomer, Stone, and Stanton. Harriet Tubman ordered these clothes; instead of her slave costume, she wore practical "Bloomers" when wandering on spy missions in South Carolina. But in her own era Amelia Bloomer was prominent for fighting alcoholism. Her friend, the Middle Westerner Gage, did not prioritize dress reform or wear the new costume, rather she pled that women should dress as they chose. For instance, in 1858, she commented that every woman should "break out of her clothes-prison. . . . Each woman [may] adjust her dress to her relations in life."[18]

It could be said that Frances Gage's public entrance into national temperance advocacy came through New York State's Susan B. Anthony. When the Quaker was angered by men's refusal to include women in temperance organizations, she did what Mott had earlier done with abolition. Anthony formed a temperance society for women in April 1853. The Rochester Temperance Convention of Susan B. Anthony invited the Ohioan to write "words of counsel and encouragement." Gage's letter combined statistics and pulpit ardor. Today her facts might be questioned, but not the tone of sincerity or competent rhetoric. She stated that nine tenths of manufacturers, drinkers, and criminals are drunkards, while women are largely their victims. Because of such men's "depraved appetites and disorganized faculties," Gage wrote, women "must refuse to live the wives of drunkards" and should petition lawmakers for redress of wrongs.[19] Anthony was impressed by this disciplined and forceful mind and invited Frances Gage to join her on New York's reform rights platforms.

In the spring 1853, New Yorker Amelia Bloomer went "West" with her husband. First they came to Mt. Vernon, Ohio and later moved on to Council Bluffs, Iowa. As Gage was courting reformers in the East, Bloomer's husband wanted to go to the West. Then so did John Gage. The husbands made the decisions, and so the Gage family was uprooted from Ohio and moved to St. Louis, Missouri. At one point, the two women met in the Gage's new St. Louis home. Since the Missouri River was too high for Bloomer to cross, Frances Gage proposed that they join forces and lecture on Temperance at St. Louis's Mercantile Library Hall, the largest venue in the city. They drew a great crowd and were applauded by Susan B. Anthony who hoped they would continue attending eastern temperance conventions.[20]

Gage and Bloomer did go to New York City for two temperance meetings in September 1853 that brought conflicting values to the fore. It was an oddly similar experience to what had happened in 1850 London to abolitionist women like Lucretia Mott and Stanton. This time, The World Temperance Convention denied delegate status to women. During the fracas, Frances Gage was boarding in New York City with Antoinette Brown. They conferred with Amelia Bloomer and Lucy Stone who, in turn, were supported by H. W. Higginson and Wendell Phillips. It was decided to challenge the "men only rule" at the World Temperance Convention. Insisting she had a right to speak, Wendell Phillips urged Brown to step up on the platform and plant her "feet upon the rights of a delegate." Rev. Antoinette Brown, an ordained Congregational minister, feigned naivety, and addressed the crowd, saying that she took the convention's title, "World" literally. Since she was Wayne County's chosen delegate to the convention, Brown felt obligated to represent women "in behalf of the cause of humanity." With some drama, Rev. Antoinette Brown was "expelled from the platform." The temperance reformers responded to this masculine slight by adopting Susan B. Anthony's idea for an alternative organization, and called it the Whole World Temperance Convention where both sexes were delegates. "Mrs. Frances Gage" was elected vice president. [21]

The negative publicity from this confrontation forced Horace Greeley and the Republican Party to abandon their defense of sex separate reform organizations. In 1854, there were no "sex segregated conventions" since the "World's" base of supporters included women. The episode illustrates the quick rise in Frances Gage's status amongst reformers. She was accepted by America's most progressive temperance leaders and claimed in her "Reminiscences," perhaps disingenuously, that Rev. Brown's rebuff was a "knock-down surprise." Repercussions that autumn followed her back to Ohio. Weary after traveling two hundred miles to a state temperance meeting in Dayton, Frances Gage rose to give her keynote speech when she was brashly interrupted by "a column of well-dressed ladies, very fashionable and precise." "They proceeded to inform us, that they were delegated by a meeting of Dayton ladies [to speak against] . . . 'the unseemly and unchristian position . . . [of our] taking our places upon the platform, and seeking notoriety by making ourselves conspicuous before men." They criticized "the disgraceful conduct of Antoinette L. Brown" at the World's Temperance Convention and marched out.

Frances Gage set aside her written remarks and extemporized a rebuttal. She mocked, "Dayton's Mrs. Grundy's," for being sexist men's cats' paws. She assured the reform minded audience that Rev. Antoinette Brown was supported by American luminaries like "William H. Channing, William Lloyd Garrison, Oliver Johnson, and Wendell Phillips, [who] stood by her, bidding her to stand firm."[22]

A year later, the Whole World's Temperance Convention found Frances Gage standing on the speakers' platform to lecture. She addressed two temperance issues, rum traffic in the South and the Maine Law. Following that gathering, she presided at their temperance banquet as an officer alongside Horace Greeley. He was an example of a man who grew to support liberal reforms, including slaves' and women's rights which he described as economic issues. Greeley wanted his newspaper to be literary, idealistic, disinterested, and supportive of working people. His *New York Tribune* began in 1845, and in 1854 became the Republican Party's unofficial national organ. By mid-century, Greeley was the country's most influential anti-slavery editor; his readership included rural northerners from the Adirondack wilderness to the Western Reserve of Ohio, from Wisconsin to Illinois.23 His Sept. 3, 1854 issue of the *Tribune* praised the women speakers at the World Temperance Convention, including Antoinette L. Brown, Lucy Stone, and Frances Dana Gage, calling them "champions of reform and humanity." Greeley's colleagueship was an invaluable endorsement for Francis Gage, a real coup. Any retrospective of her life should highlight the tale of two temperance conventions in 1853 and 1854 that demonstrates how quickly Frances Gage was catapulted into the phalanx of America's leading reformers.

Among her temperance colleagues was the highly admired reformer Lucy Stone. At an 1853 temperance meeting chaired by Rev. H. W. Higginson, for instance, Stone was a leader who focused discussion upon the apparent success of Maine's new Liquor Law. Other attendees included Antoinette Brown, Horace Greeley, and Lucretia Mott. The group passed the following resolves: total abstinence, church support, removal of wine in communion, and the cessation of liquor's manufacture.[24]

Stone and Gage hoped America could build upon the precedent of Neal Dow's 1851 Maine Law, a prohibitory statue passed to outlaw the manufacture and sale of intoxicants. After two generations of agitation, Maine was the first state in America with a statute that prohibited all sales of alcoholic beverages, except for "medicinal" purposes; it also provided for the destruction of confiscated liquor. Reformers adapted the Maine Law as a precedent in their arguments against alcohol sales. This included P. T. Barnum who hated the "liquor stores and groggeries where death was dealt out in tumblers."[25] However, eventually the hopes raised by the Maine Law were dashed because it was not enforced. Later historians described its significance as bringing "liquor into politics."[26]

Among the prominent supporters of the Maine Law was Elizabeth Cady Stanton. Her rationale was that stopping alcohol production might increase women's participation in the "public sphere," making her half right. She advocated a Maine Law in New York State and backed Susan B. Anthony, Frances Gage, and others in their door-to-door grassroots campaign; this was also supported by such men as Samuel T. Townsend, a manufacturer of sarsaparilla. Then, when the New York law was in place, Anthony and Stanton confidently turned their eyes to Ohio where they wanted to add a similar statute to Ohio's 1851 Constitution that would ban the proliferation of liquor dealers. The proposal's Article SV, Section 9 in part read, "No license to traffic in intoxicating liquors shall hereafter be granted in this state." However, recalcitrant politicians blocked the Ohio bill's passage; they were secretly funded by whisky producers. Industry lobbyists were not about to see Ohio's authorities seize and destroy liquor. Stanton soon lost interest in Ohio, although other temperance advocates continued to lobby there during the early 1850s.[27]

In 1854, Ohio voters passed a ban upon the sale of spirits for on-premises consumption. The state's civil damage clause read, "it shall be unlawful for any one person or persons, by agent or otherwise, to sell in any quantity intoxicating liquors or to be drank in, upon, or about the building of premise where sold." It also became illegal to sell to minors. It was clear that Ohio voters intended to close saloons, the "poor men's clubs," yet 98% of these establishments continued to sell spirits simply by paying higher federal taxes. This increased agitation. Three years later, Ohio's 1857 Constitution prohibited legislators from passing laws to grant licenses for the sale of intoxicating liquors, but just like earlier efforts, it was not enforced. Overall, Ohio's halting endorsements for temperance were replicated in twelve states before the Civil War. [28]

Women who were frustrated by their inability to influence male dominated temperance organizations abandoned them; this group included Elizabeth Cady Stanton, Lucretia Mott, Susan B. Anthony, and Amelia Bloomer. Even the Sons of Temperance, which had a sister organization, the Daughters of Temperance, refused to let women speak at Sons' Conventions. Susan B. Anthony's resignation from the Sons of Temperance in 1852 began the precedent of women forming their own organizations. Word got around, and on Jan. 13, 1853, the Ohio Women's Temperance Society was formed in Columbus with Frances Gage's friend, Josephine Bateman, editor of the *Ohio Cultivator's* "Home Department," serving as its first president. Its ranks were swelled by women who had gained political experience and personal confidence from Stanton's and Anthony's instruction about how to draw up petitions for electoral and referendum contests.[29]

Thus, by 1853, the tenor of the temperance movement in the Middle West was changing. It shifted from men's groups into separate organizations for each gender. The following year, the

Ohio State Women's Temperance Society held its second convention in Dayton with Frances Gage speaking. Her reformer's constancy for the cause never wavered, and she was always available to organize, attend, and speak at temperance conventions, even small ones, such as one held in Rutland, Vermont. Her hatred of alcohol is never more clearly shown than in her essay, "Aunt Fanny's Removal to the West—First Impressions of St. Louis," that described local police arresting drunks who "do unseemly things." She complained about spirits in Missouri where whiskey "barrels border the pavements" and spirits are available at "nearly every grocery and drugstore." [29] At the time, St. Louis boasted having 15 distilleries and 35 brewers. Alcohol tolerant Missouri neighbors of the Gage family complained about her participation on temperance platforms. Missourians hated "the spirit of progressive reform," calling it "northern fanaticism—a *Yankee* notion . . . a humbug."[30]

Nonetheless, Frances Gage continued to write her *Ohio Cultivator* essays like, "Chapter about the Fourth of July." It tells Cultivator Girls that their agriculture work complements men's heavy, labor, making them "feel the excitement creeping through their veins, like the effect of a glass of "Longworth's sparkling Catawba."[31] Another essay overtly demonstrates the author sputtering, "Ohio Whiskey is bringing sorrow and tribulation to the hearts and homes of the weak and wavering," and she points out that responsibility is proportionate to production because our "State [is] manufactured more barrels of whiskey than any other State in the Union."[32]

Yet, Frances Gage was essentially optimistic that demon alcohol would be defeated; an example of her optimism shows in a letter she wrote to Frederick Douglass from Rochester on Dec. 24, 1855: "I have been in New York thirty-seven days and have given thirty-three lectures; have been at taverns, hotels, private homes, and depots; rode on stages, country wagons, omnibuses, carriages, and railroad cars; met the masses of people daily, and yet have not seen one drunken man." [33]

At that point, antebellum progress against alcohol "felt" unstoppable to temperance advocates, but when the Civil War loomed, like women's rights, temperance advocacy went into abeyance. The cooler climate seems to have begun as early as 1855 when Ohio's State Temperance Alliance was unable assemble diverse temperance groups. Historians observe that women's temperance societies were short lived, partly because leaders like

Gage shifted their energies toward crucial anti-slavery work. The Civil War itself silenced temperance advocates after the Union military reinstated liquor rationing for the Army; military culture was well adapted to spirits and tolerant of drunkenness. It was patriotic to support soldiers' comforts, and distillers thrived. Following the war with its rise in alcohol consumption, another spike in temperance agitation occurred. Temperance advocates like Frances Gage resumed their campaign against drunkenness and argued that soldiers' camp life spread alcohol as a self-medication for depression, injury, and loss. They observed veterans returning with symptoms later known as shell shock or post-traumatic stress. Frances Gage thought that alcohol addicted soldiers who returned "home" were likely to continue drinking and commit domestic violence. In this sense, the Civil War raised the visibility of intemperance; it was not hard for reformers to stoke the public's worry over drunken veterans who might run amok.

As for her personal loyalties, after 1857 Frances Dana Gage supported only one temperance organization, the gender neutral Independent Order of Good Templars. She wrote it "preserves the family circle inviolate" in *The Ohio Cultivator*. Gage praised its egalitarian membership policies.[34] Templars stood for total abstinence from all intoxicating beverages, denial of new liquor licenses, and prohibition of importing, manufacturing, or selling of liquor; plus, they promoted a campaign to influence public opinion, elect sympathetic officials, and protect all citizens from the evils of alcohol. This group began in Utica, New York in 1850 and 1851 where its offices remained. Its first Ohio chapter was established in 1852; by 1856 it claimed 176 lodges. In 1865 at war's end, the organization's membership stood at 60,000.[35] When peace resumed, temperance agitation revived, and the Good Templars employed Frances Gage as a speaker. She encouraged women to support this gender-neutral temperance organization in her 1866 novel *Elsie Magoon*. Her final novel, *Steps Upward*, was initially written as a serial for a Templar's journal.

Ohio remained extremely interested in temperance, and in this state the Independent Order of Good Templars experienced explosive membership growth in the three years after the Civil War. Ohio membership jumped to 28,000 because women saw it as their "only meaningful avenue for women's temperance activity." Young women who had been employed in Civil War agencies, like the Freedmen's Bureau and Sanitary Commission, became its leaders.

These women were accustomed to the public sphere, and, like Gage's daughter, Mary, sought ways to support themselves. Thirty such women participated in Chicago's 1867 organizing meeting of the National Prohibition Party.[36]

At war's end, Frances Gage was popular at temperance meetings and conventions. Her reputation grew from the combination of two factors—the traditional role of "Aunt Fanny's" womanly roles as wife and mother, and the nontraditional public role she adopted as Superintendent of Parris Island in South Carolina. The first validated her trustworthiness; the second showed her usefulness in action as a woman leader. Together these roles combined to make Frances Dana Gage unique, a distinguished war veteran and celebrated figure. Her noteworthy speaking and writing skills brought a rare combination of talents to the table, and Frances Gage found herself in a separate category from other women reformers who lacked hands-on experience. So, Gage was repositioned among postbellum reformers and became what one modern critic calls a "rising star."[35] It was the apex of her career. Ian Tyrell calls Frances Gage an "improver," women who was eager to play new roles, help change the world, and prefigure social progress.[37]

No other woman reformer in America could compare with her credentials. Frances Gage's value for the temperance movement increased after the Civil War when she generated novels that supported its goals. When the radical decline in her health deprived Gage from maximizing her fame in the dais, she could still sit at her desk and generate novels to support the "dry" cause. Unsurprisingly, "Aunt Fanny's" indomitable spirit drew upon her feminine assets for support. She cast her mind back to the Ohio Valley of her past and adapted it to serve a simple didactic formula. This was the victimization tale, family life is ruined by an alcoholic husband—inebriates pass out or become sick, while wives and children cringe or starve. As an author, Francis Gage had become more sophisticated since writing her early short tales in tales *The Lily*. Now her vision was broader, and her analysis of domestic ideology focused upon the diminishment of woman's empowerment. Frances Gage even addressed a taboo subject, drunks can dishonor or rape their wives.

Her contributions were part of America's only social movement that emphasized the special tool of the press. For decades, The American Temperance Society published prohibitionist discourse. Their Evangelical writings often appeared as straightforward expository prose that promoted restraint and self-control. It's cheap tracts "denied individuals the right of drunkenness." Another school of temperance publications focused its attacks on "criminal" liquor traffic. However, Frances Gage was less interested in polemics based on sin or law, what she thought of as "conventional" temperance rhetoric.

Her attention was drawn to a new narrative style that historian David Reynolds calls "Dark."[38] Gage's desire to entertain and instruct adopted facets of a third steam of temperance rhetoric known as "Washingtonian." This catchy name honored America's first President, but the label had nothing to do with him. Originally, six hard drinkers met at Chase's Tavern on Liberty Street in Baltimore and agreed to remain sober by first, sharing their alcoholic experiences and second, relying upon divine help. It was the pre-war 1850s when they began to receive attention. These recovering alcoholics became popular speakers because their riveting style was based on personal and sordid experiences. Their testimony and drama of deliverance gripped audiences, and they were forgiven because they saved themselves. When polished and written down, "Washingtonian" confessions propelled temperance fiction into a new category, Best Sellers.

Gage's fiction borrowed a feature that linked alcoholism and social class; the argument was that spirit drinkers or drunks lower their social position. Abstinence is a symbol of middle-class life. Ian Tyrell explains that temperance was socially presentable; "sobriety was a central element in the ideology of self-control ' and distinguished the temperate above to the "idle" and "vicious" below."[39] This was a brilliant strategy for tempting into sobriety potentially upwardly mobile Americans. The autobiography was Washingtonian fodder, a true story that "proved" one could vanquish the serpent's hellish power and be socially rewarded.

Antebellum Washingtonian speeches, fiction, and drama were spiced with lurid and graphic details of depraved and violent lives. These cautionary tales were America's most effective media of mass persuasion. Among the era's highbrow writers, the Washingtonian influence is seen in such writers as Walt Whitman's 1842 *Franklin Evans: or, the Inebriate,* and Edgar Allen Poe's "Black Cat" and "Cask of Amontillado." Poe, a lapsed member of the Sons of Temperance, died from alcoholism.

The interest in this movement among Frances Gage's friends began in Amelia Bloomer's personal writings. Her life provides an interesting illustration of how Washingtonian influence spread. In 1840 she and her husband lived in Seneca Falls, and attended temperance meetings led by two Baltimore men named Pollard and Wright. Local men were so inspired by their "dark" and sad stories that they created an "Independent Temperance Total-Abstinence Society." Mrs. Bloomer served on committees, wrote supportive articles, and briefly produced a newspaper for them called the *Water Bucket*. However, since all women were refused membership, she turned away from the exclusive men's group and began a similar temperance organization for women. *The Lily* began as its newspaper. While neither local temperance group lasted long, her newspaper did and widened its reform focus. Thus, it could be said that Washingtonian "men only" temperance groups, like "men only" abolition and temperance groups, inadvertently added to the cultural shift that pushed women toward their own reform initiatives.

Undoubtedly, America's most influential Washingtonian author was Timothy Shay Arthur. In 1854 he published *Ten Nights in a Bar Room* which became America's most famous and influential nineteenth-century temperance story. It was our second bestselling novel, beaten out only by *Uncle Tom' Cabin*. Arthur depicted the saloon as a "bastion of maleness" with themes of—villainy, violence, and victimhood. His alcoholics die, usually after delirium tremens, a requisite in temperance tales, yet the story ends with redemption. Jeffrey Mason calls *Ten Nights in a Barroom* a "censorious temperance story" designed to horrify readers through moral instruction. Ostensibly the tale is told by a first-person, "dry" narrator who repeatedly visits a village saloon. Two characters, Joe Morgan and Slade, slide from sobriety to alcoholism; each has a disapproving wife and suffering child. This establishes a thematic pattern of reversals. The melodramatic narrative includes a series of battles between male characters—one of whom threatens the narrator; weapons include fists, a glass, a gun, a knife, and a bottle.

The structure of this "historical drama" has both overt and covert elements. Underneath the plot's melodrama, *Ten Nights* is about transformations—one alcoholic goes full circle, drunk, then shocked into recovery, and returned to the middle class. His foil goes half circle—he is unrepentant and a victim of patricide. The tale ends with a Biblical warning—a pestilence is afoot in the land that slays "the first born in our houses." Timothy Shay Arthur's moral fable shows how dire consequences follow the use of spirits—reputation, property, and innocence are lost while madness and death follow. *Ten Nights* concludes with village survivors taking a Temperance Pledge. In 1858, it was produced in a popular stage version by William W. Pratt and productions continue into the twentieth century.

In the same year that Arthur published *Ten Nights*, England's Charles Dickens visited Ohio, traveling overland from Cincinnati, to Columbus, to Sandusky. A robust man, Dickens was accustomed to consuming alcohol with gusto. He was astonished and disappointed with his Ohio lodgings in an Ohio Temperance Hotel. This is his view of Timothy Shay Arthur's ideal temperance establishment: "Nothing to drink but tea and coffee. As they are both very bad and the water is worse, I ask for brandy; but it is a Temperance Hotel, and spirits are not to be had for love nor money."[40]

Years later in 1877, the unusually thoughtful Arthur summarized his ideas about the dynamics of alcoholism in a work called *Grappling with the Monster; Or, the Curse and the Cure of Strong Drink*. Arthur posed four alternative ways to save a drunkard—prayer, self-help, taxation, and legislation. He pondered the roles of temptation, personal morality, and religion. If the issue were secular, he asked, how could society remove temptation?

Frances Gage's temperance novels were written in postbellum America during the 1860's. Her three stories confront the social significance of men consuming spirits in saloons. In *Elsie Magoon,* a young temperance advocate retrieves a drunken Irish lad from a tavern and berates its male drinkers who slink homewards. In Gage's last novel, *Steps Upward,* a realistic strategy is proposed for closing a saloon; it shifts from shaming to reforming its owners. Saloons were symbolic threats to the home, since they provided a male refuge. Reformers believed they were places where hyper masculinity cloaked immaturity. This was where men escaped their mothers, wives, and domesticity. Writers like Shaw and Gage believed men, even sober men, ought to socialize amongst family and friends in the home. To say it another way, the social institution of the tavern warped man's role as family leader and eroded the significance of woman's narrow gender sphere.

After Frances Gage studied the form of Washingtonian tales, she planned ways to adapt their formula. Her self-conscious goal was twofold, first, diminish men's compulsive drinking, and second, promote "female agency." Gage created female characters to be "agents of change, primarily through their ability to influence."[41] She also recognized that some women were sinners and built this insight into the Washingtonian formula's lurid events as subordinated subplots. There also were sober women who were cast into roles that allowed them to grow into independence from alcoholic men. Overall, these novels could be seen as anticipating another phase of temperance reform. They provide what Mary Loeffelholz calls "radical reform of property relations" in a "remarkably wide-ranging social analysis" where "progressive ideas" provide a "feminist analysis" of woman's class positions.[42]

Gage's writing was driven by financial need. She had fallen in the social scale from affluent to nearly indigent. After her carriage crash in 1864, she ironically surveyed her convalescence: too feeble to become a washerwoman," and "woman's sphere" did not serve a widow. She wrote, "three years ago I found myself without the means of life . . . placing myself in women's sphere had not brought me a dollar to pay my bills." So setting all these theories aside, I said, "I will go and lecture."[43] The plan to give salaried lectures for the Order of Good Templars was blocked when strokes immobilized her, and that left the pen. She was not ashamed or embarrassed about this exigency and threw herself into the task, which soon generated four volumes, *Poem*s and three novels.

Her publisher was J. B. Lippincott. The temperance novels each had different genesis and intention—*Elsie Magoon* was listed as "Founded upon the actual experiences of every-day life." The publisher advertised it numerous times during April and May 1867 in the *American Literary Gazette and Publication's Circular* and *Saturday Review of Politics, Finance, Literature and Society.* On May 18, *Magoon* was advertised as a "New Publication" and "A Temperance Tale," selling for a dollar fifty cents, and on June first it was "Just Issued." The *North American* reviewed the novel on May 25, calling it a vigorous narrative about the days of earnest enforcement of moral reforms; in August, *Elsie Magoon* was briefly reviewed in the *American Phrenological Journal;* it is "a powerful story, well written. . . No one can read it without deep emotion. The portraiture of character, the scenes and incidents, are too vivid to be merely imaginary." *The Ohio Farmer,* which promoted *Poems,* similarly praised *Elsie Magoon* as a "thrilling Temperance story." It was also reviewed in the *Albany Evening Journal* in 1867 and *The New York Live Stock Market* on May 23, 1868. Eventually this novel was printed in 18 editions.

Her second book, a novella called *Gertie's Sacrifice,* was written to sell for fifty cents as part of the "Sunday-School Library" published by The National Temperance Society and Publishing House which Jack Black and Neal S. Dow founded in 1865. They zealously solicited manuscripts from writers and offered prizes. The postbellum organization published three monthly periodicals and published over 2,000 books. Some historians see it as stepping into the space occupied by William Lloyd Garrison's American Anti-Slavery Society which dissolved in 1867. When Lippincott republished *Gertie's Sacrifice* under its own imprint four years later, the tale was listed on Dec. 1, 1869 in its advertisement carried by the *American Literary Gazette*. This tale was printed in 13 editions.

The final novel, *Steps Upward*, like the first, was promoted by the publisher in *American Literary Gazette, The Literary World,* and *Church Union*. This work was initially serialized by the Independent Order of Good Templars in its *Temperance Patriot.* This publishing house began in Utica, New York two years earlier in October 1867. Lippincott's first publication announcement for *Steps Upward* appeared on Oct. 15, 1870, and the *Prairie Farmer* on Oct 22 carried the following advertisement: "Recently published in the *Temperance Patriot*, is now published in book form. The Story is considered by all to the Best Effort of its Distinguished Authoress, and deserves a Place in every Family." It added that payment of a dollar and a half should go directly to the *Temperance Patriot* office in Utica, New York. Other advertisements for the book by the "author of *Elsie Magoon*" continued on Jan 2, 1871. The *Prairie Farmer* reviewed the novel on Jan 7, saying it was full of "right down good sense" and was "really the best from the author's pen." Other advertised listings appeared in *American Literary Gazette* and the *Literary World;* the *Christian Union* mentioned the novel's appearing first in the *Temperance Patriot* and added, "its popularity largely increased the circulation of that journal . . . [the novel has] unusual merit . . . nothing of the sensational order; but narrates in a truthful and appreciative style events such as may occur under the observation of any one who keeps eyes and ears on the alert."[43] *Steps* was printed in 9 editions.

Frances Gage's three cautionary novels mark the high point of her lasting contribution to America's temperance movement. The subtitle of her first novel says it all—"the Old Still-House in the Hollow." Finally, Gage could vent her irritation with Marietta pioneers' practice of building stills for their corn crops; her resentment toward the pioneers seems to have festered for a lifetime. When the hero, Elsie Magoon, is introduced, she is already disillusioned by her husband's decision to spend her dowry money to build his distillery. This wife quails at the prospect of the trouble ahead for

Richard Magoon who is patriarchal and indifferent to his wife's views. Nonetheless, she is shocked when the mill begins taking its toll. Two local men engage in a drunken brawl; one dies, and his widow goes mad. Next, the tavern has a fire that nearly engulfs the village. This leads male temperance supporters to begin to form a "dry" phalanx—Elder Peters persuades Elsie Magoon to take the Temperance Pledge. Gradually others are recruited, perhaps, even readers of the temperance journal Elsie writes for in the Ohio Valley.

The pro spirits forces include Elsie Magoon's increasingly obstreperous husband, Richard, many tippling townsmen, both high-class residents, such as Deacon Hill, and working-class characters, like an Irish workman and his wife, Pat and Nora Sweeney. Nora provides comic relief to readers for her shrewdness and articulation of a remarkable Irish viewpoint. She points out that American women are second-class citizens who accept men's' imposed limitations. Nora Sweeney argues American men have no right to be "takin' away peoples' liberties" (Ch. 7), but goes on to say women should also consume "devil's broth" because it "gives strength, which women need too!" Her idiom presents a clever kind of logic: "Baccy gives comfort, and oaths relieve a body's conscience," so does drinking spirits and fighting. She complains, "'Merican women . . . jist lit the men do as they like—drink, and swear, and chew, and smoke, and fight, and whatever else seems their pleasure, and niver ask to share a bit wid 'em." (Ch. 8)

Intemperance vitiates two generations in the novel. The weak Richard Magoo mismanages his property; the drunken Irishman drowns in a swine's slough; an Irish lad must be forcibly retrieved from a tavern, yet the second generation ends the cycle. As female heroism inverts Arthur's plot formula, daughter Elsie Magoon assumes family leadership. She dismantles the still, redeems the farm from debt, and serves as a temperance paragon for others. Her presence in the White Horse Tavern sends men slinking home. Some men are inspired by a New York City visitor who receives Gage's poem "Dare to Stand Alone" and converts to become an urban temperance leader. The doubling in her novel is "a historically prescient vision of two different generations of feminist activists."[45]

Just like Timothy Shay Arthur's still owners, intemperance affects Magoon who becomes impoverished and ill, destroyed by using his own product. On his deathbed, Richard blames the "hydra-headed monster" for his fall, rather than taking responsibility for his weakness. His daughter proves her economic value as a pragmatic leader who takes control of the Magoon property and ships their corn on flatboats down the Marietta and Ohio Rivers. This proves the lie to her father's economic justification for the distillery.

The precedents for Richard Magoon's alcoholic role in the novel are found in Frances Gage's early writing in *Pittsburgh Saturday Visiter* and Amelia Bloomer's *The Lily*. Here she first published attacks on men's "binge drinking" in her "Tales of Truth." *The Lily* stories sketch damaged wives being abused. These tales include references to infidelity, abusive violence, forced intimacy, and marital rape.[46] Another Gage commentary on this subject, published on April 14, 1855, broached a taboo—women's sexual repugnance of drunkards. She called this a secret, home-based abuse that is a "sapping poison," and a "mortification, humiliation, degradation, and abuse that the world's age will never see or hear.[47] Her novel, *Elsie Magoon*, traces the descent of such a husband into abusive violence which only ends when he is proactively imprisoned by his son and wife. One scholar called *Elsie Magoon* Frances Gage's "astute analysis of domestic abuse."[47] After Richard's death, his wife finally finds contentment. Her smart daughter, young Elsie, marries a reformed drunkard. At novel's end, the village thrives, an unrealistic and utopian antebellum vision of village life in the Ohio River Valley.

In this novel Frances Gage also touches on the national background of the temperance movement. There are campaigners for Democrat James Polk's 1844 Presidential bid who use brandy to influence voters in the White Horse Tavern. Also there are references to Gen. Samuel Fenton Cary's conservatism, while Neal S. Dow struts as the "Napoleon of Temperance," and John B. Gough gives popular temperance lectures, just as he did in Cleveland in 1850 and at the Gage's Mount Airy in 1851.

The novel also targets organized religion that refuses to condemn distillery operations. Gage write that Magoon's still sounded like "a fell demon which groaned and spouted in the hollow . . . and its abhorred, unearthly sounds might easily, by the organized fancy of the suffering, have been mistaken for the shrieks of lost souls" (Ch. 4). Conversions follow young Elsie speaking at the Methodist Church and leading a group to sign the pledge. This includes the landlord of the White Horse Tavern and Elsie's boyfriend's father, the pleasure loving Deacon Hill.

Unregenerate alcoholism is not a funny topic, yet Frances Gage's first novel includes some playfully mockery of drunken men's masochism. In particular, there is a sodden man's song about a fellow who drinks himself to death, goes to hell, and desires a repetition of the experience. He begs Charon to row him across the Styx: "I'll mind not the pain, / Row me back, row me back, let me die drunk again" (Ch. 24).

Publishers advertised the novel as founded upon "the actual experience of everyday life," though the Magoons do not resemble Frances Gage's parents. Elizabeth Dana Barker was no reformer, though her daughter's 1883 "Autobiography" credits her mother with teaching "me the hideousness of slavery and intemperance."[49] Their still was primitive: two stories of logs on brick footers, a hearth with chimney and limestone pavement. To this was added a cooking kettle and copper tubing. It was surrounded with a log wall and on top there was a suspended gable roof to speed cooling. The moonshine reduced grain crops and when decanted into wooden casks could be transported down the river. So the Barkers' still did produce income for the farm.

Frances Gage's second temperance narrative did not rely on distant history. It was written about contemporary urban life and was published by the National Temperance Society and Publication House. This fifteen-chapter novella, *Gertie's Sacrifice; or, Glimpses of Two Lives,* opposes problems caused by middle-class smugness to those created by urban poverty. It shows poverty as a cause of crime and demonstrates the limitations of individual benevolence. Also, as historian David Reynolds points out, the novel introduces a new skid row stereotype—an upper-class woman previously "invisible in temperance literature."[49]

The novella's genesis was influenced by Charles Dickens' sixth chapter of his 1842 book, *American Notes*. It describes his horror at visiting Five Points, a New York City slum located in the old Sixth Ward at Manhattan's southern tip. Five Points included twenty-two city blocks without sanitation. Its "long row of wretched tenements" had lower floors for drinking and gambling; second floors were "indecent and disgusting dungeons," of 12' square bedrooms that housed a dozen to twenty persons. Indeed, many of America's poorest immigrants, such as those who fled Ireland's Potato Famine between 1845 and 1852, lived in Five Points. It had more than 250 saloons. The slum was rife with alcoholism, disease, child mortality, prostitution, and violent crime.

Dickens protested this slum as did Gage's friend, Antoinette Brown, who was a police reporter for Horace Greeley's *New York Tribune.* She was disgusted by New York City's slums and prisons. In 1856, Brown's series of muckraking articles were published in book form as *Shadows of Our Social System.* She and Frances Gage were among the few American women who chastised city fathers for ignoring problems in Five Points.

The most visible civic response came in 1859 from a private philanthropist named Peter Cooper who gave the city a civic center in the East Village. He was a self-made man and inventor who built the Cooper Union for the advancement of Science and Art. It was revolutionary because free education was offered to all. Frances Gage was stunned by his generosity and wrote her Ohio readers about the achievement; she also touted a recent visit to a Newsboy's Night School which shared Cooper's benevolent commitment. She explained to rural Buckeye readers, "This institution will . . . improve these boys, who are soon to be our men, making them stronger and better for any position in life," and she encouraged reader donations to "redeem childhood from vice and crime."[50] Cooper's fine building brought education to the masses and lured many distinguished adults into the New York City slum. Speakers were invited to the Cooper Union where they delivered addresses and held meetings included figures like Abraham Lincoln, Henry Ward Beecher, Frederick Douglass, and Frances Gage, as well as the leaders of many progressive institutions, such as the U. S. Sanitary Commission, the Women's National Loyal League, the American Equal Rights Association, the National Women's Suffrage Society, and the American Red Cross.

In *Gertie's Sacrifice,* Cooper's building provides a backdrop for a melodramatic scene where two homeless boys, abandoned by alcoholic and deceased fathers, shelter from a snowstorm in the winter of 1857. Gage leaves her dark subject matter with humor and a "happy ending," as the boys are rescued by a benefactor. Before this occurs, the author deploys the characters' witty dialogue. One boy calls his rags remnants of three "ventilation garments." He avoids frostbite by playing a game, standing upon one foot he says things like, "now, Mr. Left Toe, you must come down in the world." Also the boy remembers his Granny's "toe story" about the pig going to   market, but grouches, "there ain't no meeting nor home nor the por-'us now'-days" (Ch. 9).

Gage reveals her penchant for recreating dialect in some women characters who discuss the onset of Gertie's "habit of tippling." Humorous dialogue also occurs from Kathleen, a reformed Irish alcoholic servant, who loves Gertie and tries to protect her from bad influences, like that of her French hairdresser. Mme. Broseau, orders "Wine for mamselle!" and must be obeyed. When Kathleen informs an older house servant, she reacts as if a finger had been put "into the very eyes." They natter on: "Bad luck to her. She's used to the likes of that. Didn't she be smacking her lips though . . . .I saw her bidding Miss Gertie, the darlint, to drink the stuff, not fit for herself" (Ch. 10).

The novella's conventional plot is a temperance tale of damnation that adapts the Washingtonian formula. The sets of characters scheme is familiar to readers. There are four youngsters who marry. Two choose sobriety and thrive, while two become drunkards and die. At the end, the pattern is tied up by two new weddings that replace the two failed ones. However, it also reverses the gender elements of Arthur's formulation. His masculine Washingtonian tale showed women as powerless victims, whereas Gage creates women characters who take initiative.

The author's third temperance novel builds upon a metaphor of vertical perspectives. In 1853, Gage had commented in an *Ohio Cultivator* "Letter" that women reformers were like "the drones in the great hive of improvement and progress." Her final novel resembles Queen Victoria's Beehive of Industry.[50] It introduces a vertical hill upon which all of the main characters live. At the top is a "Lodge" owned by the wealthy distillery owner, Judge Hancock. Halfway down the hill is the distillery superintendent's affluent home. At the bottom is the Hancock Distillery, discharging filth into the Allegheny River. Nearby are two buildings that become noteworthy, Heckel Dinmont's run-down hovel called Rocky Glen and the Frobish Tavern which markets distillery brews.

At the novel's conclusion, the vertical arrangement is rehabilitated. Everything from top to bottom is transformed. Judge Hancock is dead, the distillery is closed, Heckel Dinmont has left for Kansas, and the Frobish Tavern has metamorphosed into a temperance hotel. Only the distillery superintendent still lives in his original home midway up the hill, but his spirit is broken because his only son has drunk himself to death.

The novel's tavern at the foot of the hill is an interesting structure—a three-story frame house that at one end is mockingly called, "the very ideal of a whisky tavern." It is a place of inequity with a vile "floor painted in profuse variegation by the continual flow of tobacco juice and not infrequent deposits of the overloaded stomachs of the inebriated customers of Oxbow" (Ch. 4). This, Gage writes, is the rural equivalent of New York City's "lewd rowdyism of the Five Points (Ch. 9).

Another structuring device in *Steps Upward* is progression. This theme demands the transformation of the sleepy, alcohol tolerant village into a "dry" industrial center. The village booms after the Hancock distillery is converted into two factories. This feat is accomplished by Maxwell Carter, an outsider who comes to Oxbow as a friend of the Hancock heir. He serves as an instrument of change whose wisdom grew from his father's drunken death. The novel's unseasoned young men see in Carter a positive role model, as does his boss, Judge Hancock.

The novelist labors to realistically present physical transformations in this final novel. Viable economic alternatives are created within the hated distillery complex. It is converted into a cotton factory and paper mill. The author describes how related industries spring up nearby, including a machine shop, a rolling mill, nail factory, sawmill, planing mill, and so on, which triples the size of Oxbow's village. The distillery town's physical and moral transformation is complete when the Frobish's Tavern becomes a hospital for Union Soldiers, and Heckel Dinmont's hovel at Rocky Glen is converted into a Home for Soldiers.

Readers' attention, however, probably focuses most intently upon the growth of the story's principal female character, a conventional fictive "hero." In this idealized scenario Cinderella forgives her sisters, rehabilitates her father, educates her family, and improves the distillery owner's family, as well. She steps from unpaid to paid servant, to companion, to secretary, to wife of the Hancock heir. The female hero progression must overcome social and psychological obstacles—in this case the constraints of poverty, ignorance, and modesty. The novelist questions whether social mobility between classes is possible. Innate superiority, friendship, and love enable this transition, yet when Di's steps bring her to Washington D. C., her temperance commitment remains a lightning rod for criticism.

The storyline adapts the Washingtonian model, but relegates the story of a drunken blacksmith and his victimized family to a subplot: a drunk steals his wife's income from weaving rugs. The source of this tale was a McConnelsville experience in the 1840s that Frances Gage recounted in the *Woman's Journal.* A client asked James Gage to protect her from a drunken husband. He had to tell her there was no legal recourse if she wished to keep her children. The woman left with the knowledge that American laws were unjust, and the Gages never found out how she fared.[51]

Another facet of Timothy Shay Arthur's formula that Gage borrows is the device of contrasting two families. Those are the high class Hancocks and the low-class Frobishes. Each lineage was decimated by alcoholism—the Hancocks had a great grandfather, grandfather, and four uncles who did not "survive the riotous dissipation of youth" (Ch. 3). The Frobishes had a great grandfather, grandfather, five uncles, and four aunts who were destroyed by intemperance. At novel's end, the pattern is broken when George Hancock marries temperance advocate Di Dinmont, and Aggie Frobish weds the village's primary temperance agitator, Maxwell Carter.

The writing in this polemical novel is softened through humor and witty dialogue. The social criticism is thoughtfully realistic, emphasizing the psychology of a female who must overcome the stigma of an alcoholic father and low social class.

When her temperance novels were completed, Frances Gage was weaker and withdrawn from public life. Nonetheless, she continued her interest in reform activity in her home state and tried to support Ohio's proposed temperance legislation. In March 1870, Gage was pleased to learn that her old hometown, McConnelsville, devised, and passed its own version of the Maine Law, called the "McConnelsville Ordinance."[52] It envisioned the removal of "the evils of intemperance from our community." However, this reform, like so many others, was not to be effectively enforced. As one historian notes, villages failed to create "a new set of inner controls and external institutions to replace the old community controls"; many individuals never learned America's new requirements for sobriety or the "drinking patterns of an urban society."[53]

Gage was fascinated by Ohio's Women's Crusade of 1873-1874 when women became violent in expressing their discontent with men's intemperance. The dramatic episode proved, for one thing, that women were capable of civil disobedience. The trigger was pulled by a man named Dio Lewis who in December 1873 visited Hillsboro to lecture about his mother's successful confrontation with "rum-sellers."[54] Some called this a shot heard around the nation. Corn was Hillsboro's local crop, the home of two local distilleries, and liquor was its most important industry. Local women found alcoholism to be a significant problem in the community, so hearing Lewis's tale, they were empowered to act.

For more than 40 days, marchers protested. Some had personal motives since they were related to male relatives who drank to excess; other village women came from the wealthiest families in the village. Ohio matrons challenged the village's proprietors of drug stores and taverns, vowing to persist until the last "whiskey shop" closed. Their success was sweet, but short-lived. By Feb. 1, 1874, they closed eleven saloons. Only three remained open and one of their four drugstores.[55] The movement spread from February through late June when saloons closed in at least 59 Ohio towns. Figures vary, for example, The *Cincinnati Gazette* described 42 Crusades in Ohio; historian Jack Blocker believes that the figure is closer to 115; while another temperance historian, W. J. Rorabaugh, reckons the movement spread to 900 localities in 31 states.[56]

Then in Hillsboro, a predictable backlash occurred from liquor producers and sellers. Saloonkeepers and customers learned to ignore the protesting women and sometimes even showered them with beer. Especially in the cities, liquor dealers returned to business as usual. Temperance advocates struggled to justify themselves; for example, one temperance broadside called spirits manufacturers "OUR ENEMY" and blamed the conservatives for combining "Anti-Suffragists" and "WET' FORCES in Franklin County." It accused them of being in collusion and on the payroll of the Ohio Association Opposed to Woman's Suffrage."[57]

Indeed, opposition overcame these temperance reformers, but old time reformers like Frances Gage remained proud of this activism. Historian Ruth Bordin calls Ohio's Temperance Crusade "the first women's mass movement in American History" and "one of the major social movements of the nineteenth century."[58] The Woman's Crusade did not exactly die when Hillsboro settled down. It evolved into another reform organization, the Women's Christian Temperance Union, or WCTU, which grew into "the country's largest and most influential nineteenth-century women's organization."[59]

Frances Gage's 1884 death spared her from seeing later developments in America's temperance debates. She was proud of having supported this "vital, influential, revealing, and long-lived social issue in our history."[60] From Frances Gage's meetings in her

Mt Airy Ballroom to her speeches and novels, she consistently denigrated drunkards. They are, in her words, "senseless, helpless animals, who grovel" and yet "vote and rule the nation!"

Notes

Chapter Four

1. Frances Gage, "Autobiography of Frances D. Gage, *Woman's Journal* (March 32, 1883): 3.
2. Stephen Mintz, *Moralists and Modernizers* (Baltimore: Johns Hopkins University Press, 1995), xviii.
3. Elizabeth Cady Stanton, ed., *History of Woman's Suffrage, 1881-1902,* vol. 1 (New York: Schocken Books, 1971), 845.
4. Gage, *History*, vol. 1, 119.
5. Catharine Gilbert Murdock, *Domesticating Drink* (Baltimore: Johns Hopkins University Press, 1998), 10.
6. Jack S. Blocker, *American Temperance Movements* (Boston: Twayne Publishing Company, 1989), 6; 10.
7. Helen Waite Papashvily, *All the Happy Endings* (Port Washington: Kennikat Press, 1956), 54.
8. Julia Colman, *The Temperance Handbook for Speakers and Workers* (New York: National Temperance Society and Publication House, 1889), 22.
9. George Knepper, *Ohio and Its People* (Kent: Ken State University Press, 2003), 180.
10. Blocker, 37.
11. Ibid., 34.
12. Ibid., 37.
13. Ibid. 9.
14. Leslie Stegh, "Wet and Dry Battles in the Cradle State of Prohibition," (PhD diss., Kent State university, 1975).
15. Ibid.
16. Ibid.
17. William T. Utter, The Frontier State, 1803-1825," *History of the State of Ohio*, ed. Carl Wittke (Columbus: Ohio State Society of Archaeology and Historical Society, 1942), 5, 37.
18. Gage, *History*, vol.1, 841.

19. ___, "Letter to Rochester Women's Temperance Conference, *The Lily* (May 1853).

20. Dexter C. Bloomer, *The Life and Writing of Amelia Bloomer* (New York: Schocken Books, 1975), 21.

21. Utter, 37-38.

22. Gage, *History*, vol. 1, 842.

23. *History,* I, 152.

24. David Leigh Colvin, *Prohibition in the United States.* (New York: George H. Doran Co., 1926), 117-118.

25. P. T. Barnum, "Barnum on the Democratic Party and Temperance."<http:www.gmu.edu/lostmuseum/lm/44/7> (accessed May 10, 2008). 11.>

26. Murdock, 11.

27. Knepper, 180.

28. W. J. Rorabaugh, *The Alcoholic Republic: An American Tradition* (New York: Oxford University Press, 1989), 81.

29. Jeffrey E. Smith, "Frances Dana Gage: Turning the World Upside Down," *Feminist Frontiers, Women Who Shaped the Midwest*, ed. Yvonne Johnson, (Kirksville: Missouri: Truman State University Press, 2010, 72.

30. Gage, "Aunt Fanny's Removal to the West—First Impressions of St Louis," *Ohio Cultivator* 9, no. 2 (Jan. 15, 1853): 20.

31. "Editorial," *Weekly Herald*, St. Louis, Sept. 3, 1853.

32. ___, "Letter to Frederick Douglass," *History*, l, 843.

33. ___, "Good Templars—Hog Cholera—Ohio History," *Ohio Cultivator* 13, no. 8 (April 14, 1857): 124.

34. Barbara Leslie Epstein, *The Politics of Domesticity: Women, Evangelism, and Temperance in Nineteenth-Century America* (Middletown, Conn.: Wesleyan University Press, 1981), 37.

35. J. A. Dacus, *Battling the Demon* (St. Louis: Scammell and Company, 1877), 516.

36. Ian R. Dexter Tyrell, *Sobering Up: From Temperance to Prohibition* (Westport, Conn.: Greenwood Press, 1979), 41.

37. David S. Reynolds, "Black Cats and Delirium Tremens," *Serpent in the Cup*, eds. David S. Reynolds and

Debra J. Rosenthall (Amherst: University of Massachusetts Press, 1981): 27.

    38. Tyrell, 42.

    39. Jeffrey D. Mason, *Melodrama and the Myth of America* (Bloomington: Indiana University Press, 1993), 71.

    40. Charles Dickens, "A Jaunt," Ch. 13, *American Notes* (London: Chapman and Hall, 1842).

    41. Carol Steinhagen, "The Two Lives of Frances Dana Gage," *Ohio History* 107 (Winter-Spring 1998), 29.

    42. Mary Loeffelholz, "Subversion and Genre: The Postwar Fiction of Frances Dana Gage, *Legacy* 5, no. 2 (Fall 1988): 24.

    43. Gage, "Letter," *Ohio Cultivator* 16, no. 1(Jan. 1, 1860):173.

    44. ___, "Letter," *Lily*, April 14, 1855.

    45. Review of *Steps Upward*, *Christian Union* (1867): 102.

    46. ___, "Tales of Truth," *The Lily* 4, no. 5 (Jan. 1852): 2-3

    47. Carol Mattingly, *Well Tempered Women* (Carbondale: Southern Illinois Press, 1998), 132.

    48. ___, "Autobiography of Frances D. Gage," *Woman's Journal* (March 31, 1883): 1.

    49. Reynolds, 38.

    50. Gage, "Home Miscellany, Glimpses about New York," *Ohio Cultivator* 14, no. 11 (June 1, 1858): 173.

    51. ___, "Letter from Mrs. Gage," *Ohio Cultivator* 9, No. 6 (April 1, 1853): 109.

    52. Jed Dannenbaum, *Drink and Disorder, Temperance Reform* (Urbana: University of Illinois Press, 1984), 245.

    53. Blocker, 10.

    54. Rorabaugh, 32.

    55. Tyrell, 37.

    56. "Just Government League," (Columbus, Ohio, Aug. 14, 1890).

    57. "McConnelsville Ordinance," property of Western Reserve Historical Society (Cleveland: Ohio).

    58. Tyrell, 38.

59. Kenneth Willett Povenmire, "The Temperance Movement in Ohio, 1845-1860," (Columbus: Ohio State University Press, 1933),

60. Ruth Borden, *A Baptism of Power and Liberty, The Woman's Crusade of 1873-1874," Ohio History* 87, no. 4 (1978): 396.

61. Frances Whitaker, A History of Ohio's W.C.T.U., 1874-1920," (PhD diss., The Ohio State University, 1971) 12.

56. Gage, "Letter," *The Lily* 3 (May 6, 1851).

Chapter Five
"The Riled and Turbulent Cup,"
Gage the Writer

What kind of writer would described herself as "fretting and fuming like a barrel of new-made cider, throwing up foam and sediment to the top from morn till night" so that few would "wait for the sediment of their beverage to sink to the bottom; but they turn with loathing from the riled and turbid cup?"[1] This distinctive voice uses humor, self-mockery, and experience in rural activities to define herself for a readership that would share the unlikely analogy of temper and bubbling cider. This is one style used by a rough-hewn American author, Frances Dana Gage, who playfully chastised women for having trivial tantrums. Such exhortation, instruction, and amusement typified a unique style adopted by Frances Gage when she addressed rural Ohio women whom she believed resembled herself. Despite wide travel and growing national acclaim, this reformer never abandoned her audience of these "Buckeye girls" by becoming "hoity toity," as one of her characters labels self-importance.

It was wit and humor that allowed Gage to sidestep men's usual pejoratives about women authors being sentimental, domestic, and didactic. Her amusing 1848 cider analogy is wordy and rambling, but it can also be seen as an example of women's responses to Ralph Waldo Emerson's demand for a literature faithful to American experience. Gage's journalism drew upon her rural experiences and shrewdly avoided polemics as she undermined testy issues with wit and humor. For instance, she mocked the limited gender spheres evoked by her father. In one early anecdote, Frances Gage mocked woman's sphere as if it were a kind of carapace that a woman could accidentally break. This extended joke began in the late 1840s in an autobiographical essay published in the *Pittsburg Evening Visiter*. In January 1851, Gage added a rhapsodic setting to the account by describing "a glorious day" in April when the seven year old writer, wearing her blue calico sun-bonnet and home spun dress, was set into the side saddle by her father and told to plow a half mile cornfield. As "old, blind Dick" pulled the plow, the writer remembers the day's lyrical beauty while she was studying the wildflowers—violets, buttercups, wake-robins and blue bells that to her seemed to be singing an anthem. She returned whistles to the bob-whites, larks, blue jays, and catbirds that "were holding a stockholders meeting in the orchard." This "glorious and exciting" day was an adventure that "entailed plowing under woman's sphere and leading her toward "my home sphere. . . [so I] built my platform on Woman's Rights." [2]

Nearly two decades later in 1858 the joke resurfaced and was modified at a Women's Rights Convention. At that time, Frances Gage read a letter ostensibly from a fellow Ohio farmwoman who: "Having plowed a portion of her farm . . . lost a segment of her sphere, and never got it back. She subsequently cut through sixteen miles of ice and watered some cattle, then she lost another portion of her sphere, and has been losing it ever since." [3]

These examples place Frances Gage within a historical context of mid-century women who sought relevance in their own experiences. Scholars like Jane Tompkins explain that women's writing did "a certain kind of cultural work within a specific historical situation" and was a way of avoiding imitating men's style that favored adventure, conquest, and self-examination. If men wrote about conquering the woods and the waves, what topics were appropriate for women? Thus, writers like Gage groped toward a literature about women's experiences. [4]

Among Gage's scattered autobiographical writings are warnings from men who told her to pursue the style of writing typically found in "Lady's Books and Magazines." This crystallized her determination, "No, I will write for women and children in the country and state papers." In the 1840s, Frances Gage sent material to a variety of sources, and her journalism career was launched—notably in Jane Swisshelm's *Pittsburgh Saturday Visiter* and Amelia Bloomer's New York State based *The Lily*. By the 1850's, Gage became a regular contributor to several regional farm journals of which Michael B. Bateham's *The Ohio Cultivator* was the most important. It was published for several decades, through 1866, and combined agrarian and progressive social concerns. *The Ohio Cultivator* remained "Aunt Fanny's" most heartfelt publishing outlet. At the same time, Gage sent essays called "Letters" and poems to another Midwestern agricultural publication—*The Ohio Farmer* which commenced in 1850. She also wrote for The *Prairie Farmer,* another rural newspaper that operated out of Chicago, Illinois. It published Frances Gage's writing between 1859 and 1874 and favored fare that was traditional. In turn, these journal articles were frequently reprinted in publications like *The Maine Farmer* and *The New England Farmer*.

Frances Gage's prose style and domestic references at this time intentionally reflected Middle-Western speech patterns and drew upon a world full of rural metaphors. An early "Letter from Aunt Fanny" to Jane Gray Swisshelm's *Visiter* opened, "We were right glad" you defended the first Women's Rights Convention and "right sorry were we" to read about "tobacco chewing, swearing, whiskey-drinking Lords of creation" who insist women are "angels."[5] Such colloquial affectation gradually receded in Gage's writing. Indeed, some of her regionalisms were little jokes that only rural readers would appreciate, like when she called her sons "greengages" and commented when they moved away from McConnelsville that raising a family was like taking "care of the green Gages, but when the sprouts all grew tall and strong . . . [were] able to bear transplanting."[6] In fact, greengages were a popular variety of green plum that was introduced from France to England in 1724 by a paternal ancestor, botanist Sir William Gage.

Her worries about moving to Missouri and losing touch with Ohio's reform activities, was expressed to her *Ohio Cultivator* readers, "I would like to have a finger in the women's rights pie."[7] It clearly seems that her habits of mind functioned through such metaphors. In 1855, Gage in another country metaphor described St. Louis's alcohol tolerant culture; it was "stagnant and polluted."[8] Her imagery was not always appropriate. For example, Gage wrote of Iowa hecklers, "I met with some lions." Was it clear to readers what that meant? Also some of her referential metaphors were too abstruse; for instance, she referred to a south Asian tree, uppas, that is source for poison, like grogshops.[9] One imagines that even *The Lily's* relatively sophisticated readers would find it slow going to decipher the logic of this allusion.

More accessible are her images of flax and yeast. When Gage returned to Ohio in 1861 and took an editorial position in the *Ohio Cultivator's* offices, "Aunt Fanny's Greeting" to readers extended a metaphor based on her Washington County experiences with flax cultivation. Its analogy rendered flax as ideas, skeins as writing, and editorial work as the spinning wheel. Frances Gage wrote, "I shall be gathering the flax that is sent for my ready distaff, and spinning yarns for *Field Notes* and monthly *Cultivator*."[10]

Another rural image in her late essay, "Looking Back" likened anti-slavery agitation to yeast or leaven that makes flour rise; hence, she posed the idea that the Anti-Slavery Society's push for abolition led to the war of emancipation; the "loaf" was readied for removal from the oven.[11]

One approach to the woman behind the prose can be suggested by her use of naming. It illustrates Gage's sense of disparate identities. To the Barker family she was "France," and to her Ohio farm journal readers she was "Aunt Fanny." Reform journal readers met her as FDG, Frances Gage, Frances D. Gage, or Frances Dana Gage. What she was not known as was "the daughter of Joseph Barker" or the wife of James Lamson Gage, the subordinating "Mrs. James" Gage."

To her best adult friend, Clara Barton, she was quickly known as "Aunt Fanny" or, more intimately," mother." During the 1840s, the moniker "Aunt Fanny" introduced her literary alter ego and extended her identity onto the national dais and press. Being "Aunt Fanny" was a clever and endearing writing strategy that helped Frances Gage connect with rural, Middle Western women for whom she was a pseudo relative and knowledgeable friend. When she traveled for reform purposes, Frances Gage was a popular guest who never lacked places to stay because her readers were eager to entertain Aunt Fanny. On one occasion in the early 1850s, under the guise of Aunt Fanny who wrote "Letters from the Kitchen" for the *Ohio State Journal,* she attacked the Fugitive Slave Law. Its Whig editors learned their domestic maven, Aunt Fanny, was an abolitionist and asked for her resignation. Most periodicals welcomed Aunt Fanny in both her domestic and political roles, and many continued to carry Aunt Fanny's prose through the 1870s, such as the *Ohio Cultivator* and *Prairie Farmer.*

Yet, Aunt Fanny's persona was most apparent in the pages of *The Ohio Cultivator*, an agricultural newspaper founded in Columbus on January 1, 1845 by Michael B. Bateham. Gage explained the origin of her penname to *The Ohio Cultivator*'s readers in its January 1852 issue. "New Year's letter from Aunt Fanny" appended the following, "P.S. I have been asked why I call myself Aunt Fanny! Because I have been in deed and in truth the Aunt of over 50 men, women, and children."[12] Between 1845 and 1862, "Aunt Fanny's Girls," or as she sometimes called them "Nieces," constituted a loyal audience for *The Ohio Cultivator's* "Home Department." Her domestic advice included such matters as health, home, and dress. In effect, she combined attributes a later century found in such personages as Martha Stewart, Heloise, and Abbey Van Buren. As time passed, Aunt Fanny's "Letters" expanded to describe Frances Gage's work as a reform speaker in the deep Midwest and travels in the West Indies, as well as her war correspondence from South Carolina's Sea Islands. These writings in farm journals were unprotected by copyright laws and were freely reprinted across the nation. Unbeknownst to Gage, this created a broad national audience that was not recognized until Aunt Fanny collapsed. In the summer of 1867, sympathy notices were published from as far away as California.

Her pseudonym also softened Gage's identity as a fiery abolitionist and temperance reformer. Early speaking engagements in villages like McConnelsville, Salem, and Chesterfield prepared her for later moves into states like Iowa. Here just one lecture tour included twenty-five programs. Aunt Fanny carefully packaged her doses of liberal human rights' ideology for different audiences. These rural engagements spread her reputation as a wise, kindly leader and helped make Frances Gage a "draw" at large rights assemblies in cities like Chicago, Philadelphia, and New York. Her podium style was lauded for being nonthreatening, persuasive, and effective. She trusted this helped open the path for later women speakers.

The Ohio Cultivator represents a keystone to her journalism. It became a significant publication at a time when the "United States was primarily an agricultural nation with over 400 agricultural periodicals. Like many of these, the *Cultivator* included women's issues and developed "a special relationship with the reading public which extended far beyond the rural household."[13] Bateham's editorial work included a commitment to serve Ohio's women. He originally promised a "Ladies Department" which was to be edited by his wife Mrs. Louisa Jane Lovell who wished to call the column the "Housewife's Department." Her death led to a hardier second wife, Josephine Penfield Cushman Bateham, who took over the department, shrewdly renaming it "Home Department." Josephine Bateham was an Oberlin College graduate who served as a missionary in the West Indies and expressed a kinship with Frances Gage on issues like temperance and women's education. From 1851 through 1855 she edited the Women's Department. The bimonthly *Ohio Cultivator* was read by both farmers and their wives. With a circulation of 10,000, it was "one of the most widely read of the agricultural journals in the Midwest."[14]

During the years of Michael B. Bateham's editorial control, Gage was a popular and frequent contributor; for example, in 1855 the journal printed sixty-two of her articles, such as essays about the needs of the poor and schools for truant boys, plus poems, including two of her most popular and widely reprinted verses, "The Perplexed Housekeeper's Soliloquy" and "The Sounds of Industry." In 1862, the Batehams retired and S. D. Harris became editor of *The Ohio Cultivator*. He wanted articles on health, children, fashion, and Ohio agriculture. For a time, Harris limited Frances Gage's contributions to hearth and home.

She was assigned to promote rural events like county and state fairs where country folk assembled for farm-based displays, instruction, competition, and entertainment. Harris was delighted when the Ohio State Fair became one of America's largest. The ever-obliging Gage shared his enthusiasm about these gatherings and good naturedly tailored essays for their promotion. Sometimes Gage did not restrain her wit as when she quipped in an 1850 essay that the Fair ought to have a competition to see which woman could embroider the best caricature of Henry Clay.[15] However, when S. D. Harris was her employer, she had to subordinate her humor. For example, she was told to promote the state fair and composed four poems called, "Ben Fisher, Home Pictures," that in some quarters became seen as American classics. This narrative traced one Ohio family's rising appreciation of the Ohio State Fair and constituted a hearty endorsement of the event's positive influence on farm families.

During four months in the spring of 1860, Gage's journalism shifted into a new mode, the role of "foreign correspondent" for *The Ohio Cultivator* and *The Ohio Farmer*.[16] This was when she forwarded essays from the West Indies, including Cuba, St. Croix, and Jamaica. Simultaneously, she also wrote "Letters from Mrs. F. D. Gage" to such national reform papers as William Lloyd Garrison's *Liberator* and the *National Anti-Slavery Standard*. This journalism widened her national reputation and increased S. D. Harris's respect. As a consequence, late in 1860, he became reconciled with her interest "in women's issues," and gave her freer rein for topics in the "Home Department."[17] The following year he appointed Gage to be the salaried Associate Editor of the *Cultivator*, a title she enjoyed through 1862 when the paper to left Columbus for Cleveland. This led S. D. Harris' to publish a new weekly farm journal called *Field Notes* where Francis Gage again was employed. She edited its "Home Department" and wrote a regular column called

"Every Day of the Week," that covered topical, rural issues. She also contributed short stories in a section called "Home Fireside," tales by Aunt Fanny written "For the Young Folks," plus a column of domestic tips called "The Housekeeper." [18]

Unfortunately, *Field Notes* closed down in 1862. The war took men away from farms, and this affected subscriptions to farm journals. S. D. Harris did not forget the labors of Frances Dana Gage and when her volume, *Poems* appeared in 1866 he promoted the book in Ohio, collected its sales receipts, and forwarded the income to Gage in New York City. It was the Civil War that sounded the death knell for many journals like *The Cultivator* that ended its run in 1866. Postbellum taste moved toward publications with abundant advertising and national, rather than regional, scope.

During the decades when she wrote for farm journals, Aunt Fanny sustained a strong following amongst Ohio women, whether she lived in Missouri, Indiana, or New Jersey.[19] Certain themes reoccur, such as the condition of her plantings. The gardens changed, but readers could trace her enjoyment in nurturing a garden from her glorious flower garden at Mount Airy, to her struggling plantings in St. Louis, to the marvelous old flower gardens on Parris Island, to her flourishing vegetable garden in New Jersey. Having her hands in the dirt rejuvenated Gage as she explained, "No labor of my life, simply as labor, has yielded me such true enjoyment. . . . Day by day the vigor of other days came back; my sleep grew sweet and sound, my digestion capital, my spirit buoyant, and my heart was full of thankfulness." Her widow's letter to the "thousand readers" of the *Ohio Farmer* in August 1865 began by mentioning her broken shoulder and ribs, long confinement that weakened her nervous system, and consequent sleeplessness, painful breathing, and dyspepsia. Then it shifted to her real topic, a joyful description of her potato patch, beets, peas, lettuce, cucumbers, melons, corn, green beans, and strawberries—all cultivated before breakfast. This was how Aunt Fanny transformed her medical ordeal into suggested remedies for others—health advice about the therapeutic effects of gardening. Her epistle is signed, "Ever the Friend of the Working Woman."[20]

A third farm journal, *Prairie Farmer*, hired her between 1859 and 1874. This became the Midwest's leading agricultural magazine. It was printed monthly by Chicago's Union Agricultural Society and started carrying Gage's work after she left Missouri. The crudeness of prairie farm country reawakened Gage's desire to assist farm-bound housewives and led her to submit essays on practical topics like bread baking, child rearing, and housekeeping. She also shrewdly integrated two women's rights' essays, "The Wants of Women" and "Women's Rights." The tone of these submissions is more subdued than the intimacy of her "Buckeye Girls'" missives to the *Ohio Cultivator*. Other farm journals also carried her poems, such as the *Maine Farmer* and *The New England Farmer*. Even in the ultra-conservative *The Valley Farmer* published in St. Louis, Missouri, Aunt Fanny had several domestic poems appear, an *Ohio Cultivator* essay, and an article about its editors meeting her as a noteworthy person in July 1853, which was the year this lackluster farm journal ceased publication.[21]

The indefatigable Gage also sent material to a variety of other periodicals during the 1850s, including regional publications like the *Morgan Herald, The Anti-Slavery Bugle, The Ladies Repository and Gatherings of the West*, and Rochester, New York's *Frederick Douglass' Paper* which appeared between 1851 and 1855. Beyond such antebellum writing for reform and farm publications, Gage also sent material to literary journals. Among them was the *Western Literary Magazine* where after 1851 Gage published poems, essays, and some book reviews.

One example was her critique of Caroline Kirkland's *Western Clearings* (1845). Seven years earlier, the Kirklands left New York to settle in Pinckney, Michigan where they labored for six years. Her popular book about that experience challenged Easterners to become pioneers and has been called America's first, well-known story about the development of a western settlement. The title was a rhetorical question: *A New Home Who'll Follow?* Caroline Kirkland's subsequent book, *Western Clearings,* in 1845 was composed as a sequel. This book consisted of satirical essays about local settlers. Edgar Allen Poe in the *United States Democratic Review* positively reviewed the volume. However, genuine pioneers, like Frances Gage, disapproved of Kirkland's patronizing attitude, which she complained about in a negative review published by the *Western Literary Magazine*. In fact, the Kirklands soon tired of Michigan's frontier, and in 1843 returned to New York City where he edited and she taught, raised five children, and wrote for publications like the sensational *New York Mirror*.

From the late 1840s through the mid 1850s, Frances Gage's poetry remained popular. In the summer of 1850, Cincinnati's *The Literary World* reviewed Ohio authors' writings in order to encourage poets; it wrote, "Among the writers most popular . . . is the poetess Mrs. F. D. Gage" who it placed second on its list of important writers.[22] This was when Gage's prose began appearing in some eastern reform journals, like Jane Grey Swisshelm's *Pittsburgh Saturday Evening Visiter* and Amelia Bloomer's *The Lily*. The reform "self pollination" was strong as reprinted Gage articles like "Woman's Sphere" from the *Visiter* soon appeared in *The Lily*. This was a humorous article about Gage's childhood and the self-destruction of her "sphere." *The Lily* for many years continued to publish of Frances Gage's thoughtful "Letters" and short tales that combined temperance and women's rights concerns. For example, *The Lily* published two stories entitled "Tales of Truth" in January and March 1852. After 1854 when Mrs. Birdsall of Richmond, Indiana for two years edited the publication, Frances Gage continued submitting material, including a serialized story called "Our Joette" that appeared in ten installments between March 1 and December 25, 1855. The following year *The Lily* published an earlier Gage "Letter," calling for women to find balance in their lives that was reprinted from State's *Cauga Chief*, a weekly paper published in Weedsport, New York between 1849 and 1857.

When another women's rights paper appeared in 1853 called *The Una*, Gage wrote to encourage its new editor, Mrs. Paulina Wright Davis of Providence, Rhode Island. This feminist sought a broad audience and in 1853 began publishing a clever woman's monthly newspaper dedicated to "women as human beings." It summarized convention activities and offered women's history, book reviews, and literature. Reformers like Frances Gage supported the publication. For instance, in its October 1854 issue, she contributed a poem in a popular style that epitomized what might be called her lifelong literary theme—strong women can bear trials and overcome the constraints of social convention. "The Market Woman" illustrated a practical woman's independence and courage:" She stands behind her market stall . . ./ Go to, ye prating ones, and learn/ That woman's holiest sphere,/ Is only filled by duty done,/ Without remorse or fear." Gage concluded the poem by saying that a "mother working for her child," will "never leave her woman's sphere."[23]

This note was famously struck by Margaret Fuller in her influential 1845 study, *Woman in the Nineteenth Century*, and elaborated upon by Frances Gage in Bloomer's *The Lily* seven years later.[24] *The Una* also published Frances Gage's essay, "How Fares Our Cause," a survey of how popular journals' viewed the "Woman's

Rights" movement.[25] It included an indictment of masculine arrogance in *Harpers*. Despite reform women's support, Davis's newspaper only remained in print for two years, between Feb. 1853 and Oct. 1855.

Eastern reform publications provided Frances Gage an occasional but sustained presence for several decades. Her friendship with abolitionist William Lloyd Garrison, publisher of Boston's *Liberator* for the Anti-Slavery Society, also led to a broader readership for Gage. Its circulation of 3,000 subscribers included many African Americans. Garrison's reputation for uncompromising advocacy against slavers brought nationwide notoriety and set the tone for other abolition publications. A representative example of Mrs. F. D. Gage's journalism in the newspaper was her 1859 essay analyzing the comparative effects of slavery and emancipation in the West Indies. Antoinette Brown in 1850 called *Liberator* the "thermometer of the public pulse."[26]

The American Anti-Slavery Society's 1861 "Annual Report" included a section called "Foreign Intelligence" that complimented Gage for dwelling "with lively satisfaction on various tokens of the happy influence of freedom upon the condition of the island"; it summarized her description of Santa Cruz's freed children being smarter and better looking "than slave children"; the laborers were well treated—had limited hours, fair pay, no beatings, and gender equity, "the same price for the same labor."[27] The Society's two newspapers were eager to carry Frances Gage's war missives from South Carolina that updated Edward L. Pierce's Sea Island's Experiment, such as her essay, "Education of the Freedmen." During the war years, communications to the peripetic Frances Gage were forwarded from the National Anti-Slavery Society in care of the *Standard* at 45 Beekman Street, New York City.

There were other reform minded eastern newspapers that occasionally published Frances Gage's essays and poems. This included Gamaliel Bailey's weekly *National Era* based in Washington, D.C, and the Congregationalist's *Independent* in New York City. The *Era* ended in 1860 after Bailey left the United States and died; the *Independent* ran from 1848 past the end of the century. The most prominent reform newspaper was Horace Greeley's *New York Tribune*. He introduced the paper in 1841 and edited it for over thirty years. The *Tribune*, like the *Independent*, continued past century's end. Greeley evolved politically—beginning as a Whig, becoming a Free Soil man, and then helping form the Republican Party. His legendary career ended in 1872 after he lost a Presidential bid against Ulysses S. Grant.

Two decades earlier, in the 1850s, Horace Greeley had come to know and appreciate Frances Gage through her work with temperance and woman's rights advocacy alongside Mott, Anthony, and Stanton. Frances Gage's labors were covered by his paper during Civil War years. His *Tribune* supported abolition and woman's rights, and Greeley aimed to promote healthy post-war Reconstruction.

The years between 1860 and 1867 were fraught with change for Frances Gage. No longer saddled with dependent family members, she was welcomed in many quarters. As the Civil War slammed some doors shut, it also opened others. Even after her early paralysis, Frances Gage's writing continued. For example, other than the volume of poems and three novels, she produced what might be called occasional pieces, like an article on "Early Times in Ohio" for a children's magazine called *Little Corporal*. Gage also sent tales to a similar publication, *The Little Pilgrim*. Her writing at this time included a children's column written under the pseudonym "Grandma" in the *Independent*. One of these was an autobiographical essay, "The Russet Apple Story, How Mischief Punishes Itself," that comically recounts her embarrassment as a farm girl. "France" got stuck inside a keg while stealing an apple; her father hauled her out of the keg and kept his promise not to "tell" the family. Writing this confession years later, allowed her to expunge secret guilt over being a "naughty girl."[28] Gage's literary technique used her personal history to make a moral point. "The Russet Apple Story's" moral for children relates the virtue of obeying the rules and also, perhaps, it speaks to adults about sensitive parenting.

During the mid 1860s, her friend Henry Ward Beecher was editor of *The Independent* and appreciated her contributions. The paper sadly notified readers of Gage's stroke in 1867, calling her "a writer of both poetry and prose who has "carried joy to thousands of families" and added, "news of the calamity that now has befallen her will be heard with a pang and awaken emotions of tenderest sympathy."[29]

At this juncture, Frances Gage's correspondence shows her increasingly thinking about personal concerns, like her friend Clara Barton's pending return from Europe; she ponders how one supports a friend's promotion at Howard University and the welfare of her children. In 1869, she rallied enough to send short pieces to the *Independent*, Cincinnati's *Herald for Health*, and the *Saturday*

Evening Post. Frances Gage had planned to write for other journals, including William P. Tomlinson's *The Woman's Advocate* which was to be "frank, outspoken, earnest champion of woman's cause." She encouraged this publication by forwarding a number of her favorite poems. The *Advocate's* first volume opened with Frances Gage's retrospective essay, "Looking Back," and printed two versions of her poem "A New Song to an Old Tune." The second poem was adapted by Joshua Hutchinson and became famous as, "One Hundred Years Hence." The *Advocate's* second issue included several reprinted Gage poems and two essays; one of these, "Tulliver's Philosophy," compared George Eliot's female hero to women like herself who experienced gender discrimination. *The Woman's Advocate*'s final volume was abbreviated, including Frances Gage's "invalid" letter to Cleveland's American Woman's Suffrage Association, and a sad note from Brooklyn announcing another immobilization that kept her at home. In 1870, the *Advocate* was absorbed into Lucy Stone's *The Woman's Journal*, the new publication of the American Equal Rights Association.[30]

During her lifetime, many America readers knew Frances Gage only as a poet. She enjoyed the form's condensed self-expression and tried to avoid imitating the grandiose models she parsed amongst her father's books. After age twelve, she was writing verses that were characteristic of the period's style. She found it easy to make rhymes and often wrote the blank verse that William Wordsworth popularized. During the Civil War while billeted at the ruined plantation on Parris Island, she never stopped making rhymes. Daughter Mary and friend Clara Barton marveled over Aunt Fanny's quick composing of occasional verse, as Barton recorded.[31]

From the beginning of her poetry submissions, Frances Gage did not fear being controversial. Her poetry sometimes addressed political challenges, most notably her 1848 poem written to Salmon P. Chase. He made the mistake of promising her husband a Congressional seat in exchange for his Whig support. The wife's reaction to Chase's "tergiversations" was quickly scribbling a poem on a scrap of paper and showing it to him. This was "Dare to Stand Alone." Chase later said this poem convinced him to leave the Whig Party and coin the phrase "Free Soil Party." It became easier for him to help create "the present triumphant Republican party."[32] "Dare to Stand Alone" includes powerful rhetoric and was first printed in a local newspaper, the *Morgan Herald* on June 13, 1850. It pleased the audience and poet, becoming Gage's anthem. She urges the faint hearted to be bold and true. It is included in her anthology, *Poems,* and is also embedded in her novel, *Elsie Magoon.*

Another illustration of her feistiness appears in Frances Gage's 1849 poem, "The Dissatisfied," that was published in Gamaliel Bailey's abolitionist weekly, *National Era.* The Mount Airy matron reacted to Alice Cary's poem "Hope" in Cincinnati's *Sentinel* and the *Ladies' Repository.* It used the metaphor that life is "a ship unmasted." Such pessimism irked Gage who lived amid her sons' domestic upheaval. Perhaps, at the time she may have envied the unmarried Cary's thriving professional life. The Mount Healthy poet was included in Rufus Griswold's 1849 anthology, *The Female Poets of America,* published a volume of her own poetry in 1850, and was a contributor to the *National Era.* Frances Gage's response asked Cary twelve rhetorical questions that essentially told her to stop being sad; "could the cause be disappointments and unmet desires," she asked.[33] The naïve Gage thus lectured Alice Cary about how to repudiate sadness. Her anti melancholy formula suggested taking on fulfilling duties, mingling "hope and love" in each "lay," and "greeting with a cheerful song the social hearth."

No response from Alice Cary was forthcoming. Two years later, in May 1851, Frances Gage again mentioned Cary in a "Letter" to *The Lily*. She worried that Alice Cary's response to a negative *Westminster Review*'s criticism might sadden her and impede Cary's "upward flight." Indeed, the Mount Healthy author had flown from provincial Ohio in 1850 and moved with her sister to 20th Street, New York City where for fifteen years they became famous for holding Sunday evening Salons. Literati flocked to these soirees, including writers and reformers like John Greenleaf Whittier, William Lloyd Garrison, Horace Greeley, and Elizabeth Cady Stanton. Gage did not live there, but if she hoped to be invited to the Carys' Sunday gatherings, this did not happen.

After Alice Cary's death in 1871, the home was bought by an Ohio acquaintance who was the sister-in-law of Lucy Stone and Antoinette Brown—Dr. Emily Blackwell. She was an English-born 1854 graduate of Cleveland, Ohio's Western Reserve University's medical school and for over forty years ran an Infirmary for Indigent Women in Children in New York City. During the Civil War, Dr. Emily Blackwell trained nurses and helped establish the United States Sanitary Commission. In 1868, she opened a women's medical college.

When Gage later lived in the East, she expressed fellow feeling for Ohio writers who she called the "Great *Cultivator* family." For instance, one woman she saw in this light was Metta Victoria Victor who had moved to Hohokas, New Jersey, which was near Lucy Stone's home. Victor was a prolific and clever writer who, like Gage and Beecher, broached temperance and anti-slavery concerns. The two reform women had much in common. Victor's work included two popular reform novels—in 1851, *The Senator's Son; or the Maine Law, a Last Refuge,* and a decade later, *Maum Guinea.* Her husband, Orville J. Victor, had been editor of Sandusky Ohio's *Daily Register,* and after marriage, the couple moved east where he became a noted editor of "dime novels," a sensational, western-styled genre that Metta Victoria Victor mastered. There is no record of the two women meeting.

Frances Gage's laudatory addresses were often directed toward her friend, Clara Barton. She is also referred to in two of Gage's novels. In one, Barton is the messenger who delivers a posthumous epistle to a soldier's family, and in her last novel Clara Barton teaches nursing to the inexperienced protagonist in a Union hospital. The nurse received many handwritten, unpublished poems that she put in a folder titled, "Poems,—by Mrs. F. D. Gage, Addressed to me at Hilton Head, S. C. during the summer and autumn of 1863. Clara Barton."

Deciphering Gage's handwriting is a challenge; in fact, a decade earlier in 1856, Gage admitted in the *Boston Evening Transcript* that her handwriting was little schooled and even she found it difficult to read.[34] The following year, she humorously admitted the same problem in the *Woman's Advocate*, "I write the worst hand in the world; can't read it myself when it gets dry—/The T's are not crossed, the Is are not dotted, / Some words are expunged, and others are blotted,/ And some are spelled wrong, or letters are left out;/One scarcely can tell what I am writing about." [35]

Frances Gage's occasional poems to Barton in South Carolina are uneven. The first, dated May 28, is a thank you note: "Dear Clara, since you've fixed me a nice little place to write, I'll write you a nice little rhyme, Just to make you remember, some other night, this one strange hour of time." Then one of Gage's "Impromptus" follows in which she muses over life's chance encounters; it compares outside and inside storms, and expresses a hope Barton may preserve happy memories for the future. Aunt Fanny asks, "Will you not give a brief thought to me, and to Carolina's shore," because Gage knows that, "Our few brief hours together will be a joy to my spirit until I pass life's stormy weather." She ends the poem by wishing the "war storm soon may end" and her friend, "Be blest forever more."

A second "Impromptu" salutes and teases the serious minded nurse, "Think of a heroine who fields of battle could march unflinchingly, and stand amid its fiercest roar and rattle to do her charity. Think of her among the dead and dying . . . Staining her soft white fingers with the flower of some hero's blood." This missive is signed F. D. G. and ends with a joke, "it seems sacrilege to call her human/ Fretting about a flea."

The remaining poems are untitled and were composed during the fall after James Gage's death and the atrocities at the Battle of Fort Wagner. On Oct. 22, Gage offered solace, if "ever a dark cloud of blue rest above thee," you should "think for a moment how dearly I love thee." Another humorous poem opens with Gage's middle-western and colloquial style, promising, "to send ya a 'How'dye' and waft you a kiss." Aunt Fanny's effort to be light hearted is darkened by references to "bloody hands" and the "cannon's roar, Death freighted, carrying sounds of war to every ear." Another of Gage's October poems marvels about the irony of a place being as beautiful as the Sea Islands and yet accursed by evil slavery. The poet wonders when freedmen will share the fruits of victory. Her final October poem speaks of autumn crops being gathered, freedmen's songs, the foaming sea, and time speeding past.

The published poems reflect contemporary readers' taste in poetry. This was shaped by popular anthologists like Rufus Griswold who preferred genteel lyrics. Literary historian Elaine Showalter points out that America's nineteenth-century women poets were expected to be either sentimental or morally instructive, a righteous strain of poetry traceable to Mary Wollstonecraft and preoccupied by questions of equality and liberty. This style tended to be cerebral, carefully structured, and witty.[36]

A mind that could visualize pieces of busted woman's sphere falling through the Barker's inch thick Marietta River ice was well disposed to take the imaginative leaps demanded by poetry. Gage wrote abundant poetry but dreaded organizing the publicly successful or "personal best" poems for inclusion; this required jettisoning much of her life's work. However, the volume was warmly promoted in *The Ohio Farmer* on Oct. 20: "Ohio's glorious Aunt Fanny, the Poet of the People and of Humanity" will be publishing her best poems; it asked readers if they wished to buy a copy "as a souvenir of their friend."[37] The journal sold the volumes for $1.50 each, and the proceeds were sent to her as a "New Year's offering to Aunt Fanny Gage, a token of remembrance from her western friends." Other publications also advertised the anthology, including *The Nation* then edited by her friend, William Lloyd Garrison, which on July 11, 1867 included her book in its brief review, "Mrs. Hewett, Mrs. Gage and Others."

Female readers appreciated Gage's poems that reflected their domestic lives. One example was her 1851 "A Home Picture," that first appeared in the *Ohio Cultivator* and was soon reprinted in the *American Phrenological Journal* and elsewhere. Gage extended the original "state fair" poem to four numbered segments, "Ben Fisher, Home Pictures," tells the story of how a young husband's restless itch for adventure is curbed by his attendance at Ohio's State Fair.[38] This widely popular narrative was set to music in 1853 by Boston publisher Oliver Ditson with music by L.V. H. Crosby.

Rufus Griswold, the eastern anthologizer of *Poets and Poetry of America* (1842) and *The Female Poets of America* (1848) believed many women poets experienced a conflict between reformer's passion and art instinct.[39] Frances Gage's *Poems* presents exactly this dilemma. She saw the problem and wrote about her "two lives"—political and personal. Her dominant note is personal ruminations, that is domestic and sentimental "home thoughts." In fact, the anthology is dedicated to her descendants—children and grandchildren. Its homespun productions serve as a kind of memoir setting the stage for how she wishes to be remembered.

Its opening poems ponder living half a century and facing old age. Following are a variety of personal experiences, such as being a pioneer child, talking with her grandmother, becoming a young matron, watching her daughter start teaching, and leaving Ohio. The second section shifts toward the philosophical, like "The Web of Life," and darker, such as "Lines, the Convict to His Mother" and "The Maniac Wife."

The intentional shift in tone reflects how Gage's life widened in the 1850s when her "Two Lives" strongly conflicted. The May, 1853 cautionary poem "Don't Run in Debt" appeared in the *Liberator*.[40] That was the year her husband altered his career and their domicile. Her second cautionary poem, "Don't Go to California," argues for Ohio's superiority based on geography. Its teeming valleys, herds, dark forests, craggy hillsides, and even railroads represent "wealth"; she repeats, "stay at home, oh! stay at home" because "There's gold in our dancing rills, boys, Oh! gather it while you may." The conclusion thus is a rollicking adaptation of the "carpe diem" or "gather ye rosebuds while you may" theme. Gage uses hyperbole to flatter Ohioans, who possess "true wealth." And she adds that true value is only found in human connections, so "Don't barter life's loves away!" Western migration, she writes, may interfere with "true wealth," but the Gage family abandons the Ohio Valley.

    Other life experiences included in Frances Gage's collection include her sailing to St. Domingo in 1860 and relishing South Carolina's beauties in the fall of 1862. Also several imaginative tribute poems are addressed to her elders, Rufus Putnam's pioneers who "conquered" the Northwest Territory's wilderness. "When This Old Ring Was New" considers her mother's wedding band. It first appeared in the *Missouri Republican* on May 29, 1853 and uses informal vernacular style. The narrator imagines her newlywed mother traveling by foot and wagon from New Hampshire's "Granite Hills" and across the Alleghenies when "*Ohio* then was '*West.*'" The young woman faced the "redman in his wrath [who] lay coiling like a rattlesnake" and heard native's war whoops, wolves' howls, and panthers' screams. After this introduction, the poet glorifies Putnam's "band of brothers" with fortitude that "never heard of *humbug* yet." There is a third shift in tone when Gage cites her pleasant memories—making bread, spinning wool, weaving linsey-woolsey, and sewing simple clothing, such as handmade knit stockings and calfskin shoes that pioneer females wore while they danced the reel. The poem's final shift draws the modern contrast. By the era of the Civil War, Ohio was transformed into "'way down East," and the poet's "poor muse" gives up on a story that "hath no end."

    Two additional tribute poems are dedicated to Putnam's settlers; each avoids whimsy. "Landing of the Pioneers" repeats the refrain, "just 60 years ago." The poem praises the "adventurous band" that cut trees, built cabins, and shared the "social joys of life." Today the land is tamed, the wilderness blossoms; the West is over for Ohio residents, but they should still emulate the pioneers' "well spent lives." The second poem "Lines," is also dedicated to survivors of Rufus Putnam's Ohio Company. It describes Frances Gage's 1869 visit to Marietta and her parents' "manse." A surviving elder speaks about life 70 years earlier on "La Belle Riviere." The

Barker's Marietta mansion was inherited by the Joseph, the eldest son in 1843, and is now fitted up with fancy mirrors and carpets for his family; she calls it a "monument" to progress. His feet that once trod their log cabin's "puncheon floors," now walk on marble in the State House. The panegyric stiffly concludes, "All honor to the heroes." Another visit is described in a final poem about her childhood in Marietta; in "Impromptu" the poet notices a picket fence that now surrounds the "stately dwelling," but her interest is in their original log cabin where she was born, "picked the fleece," "spun the rolls," and "turned the cheese." Gage concludes simply, "That old homestead of my childhood is earth's dearest spot to me."

    The implicit double nature of such narratives is finally clearly labeled—her dual identity is articulated in the poem "I Live Two Lives," first published in the *National Anti-Slavery Standard* on Feb. 7, 1862. It explains her domestic incarnation is a Pollyanna who looks "above life's sorrows and sadness." The darker half of Frances Gage, on the other hand, is the serious minded reformer who sees life's "pain and sadness." She depicts intemperance through the image of "a red-eyed monster slyly creeping" and complains that most women hide their "talents 'neath plumes and flower." Her public voice occasionally drifts into self-righteousness that threatens to alienate peers. For example, she once attacked Lydia Sigourney for not joining her in public opposition to intemperance and slavery. Gage's 1850 "Impromptu" is a challenge to timid women who should battle slavery and attack the Fugitive Slave Law. She writes, "Up, women, to your duty now . . . For freedom, truth, and right . . . . Save Ohio's name from shame and taunt and scorn."

    Sometimes the poet wrote about prospective joys as in another widely popular poem, "One Hundred Years Hence," ostensibly written on July 4, 1875, set to music by John W. Hutchinson, and arranged by James R. Murray. It was performed in 1876 by the famous Hutchinson family singers of New Hampshire at the rousing conclusion of the National Women's Suffrage Association convention.[41] Half a century later, the poem was adapted by Charlotte Perkins Gilman and sung on Jan. 17, 1934 for the Ninth Conference on the Causes and Cure of War.

    Gage's treatment of history reveals her most referential, concrete, and didactic side. She indicts Revolutionary War heroes who fell from their pedestals because of supporting slavery. These include Winfield Scott, Daniel Webster, and Henry Clay. "Lines on

Reading Webster's Speech" is based on Winfield Scott's pro-slavery letter to President Polk dated Feb. 9, 1843. Gage imagines his blustery apostrophe to abolitionists: "let the bondman bear his burden." Yet, this hyperbole distorts his letter because Gage omits Scott's wish that he could "meliorate slavery even to [its] extermination." Daniel Webster and Henry Clay both promoted the Missouri Compromise in 1850 that included the Fugitive Slave Act. "Lines on Reading Webster's Speech," was published in 1850 in the *Ohio Journal* and reprinted in the *Liberator*. [42] It is an anti-slavery diatribe against Daniel Webster's 1850 Missouri Compromise and opens by reminding readers that he fought with General Rufus Putnam at Bunker Hill. The poet repeats that Webster was unworthy of Putnam's company. Frances Gage asks rhetorically, "Does such a man as Webster think the tingeing, That Nature's law has given to the skin, Can make the spirit bow with servile cringing, And shut out all the God-like from within?"

Two poems directly attack the Fugitive Slave Bill and share similar titles, "Lines on Reading of the Fugitive Slave Bill" and "Lines on the Passage of the Fugitive Slave Bill." Their strategies differ. The first addresses, "fathers and mothers" with the "conceit" that readers imagine being parents of a stolen child. Gage asks if extricating a child should be grounds for civil disobedience. Northern politicians are accused of selling themselves to slavers. Her other anti-Fugitive Slave Law poem, subtitled "In Reply to a Friend," imagines an interlocutor raising questions, "Is the Negro a Man?" The poem concludes with another accusation that pro-slavery supporters are thralls of southern slaveholders.

Among the anthology's concluding poems are its most artistically rendered, probably because they blend her personal and political voices. Among these is "Sunrise Chimes," which reflects Lord Alfred Tennyson's New Year's Eve paean, the Bells section of "In Memoriam," and Edgar Allen Poe's "The Bells," each of which was published in 1849. Gage's five-stanza poem opens with church bells ringing in Beaufort, South Carolina. Their Southern message is strange to her ears: "Slavery, Intemp'rance, Want, and Crime." The men in the village's licensed grog-shop ignore the bells since, "what care they for grog-shop crimes?" But, the reader is told to "list" because tomorrow slaves will be auctioned at the Court House. The saddened narrator imagines a day when a different message will come from the church's bells, a prophecy of change when grog-shops and slavery will both be abolished. Then the bells' refrain shall be, "Peace on earth, good will to man."

Another fine regional poem is "The Fisherman of Beaufort." Its first four stanzas commence with "The tide comes up and the tide goes down," that establishes the rhythm of the ocean's cycles. Against this backdrop are set two local characters, a Sea Island's fisherman and oysterman who value their new freedom; they speak in Gullah dialect as the first says fish eagerly jump into "de nets ob de free." The oysterman adds that he fears no punishment if he leaves with empty hands. The song of these freedmen is directed to "massa white man," who is asked, "gib him de work and gib him de pay." Though the Emancipation Proclamation declared their freedom, Frances Gage asks if African Americans will get paid work so they won't "never him trouble de icy Norf."

The concluding poem is the "Ballad of Port Royal, South Carolina;" it recreates New Year's Day, 1863 when Frances Gage was on the speakers' platform at Brigadier General Saxton's extravagant Port Royal gathering to celebrate the Emancipation Proclamation. There are speeches, and the high point is Col. H.W. Higginson's address to his First South Carolina Regiment. As an aside, Frances Gage imagines a conversation between two white soldiers who sneer at the "nigger show." Events hinge upon their changing reactions to the ceremony—the chaplain prays, Saxton's reads Abraham Lincoln's Proclamation that frees African Americans, shouts arise, and a freed woman leads an impromptu national anthem, "My Country, Tis of Thee." Col. Higginson presents the regimental flagstaff to freedman Sgt. Rivers who promises his scarred body will bear this Union flag until fallen in battle.

At this high point of the ceremony, the author reveals that the white Union soldiers are converted into respect for the freedmen. Her poem's epilogue describes the next two years' service of the First South Carolina Regiment. It served valiantly at battles such as Fort Wagner, Jacksonville, Port Hudson, and Fort Pillow. This, indeed, proved African Americans are truly men, not "half bound slaves." At the poem's conclusion, Gage prophetically warns—pardoning white rebels will offend honorable, black-skinned veterans. The poem also salutes the "ghosts of half a million" dead soldiers, and offers tribute to their widows and orphans. Thus, "The Ballad of Port Royal" is a powerful historical narrative that confirms America's promise to freedmen.

In 1860, William Turner Coggeshall included Frances Gage in his anthology, *The Poets and Poetry of the West*, and praised her sentiments, character, and reputation as a poet.[43] In 1891, S. H. Venable in his study of Ohio Valley Culture praised her as a "womanly woman" and poet; he admired her political journalism, too, and wrote that she was one of the ablest advocates of reform known to the Press."[44] She traveled in good company in the years between 1850 and 1865 with her poetry appearing in Bailey's *National Era,* Garrison's *Liberator*, and a variety of journals, ranging from the *Herald of Truth* and even women's fashion magazines like *Godey's Lady's Book*. Her reputation as a poet was spread through the era's practice of reprinting material; one critic who discusses this pre-copyright publishing activity calls it a "common industry practice" to "pirate" or "pilfer" copy.[45]

The same thing occurred with Frances Gage's prose between 1850 and 1870. Her essays and stories appeared in a wide variety of publications; for example, a "Letter" she sent to the *Liberator* was reprinted by the *Pennsylvania Freeman*. Such dissemination had the effect of spreading her words to a wide cross-section of American readers in Pennsylvania, Massachusetts, New Jersey, Wisconsin, Illinois, and, even, California. An alphabetical sampling of publications which Frances Gage did not "write for" but was "published in" follows: *Cincinnati Daily Gazette,* Cleveland's *Critic Record, the Farmer's Cabinet, Lowell Daily Citizen & News, The Northern Christian Advocate, North American, Ohio State Journal,* the *Philadelphia Inquirer, The Springfield Republican, Saturday Evening Post, Trenton State Gazette,* the *Weekly Wisconsin Patriot*, the *Wisconsin Chief,* and *Wisconsin Free Democrat.* Even the Pacific coast's *San Francisco Bulletin* reprinted Frances Gage's articles, gathered from sources like the *Ohio State Journal.*

Of course, Frances Gage was not paid for most of this work.[46] Like other women authors of the era, she found writing to be a risky career, but when the occasion demanded it, a few literary women could support themselves. A famous example was Lydia Sigourney (1791-1865), who after her husband's business failed earned money from her novels and editing *Godey's Lady's Book.* Another was Mrs. E.D.E.N Southworth (1819-1899) whose husband deserted her, yet she became wealthy from writing domestic novels. A third example was the unmarried Louisa M. Alcott whose fame came from *Little Women* in 1868, and she covertly added to her income by selling potboilers under a pseudonym.

Victorian culture was a pre-specialist era when many writers composed in a variety of genres, whether cookbooks, poetry, novels or children's literature. Both popular and profitable were children's books that adults bought for their common sense, practical advice, and entertainment value. Frances Gage's children's stories used a style that was characteristic of the day. For example, her 1850 volume *Aunt Fanny's Story—Book, Christmas Stories* included three tales: "The Spider," The Dentist," and The Apple-Dumpling." The first two demonstrate children conquering fear; there is a boy who can't escape fear; the second role model is a brave girl who in order to protect her quivering grandmother doesn't scream while her teeth are being pulled. More charming for modern readers are Gage's quirky tales that make fun of adults, like the old woman in "The Apple-Dumpling" whose spectacles fall into her dumpling four times before she concludes, "I must get a new nose."[47]

Two of Frances Gage's earliest tales for children were published in 1840 by the American Sunday-School Union of Philadelphia, "Aunt Fanny's Story," and "The Danger of Riches," a tale that adapted Matthew's Gospel 19:23-30 regarding rich men's problems finding salvation. The Union between 1817 and 1865 generated numerous penny texts to foster literacy and teach moral conduct; after 1830, the Union's "Mississippi Valley expansion" program included Ohio. Many of Gage's children's works were published by D. Appleton and Company under her pen name "Aunt Fanny," including *Aunt Fanny's Story-Book* (1850). Other publishers later presented her children's stories: for instance, in 1864, Sheldon and Company in New York City published six of Gage's *Pop-Gun* tales. In 1866, Breed, Butler & Co. in Buffalo, New York published five of Frances Gage's books, including *Fanny at School, Fanny's Fair, Fanny's Picnic*, and *Fanny's Birthday*. This publisher also printed her moral tale, "Miss Nason's Story," about a child who dies from a drunken mother's abuse.

It was unfortunate that after 1870 a second writer of children's tales adopted Frances Gage's pseudonym "Aunt Fanny," causing confusion about attribution. Fanny Barrow (1822-1894) was a wealthy dilettante who lived in New York City and traveled widely. She was affluent and sophisticated; her series for children covered simple subjects like mittens, nightcaps, and little pets.

Quaker Joshua Lippincott was the dominant publisher for Frances Gage's poetry and prose. His business grew in the 1850s from prayer books and Bibles, and then expanded into history and fiction. J. B. Lippincott was considered "one of the great publishing houses of the country."[46] In 1867, it published her mature volumes, *Poems,* and the novel, *Elsie Magoon; or, The Old Still-House in the Hollow a Tale of the Past.* Two years later in 1869, it reprinted *Gertie's Sacrifice; or, Glimpses at Two Lives* which was first released by the National Temperance Society and Publication House. Then in 1871, Lippincott also published *Steps Upward,* which first appeared in 1870 as a weekly serial in the *Temperance Patriot.* Frances Gage was fortunate to rely upon a variety of commercial and nonprofit publishing houses. Commentator Nel Irvin Painter sees Frances Gage's different publishers as a reflection of her belief in the power of the pen to reach the widest possible audience. Painter writes, "Throughout her life, she remained with the religious and feminist press. Among her 11 books of fiction, those published for temperance organizations predominate.[48]

Between 1866 and 1870, a burst of post war creative energy enabled Frances Gage to published her poetry anthology and three novels; it must have seemed a kind of "annus mirabilis," a miracle time of crowning accomplishment that capped off decades of her writing career. For her the new challenge was undertaking novels. Gage did not frequently read fiction and probably was not fully conversant with contemporaries' narrative techniques. Indeed, her third novel includes a warning that women should not to waste time doing frivolous reading, such as *Godey's Ladies Book,* the *Ledger,* and "novels of the day." These choices were, indeed, apt. *Godey's,* edited after 1830 by Sara Josepha Hale built its fame and circulation by including fashion plates. Robert Bonner's New York's *Ledger* provided a racy kind of escape; it was a sensational six cent weekly "story paper." Frances Gage's narrator tells women to prioritize their energies toward serious reading.

Her novels share a number of practices with other contemporary novelists. Her storylines are organized by chronology, characters either charmed or repelled, challenges were met and overcome, and happy endings occur. As was the popular convention, each of Gage's novels introduced a troubled "heroine," who proves her merit through deeds, and reknits a healthier social order. Furthermore, an intruded narrator controls each novel's expository background and theme.

Post war novels were often titled with women's names and introduced female characters with whom readers could identify. Frances Gage's protagonists' are—Gertrude, a saint who prayed for souls in purgatory, Elsie, a variant of Elisabeth, which in Hebrew means God's Promise or God's abundance, and Diana, the goddess of chastity. These were heroines with apt names, and of all of them, "Elsie" remained popular in book titles through the 1880's when it became America's most popular name for baby girls.

These novels include much of period interest—there is a vibrant picture of the Ohio Valley's pioneer settlement, a gritty depiction of New York City's seamy side, and a politically evocative scene in Washington D. C. Temperance remained Gage's theme; each novel presents a female protagonist who confronts the coiling serpent. The novels sum up her lifetime's concerns. The definitive work is *Elsie Magoon* which traces a quarter of a century's damage caused by alcohol from one Ohio Valley still. In this tale, two women, a mother and daughter, supersede social conventions. The novella *Gertie's Sacrifice* introduces other questions about social privilege and gender. Its title character descends into drunkenness that proves that neither gender nor social class protects one from alcoholism. The last novel, *Steps Upward,* revisits the question of rural alcohol production via a huge commercial distillery whose tentacles reach throughout the nation.

A supporting theme is aberrant or hyper masculinity. In Gage's novels weak men do bad things. For example, Richard Magoon knows he is legally and socially superior to his wife, Elsie, and falsely assumes he is morally superior, as well. Sadly, he is simply selfish and has married a wealthy woman. His moral errors are replicated by other men in the novel. Her second novel shows weakness in both sexes; one man rejuvenates himself, while the female protagonist reverses the Washingtonian pattern and dies a drunkard. The final novel includes both strong and weak men, but its husbands are solipsistic—especially the distillery and tavern owners.

Gage's plots do, of course, generate happy endings. The mother and daughter named Elsie find contentment, one as a widow who has done her duty, and the other as a worker who wins a regenerated husband. The happy ending in *Gertie's Sacrifice* is muted; its "naming" character experiences delirium tremens and dies. Two marriages follow as a reward to those who escape alcohol's clutches. It is interesting that Gage's final novel complicates the formula of "married and lived happily ever after" endings. However, *Steps Upward* legitimizes the heroine and creates a healthier community.

This novel's conclusion is abrupt, perhaps, because serialization affects form. Its competing themes include a call for "True Women" in a village and "New Women" in an urban environment. A generation ahead of their time, Frances Gage's novels anticipate the social movement historians label, "New Womanhood." [49] It was true in the 1880s and 1890s that a new breed of females in America began carrying Gage's ideas forward; this generation challenged society about narrow feminine identity and demanded opportunities for economic independence.

Gage's mature thought on gender identity is introduced in *Elsie Magoon* with a mother and daughter who discuss the pitfalls of marriage. The daughter has observed her father's drunken abuse, and argues—women's motto should be, "Do not wed." Yet desiring love and children, she marries. Gage's narrator protests the waste of women's potential, "women are born to the heritage of brains, with faculties for planning and organizing, and powers for executing that might. . . have fitted them for spheres of action as wide and deep as the world offers to the human soul" (Ch. 15). This novel demonstrates what Annette Kolodny, a modern literary critic, labels "vitiating rural public opinion;" outstanding females like young Elsie Magoon must survive "the suspicion that women become desiccated or masculinized (or both) on the frontier."[50] Gage's final novel, *Steps Upward,* wrestles with the conundrum of women's social and economic issues; furthermore, she raises unanswerable questions—post-wedding ceremony issues. What happens if a decent and wealthy husband turns out to be less intelligent than his wife, could she still be fulfilled? Or, should husbands "allow" their wives to balance matrimonial duties with growth through travel and work? If they did not, could women escape social censure and move beyond oppressive families?

A commitment to gender equality was embedded in much of this author's work from the 1850s when she wrote in the *Ohio State Journal* that women's kindnesses to men should earn them respect; her example was giving up her train seat to an elderly man.[51] This is what a "true woman" should do. She resented any unnatural philosophy that separated men's and women's gender spheres. It was unfair that only the masculine were entitled to public life and excluded all others who had the misfortune of being born female. She believed this separatism between the sexes was bad for men, too; proscribed hyper masculinity often did not suit individuals' innate natures. Unrestricted hyper masculinity could even lead to violence and the carnage of war with which she was engulfed in South Carolina.

Moreover, Frances Gage observed that women of achievement were universally criticized; it took real initiative for them to oppose convention. Shaming, mockery, or overt criticism were employed —Amelia Bloomer freeing clothing, Lucy Stone working her way through college, or Sojourner Truth lecturing. The viciousness of attacks on strong women was not so easily shown as when in 1858 Sojourner Truth proved she was not a man by baring her breasts. Indeed, the era's reform minded women, like Francis Gage, did not wish to emulate men. As a recent commentator notes, women reformers did not wish to impinge on men's sphere by smoking, chewing tobacco, swearing, drinking, becoming corpulent, or hanging out in saloons.[52]

The roots of Frances Gage's gender philosophy sprang from childhood accusations about being called a "masculine" girl with "mechanical" aptitude. She refused to believe innate talent could unsex anyone. This was why Frances Barker joked about breaking her sphere. Maturity added evidence of her egalitarian ideal; women like Clara Barton and other reformers proved "separate spheres" was an invalid metaphor. It damaged the brightest and best women who had "superior" qualities. The longer she lived, the more Gage admired androgynous women of accomplishment. Her 1858 essay, "Masculine Women," supported women's right to achieve in a public life. She endorsed a variety of contemporary achievers, including sculpture Harriet Hosner, painter Rosa Bonheur, and such writers as Harriet Beecher Stowe, Elizabeth Barrett Browning, Currer Bell (Charlotte Bronte). She also praised the singer Jenny Lind, reformer Lucy Stone, scholar Miss Peabody, astronomer Mrs. Somerville, Dr. Elizabeth Blackwell and contemporary heroes Mrs. Patton and Mrs. Clemors, each of whom employed "the talents God gave her." They illustrated her belief that "Every woman should make the very most of herself, and be able to act her part well in whatever circumstances of life she may be placed."[53]

A final context deserving mention is "regionalism." In the 1830s and 1840s men like William Davis Gallagher were cheerleaders for romantic depictions of pioneer life. They celebrated independence, earnestness, individualism, all of which were seen as masculine traits at the time. He saw the Old Northwest as a social experiment in reform that led pioneers to material, moral, and intellectual progress. Indeed, this was Gallagher's Ohio version of the "Jeffersonian Persuasion" that connected "Westerners to the republican principles of the American Revolution."[54] This anticipated the influential historical theories of Frederick Jackson Turner in the twentieth century.

Frances Dana Gage was not from Cincinnati where Gallagher generated his influence and promulgated his definition of pioneer writers who were committed to the defense of human rights.[53] She was not the kind of ardent "Westerner" that men like Venable, Gallagher, and Coggeshall called for. Nonetheless, Frances Gage produced valuable retrospectives of "regional" life on the Ohio, Muskingum, and Allegheny Rivers. She was enormously proud of being born among the region's pioneers. What was different about her was a womanly intelligence and travel that widened Gage's perspective. She respected others' regions too. It was a unique and rare sentiment we might call rural-based humanism. This is what George Stuart calls "intelligent provincialism."[55]

Following the Civil War, the aged widow reconsidered her background and role in America's "history." Without a husband or home in the Middle West, facing old age and debility, Frances Gage drew on the past as a resource for a variety of poems, stories, and novels. Her novels aim to rise above regional partisanship and reconcile her pioneer life on the Middle West frontier with her adult experiences in the East. Frances Gage's reflections produced a maturity of vision that remains an uncommon achievement.

Notes

Chapter Five

1. Gage, "Letter," *The Herald*, 141.
2. _____, "Woman's Sphere," *Ohio Cultivator* 7, no. 1 (Jan. 1. 1851): 15.
3. _____, "Speech, Woman's Rights Convention, 1858." in *History* 1, 152.
4. Jane Tompkins, *Sensational Designs, the Cultural Work of American Fiction, 1790-1860,* (New York: Ohio University Press, 1985), 200.
5. Gage, "Letter from Aunt Fanny," *Pittsburgh Saturday Visiter* (Nov. 16, 1850): 174.
6. _____, "Aunt Fanny's Husband," *Ohio Cultivator* 9, no. 5 (March 1, 1853): 74.
7. _____, "Letter from Mrs. Gage," *Ohio Cultivator* 9, no. 6 (April 1, 1853): 109.
8. _____, "Untitled," *The Lily*, 7 (Dec. 15, 1855): 181.
9. _____, "A Letter from Mrs. Gage," *The Lily*, 7 (July 15, 1854): 104.
10. _____, "Aunt Fanny's Greeting," *Ohio Cultivator*, 17, no. 1 (January 1, 1861): 24.
11. _____, "Looking Back,: *The Woman's Advocate* 1 (January, 1869) 4.
12. _____, "New Year's Letter from Aunt Fanny," *Ohio Cultivator* 8, no. 1 (January 1, 1852): 12.
13. Norma J. Bruce, "A Commitment to Women—The *Ohio Cultivator* and *The Ohio Farmer* of the Nineteenth Century," *The Serials Librarian* 37, no. 2 (1999): 15.
14. Terzian, 111.
15. Gage, "Mrs. Jones Experience," *Ohio Cultivator* 3, no. 4 (Dec. 1850): 132.
16 Bruce, 21
17. _____, 22.
18. Frances W. Kayes, "The Ladies Department of the *Ohio Cultivator*, 1845-1855: A Feminist Forum," *Agricultural History* 50 (April 1876): 416.
19. Bruce, 18.

20. Gage, "Letter from Mrs. Gage," *Ohio Farmer* 14, no. 16 (August 1865).

21. ____, "Sigersons," *Valley Farmer*, 5, no. 7 (July 1853): 264.

22. "Our Authors," *The Literary World*, Cincinnati, 1850.

23. Gage, "Market Woman," *Una* (Oct. 1854).

24. ____, "Letter from Mrs. Gage," *The Lily*, no. 8 (August, 1852): 66.

25. Gage, "How Fares Our Cause," *Una* 4, no. 8 (August, 1852): 246.

26. Antoinette Brown, "Letter to Lucy Stone," *Friends and Sisters: Letters Between Lucy Stone and Antoinette Brown Blackwell* (Urbana: University of Illinois Press, 1987), 93.

27. Executive Committee, "The Anti-Slavery History of the John Brown Year, Twenty Seventh Annual Report of the American Anti-Slavery Society, 1861," 310.

28. Gage, "The Children's Column, The Russet Apple Story, How Mischief Punishes Itself," *The Independent* 18, no. 921 (July 26, 1866): 6.

29. "Persona," *The Independent* 19, no. 977 (Aug. 22, 1867), 4.

30. ____, "Letter to the American Woman Suffrage Association, (Jan 1869). Emory University, Woman's Advocacy Collection. http:222.bingle.nu/results.pp?type=www&query=Frances GagePoems>

31. Oates, 192.

32. Brockett, 685-686.

33. Gage, "To Miss Alice Cary, 'The Dissatisfied'" *National Era* 3, no 50 (Dec. 13, 1849): 197.

34. ____, "Excellent," *Boston Evening Transcript* (August 4, 1856).

35. ____, "Letter to *Woman's Advocate*," reprinted in *American Phrenological Journal* 25, no. 4 (April 1857) 82.

36. Elaine Showalter, *A Jury of Her Peers* (New York: Alfred A. Knopf, 2010), 62.

37. Gage, "Notes," *The Ohio Farmer* 15, no., 421 (October 20, 1866): 329.

38. ____, "A Home Picture," *Ohio Cultivator* 7, no. 16 (August 15, 1851): 254.

39. Rufus Griswold, *The Female Poets of America* (Philadelphia: Carey and Hart, 1848): Introduction to Frances Dana Gage.

40. Gage, "Don't Run in Debt," *Liberator* 23, no. 20 (May 20, 1853): 90.

41. Linda Moody, "Frances Dana Gage, <http://www.jaushead.oorg/JHSumm99/moody.cfm>

42. Gage, "Lines on Reading," *Ohio Journal* 20, no. 28 (July 12, 1850): 112.

43. William Turner Coggeshall, *The Poets and Poetry of the West* (New York: Arno Press), 394.

44. W. H. Venable, *Beginnings of Literary Culture in the Ohio Valley* (Cincinnati: Robert Clarke, 1891): 273.

45. Coggeshall, 393.

46. Amy B. Aronson, *Taking Liberties: Early American Women's Magazines and Their Readers* (Westport, Conn.: Praeger Publishers, 2002), 133.

47. Gage, "The Apple Dumpling," *Aunt Fanny's Story Book* (New York: Jon Wiley & Sons, Inc., 1932), 95

48. Henry Walcott Boynton, *Annals of American Bookselling, 1638-1850)* (New York: John Wiley & Sons, Inc., 1932), 95.

49. Nel Irvin Painter, *Sojourner Truth, A Life, A Symbol* (New York: W.W. Norton, 1996), 177.

50. Annette Kolodny, *The Land Before Us* (Chapel Hill: University of North Carolina Press, 1975), 791.

51. Gage, "Letter," *Ohio State Journal* (August 1850), 177.

52. Smith, 10.

53. ___, "Masculine Women," *Liberator* 15 (Jan. 1858): 12.

54. Terry A. Barnhart, "The Partisan, William Davis Gallagher and the Case of Western Literature, *Ohio History* 115 (2008): 115.

55. George Stewart, "Western Writings," *Regional Approach to Literature*, ed. Gerald Haslan (Albuquerque: University of New Mexico Press, 1948), 47.

Epilogue, a Reassessment

What Frederick Jackson Turner described as the "winning" of the West was exemplified by Rufus Putnam's pioneers with the Ohio Company late in the 1700s. After the Fallen Timbers battle of 1794, post-Appalachian American expansion into Native American hunting grounds became inevitable. Orderly distribution of "public land" in the Northwest Territory led colonizers to follow soldiers. "Frontier" means perimeter, and pioneers moved west of the Appalachians after 1794 with unanticipated velocity. Putnam's Ohio Company largely consisted of hardy men who were both fighters and settlers. They knew that their conquest wiped out the culture that preceded them. With a gun in one hand and an ax in the other, they depleted wildlife and altered the ecology of the land. Frederick Jackson Turner celebrated this process of Anglo-American colonization as "progress," which meant destroying, disturbing, and despoiling. Revisionist historians qualify this orthodoxy, though it has many germs of truth.

The "hyper masculine" Ohio frontiersmen have been further studied by historians like John Mack Faragher, Stephen Aron, and Nicole Etcheson. Their clarification of "manliness" in the Old Northwest emphasizes that it valued action, strength, and the suppression of emotion. Its frontier culture consolidated a new set of cultural values, and as early as the 1820s political authority was relegated to men of the "better sort," that is men to whom the rank and file deferred, men like Col. Joseph Barker.[1]

His youngest daughter, Frances Barker grew up in a world of conflicting possibilities. Being born to straddle these divides, she was poised between the calls of frontier and pioneer, North and South, antebellum and postbellum, traditional and progressive. When she was a child, the scars wrought by Indians were still vivid in her elders. No one would have thought that some women's view of wrenching the land away from its ancient owners would eventually find expression. One baby from Putnam's settlement knew that her father was murdered by the natives, yet as an adult wrote a hagiography of Tecumseh. While ambivalent about the eradication of native peoples, Julia L. Dumont's romantic efforts also praised Daniel Boone and other frontiersmen.

As the passage of time would show, the effect of this hyper masculine culture was going to be subject to alteration. After two decades Frances Barker escaped from the Marietta farm in order to live with a different kind of man. James Lamson Gage was an educated easterner, an abolitionist who sought a helpmate to share his values. Their companionate marriage released Frances Barker to dedicate herself to assist escaping African American slaves, for instance by attacking the Fugitive Slave Law.[2]

The Marietta native was dutiful but rejected her father's last name. In adulthood she rarely visited the family property, now occupied by her eldest brother. He embellished the "manse" and stepped into his father's shoes in state government. Frances Gage's sentimental attachment was tied to some elderly women who still lived in Belpre and Marietta. Considered in the light of Faragher's frontier paradigm, these villagers could serve as examples of women's disempowerment. They remained in a post-frontier world of "hearths and trammels, piggins and noggins" that is fireplace hooks, pails and cups.[3] Frances Gage joined them by transforming herself into "Aunt Fanny," a friend who fused lonely rural women into a community of value. Her perspective was broad and deep. Perhaps she was also motivated by a kind of payback for being forbidden to "scribble."

As John Mack Faragher and others raised consciousness of changes in nineteenth-century culture in America, they examined the morphing of separate sphere stereotypes. Men had freedom in the public world and were the beneficiaries of women's labor. If masculinity is defined as action, women's purview is "verbal" and led to same sex bonding.[4] Language was women's greatest asset, an asset that Frances Gage developed throughout her adult life.

Frontier women built extended kinship networks, and reform work extended those bonds beyond the family. Reform women sought out men who represented alternative versions of masculinity, for example men like Frederick Douglass, William Lloyd Garrison, Salmon P. Chase, Thomas Wentworth Higginson, Theodore Tilton, and Edward L. Pierce. Women too began experiencing a gender reality that allowed variations, and Frances Gage drew attention to nonconforming women who were, for instance, "mechanical."

Frances Gage was the product of diverse experiences. There were slave and non-slave villages where she lived in the West and South. Historian Stephen Aron comments that her travels as a reformer gave her what he calls a "broad spectrum view." In contrast, more staid women like Elizabeth Cady Stanton clung to a limited perspective. Biographer Lori Ginzburg describes her as elitist and racist.

If history is what one chooses to tell, then Stanton and two associates created history in the multi-volume *History of Woman Suffrage Movement* that was published in 1881-1882; it serves the public a comprehensive record. Its editors included Stanton's cohort, Susan B. Anthony and Matilda Gage.[5] All were raised in New York State. Matilda Gage, the books' historical scholar, attended the Clinton Liberal Institute; Stanton was educated at Emma Willard's Troy Female Seminary, and Anthony attended a Philadelphia boarding school. They brought the coloring of their values to depictions of other reformers.

As Gail Parker, a twentieth-century editor of *Eighty Years and More*, warns in her "Introduction," there is something repellant about Elizabeth Cady Stanton's superiority complex.[6] A good example of this is seen in *History's* approach to Frances Dana Gage. The editors' perspective is critical of her frontier background. She was seen as an able foot soldier and is patronized for having risen above arduous domestic life of mother and housekeeper, who remarkably presided over Akron's 1851 Convention with "an easy manner of graceful and appropriate extemporaneous speech." Frances Gage saw her pioneer challenges as a source of grit, self-sufficiency, and independence. Ohio's "wild west" culture produced her strength.

By the time *History* was written, the "spirit of the age" was profoundly altered. Abraham Lincoln was dead. Reformers like Henry Ward Beecher, Theodore Tilton, Susan B., Anthony and Elizabeth Cady Stanton were diminished by scandals. Anthony and Stanton defied the new era's commitment to give African American men citizenship rights and opposed Constitutional Amendments. William Lloyd Garrison retired after the Civil War. Theodore Tilton was self-exiled in Paris, and Henry Ward Beecher gave up newspaper work.

Gage's reform colleagues were diminished by age. The rich and interesting community of women that had been melded by reform movements was decimated. Lucretia Mott died in 1880; Sojourner Truth passed away in 1883; Frances Gage was gone in 1884; Lucy Stone drifted off in 1893, and Amelia Bloomer died a year later. Elizabeth Cady Stanton hung on until 1902; her friend,

Susan B. Anthony, lived four years longer. Clara Barton, nearly "the last leaf on the tree," passed away in 1912. Antoinette Brown Blackwell, the only survivor of the 1850 first Woman's Rights Convention in Worcester, Mass, lived to enjoy the franchise and vote in a presidential election.

After Gage's death in 1884 the "triad" causes that inspired Frances Gage ran their course. Slavery was abolished but neither black nor white women could vote. Temperance continued to animate Americans because alcoholism led to the abuse of women and children.

Frances Gage's final years of widowhood were supported by several adult children. Her loyalty to Clara Barton continued, and Barton was so shocked by her death that she delayed sending condolence notes to Mary, Sarah, and Joseph Gage.[7] When she wrote it was to celebrate their mother's loyalty and "faithful, strong loving letters full of faith and trust . . . grand strong loving Mother." In 1892 the nurse eulogized her friend at the final meeting of the Potomac Corps of the Women's Relief Corps. The Women Who Went to the Field" was dedicated to all Civil War "sisters in mercy," and included Aunt Fanny who had the "courage to scoff at fear."[8]

Was Frances Gage afraid of anything? Would she have lived her life differently if she could have imagined where it would take her? The answer drawn from all of her written evidence is: no. She faced all sorts of awful things—a maddened and rearing horse that almost trampled a nephew, personal and family debilitating illnesses, arson, catcalls, regional animosity, the deafening noise of bombardment, the pitiful freedmen and wounded soldiers. Would anything have happened differently if Frances Gage in July 1867 was not forced off the public stage? No, because her efforts, in the grand scheme of things, were small and even a healthy Frances Gage could not have made a difference to these waning rights issues. She was forced to retire in one day but could always remember her contributions—from helping bandage slaves, to attacking the Fugitive Slave Act, to fighting for legislation to improve the rights of married women, to working as a Superintendent on Parris Island. She celebrated the gatherings she had instigated and the friendships she had developed. It was all done in the name of duty, leaving her no regrets about what was accomplished in the public sphere.

A recent literary critic warns, "What authors have survived their time and which have not" depends on who "noticed them and chose to record that notice."[9] Unfortunately, Frances Gage has not survived. She did not leave behind much of a photographic record. There are two classic engravings of her in Congressional archives which convey a rigid visage. Her appearance generates an impression of endurance and strength. Susan B. Anthony wrote a short poem about Frances Gage that is unflattering. The Quaker describes her as being tall and solid with coarse features; Frances Gage had gray hair, a narrow forehead, flat nose, thick lips and large mouth. Thus, Anthony complained that she was not pretty and gave the impression of willfulness. On the other hand, she recognized that the Ohioan as had kind and tender feelings, common sense, a quick tongue, merry laugh, and love-craving heart.

Surveying Frances Dana Gage's contributions to her culture takes a reader to the "Ohio from 1850-1861" chapter in E. C. Stanton, S. B. Anthony, and Matilda Gage's *History of the Woman Suffrage Movement*. Its editors stress Gage's limiting pioneer roots in "arduous domestic life, of mother and housekeeper, in a new country." They praise her "easy manner of graceful and appropriate extemporaneous speech" at Akron's 1851 Convention and include a number of her recorded speeches, among these the 1851 Second Ohio Woman's Rights Conference in Akron, the 1852 Ohio Woman's Rights Convention, and Cincinnati's 1855 National Woman's Rights Convention. *The New York Times* called this "The great speech of the Convention; it was remarkable for its high-toned morality, its truthfulness and eloquence."

The records of these gatherings trace her panache in stories that reveal a quick mind and fresh wit. For instance at the 1852 Rights Conference, Gage tempered her idealistic anger with humor and irony as she assailed those who attacked woman's rights advocates. There is a memorable verbal duel she had with a McConnelsville judge who sneered at women's petitions to close grog shops. The law was on his side, but logic was not. The judge wanted women to remain in the nursery and parlor; he blamed mothers for their son's failures. Gage retorted, "What mother ever taught her son to drink rum, gamble, swear, smoke, and chew tobacco?" The patriarch was warned that mothers cannot impose moral standards in sons that their fathers will not follow. Her argument concluded that sons who are taught that their mothers are inferior will find it unmanly to obey her guidelines. The judge grew silent. In this way, Gage's reputation for firm public stands on woman's issues grew in McConnelsville.

Among the public figures who recorded positive comments about Frances Gage is James Parton, husband of Fanny Fern, and the editor of *Eminent Women of the Age* who described Gage as vigorous with a good and benevolent face; he emphasized her easy manners, fund of varied conversation, and successful platform style of a "talker, rather than an orator."[10] Historian, W.T. Coggeshall placed her among the "first rank of social female orators."[11] W. H. Venable, another early cultural historian of Ohio Valley culture, called Gage "one of the ablest advocates of reform known to the Press.[12] Urban newspapers in places like Cleveland, Syracuse and New Orleans praised her demeanor and delivery, giving her "high visibility in major reform causes" as organizer, speaker and activist. Among her close cohorts and friends in Ohio, Frances Dana Gage was especially esteemed; Hannah Tracy Cutler emphasized her "intellectuality" and "sparkling wit and humor"; she believed her "interior springs of thought and feeling surpass. . . the scholar. . . even Miss Stone."[13] Others repeatedly praised her reliability and a few over valued her writing with comparisons to Harriet Beecher Stowe and Elizabeth Barrett Browning.

Indeed, "Aunt Fanny" promoted her viewpoints, but did not search for fame. She attacked "bad laws and customs of society," which become "dated." Jeffrey E. Smith notes that reputations are fragile and here drew less attention because "she spent much of her life in the field."[10] Also, contemporary Victorian paradigms fit her badly. She promoted domesticity and raised a large family, but was not really domestic, except for her love of gardening. Frances Gage was interested in everything; an older sister commented that as a youth she wanted to know it all, including "the concert of the blind and the ball of the lunatics." She added that France wanted to ride sidesaddle on a comet's tail. These were childish and comic exaggerations, but as an adult she performed on a prodigious level. Her commitment to work and friendship, the juggling of family and career, the disillusionment with religion and government, the use of humor, wit, and irony—all served to distinguish Gage from more typical women of the era.

Once Gage described a particular woman as "having a mind that sees both far and near." Occasionally someone is born with this gift and the phrase aptly fits her. She argued there should be a "metempsychosis" or change in the soul of things, no small order. Frances Gage also recognized that reforms will inevitably have limitations; nonetheless, she said, "there will yet be reforms and reformers." Her appeals are timeless—turn anger over injustice into a plan for active good; work to create a broad, inclusive sense of community; exercise your imagination and creativity; cultivate deep roots, yet seek a diversity of experiences.

Those who knew her best recognized Gage's rare capacity to rise above the role of reformer to that of seer. Beyond the inevitable success of her three reform causes, Gage foresaw that women's rights would include the option of women channeling their energies into different kinds of lives. Her late career evocation of "New Women" and praise of nontraditional female achievers was precocious.

Traditional religion disappointed Frances Dana Gage. During her 22 years living in McConnelsville, she often boarded preachers at Mount Airy, but when the Gages asked churchmen why they avoided becoming involved with rights issues, they parted company. In 1882 a Universalist publication carried an article in which she explained her "faith": "I have read much, thought much, and feel that life is too precious to be given to doctrines." She aimed to preserve history and wished to have "added my mite to the world's good." When asked about an overall goal, Frances Gage responded simply, "We ask equality with men."

Her dynamic messages were often embodied in an anecdote. Gage charmed the audience at the 1866 Eleventh National Women's Rights Convention with an experience from five years earlier in the West Indies. She stood amidst the ruins of Christopher Columbus's brother's home, now only magnificent ruins. Gage eyed at a small plant growing atop a ruined wall and learned its translated name was Rock Splitter. She mused, "its little roots [go] down into and disintegrate the coralline rock," So, "by its own inherent force it had riven those old walls asunder . . . and made an utter ruin." Gage's moral was that reform's seeds of truth will destroy "old walls of tyranny, superstition, custom, and oppression." In other words, devastation is a stage amongst progressions. Like the pretty Rock Splitter, Frances Dana Gage wished to destroy "old ruins and clothe them with verdure and beauty." Applause twice interrupted this speech.

When a final stroke quenched the spirit of Frances Dana Gage in 1884, her daughter Mary and youngest son were there to follow her wishes and inter her locally. The Ohio Company's literal story ends there, back in New England. Retrospectively, it is undeniable that the currents of history were affected by slavery, alcohol, and women's rights. Those who pushed these ideas to the fore did not make themselves popular, but they enjoyed their comradeship and were energized by small successes. A humble reformer like Frances Dana Gage was a pioneer product who truly left a mark on American culture.

Epilogue

NOTES

1. John Mack Faragher, *Sugar Creek, Life on the Prairies*, (New Haven, Yale UP, 1988) 41.

2. Nicole Etcheson, "Manliness and the Political Culture of the Old Northwest, 1790-1860," *Journal of the Early Republic* 15 (Spring 1995): 559-577.

3. Faragher, "History from the Inside Out: Writing the History of Women in Rural America," *American Quarterly* (1981) 33: 148.

4. _____, 148.

5. Elizabeth Cady Stanton, et al. *History of Woman Suffrage, 1881-1902* 4, (New York: Schocken Books, 1971), 429.

6. Gail Parker, "Introduction," *Elizabeth Cady Stanton, Eighty Years and More.* (New York: Schocken Books, 1971), xviii.

7. Clara Barton, Papers of Clara Barton, Library of Congress, Manuscript Division.

8. _____, "Women Who Went to the Field." Papers of Clara Barton, Library of Congress, Manuscript Division.

9. Jeffrey E. Smith, "Frances Dana Gage "Frances Dana Gage: Turning the World Upside Down, *Feminist Frontiers, Women Who Shaped the Midwest*, ed. Yvonne Jonson (Kirksville, Missouri: Truman State University Press, 2010), 35.

10. James Parton, "Frances D. Gage, *Eminent Women of the Age* (Hartford: S. M. Betts &. Co., 868), 383.

11. W. T. Coggeshall, *Poets and Poetry of the West* (New York: Arno Press, 1975): 393.

12. W. H. Venable, *Beginnings of Literary Culture of the Ohio Valley.* (New York: Peer Smith, 1949): 74.

13. Hannah Tracy Cutler, "Eulogy," *Woman's Journal*, 4.

LIST OF WORKS CONSULTED

Frances Gage Books

Gage, Frances. *Aunt Fanny's Story-Book—Christmas Stories.* New York: D. Appleton & Company, 1850.

___. *Elsie Magoon; or the Old Still-House in the Hollow.* Philadelphia: J. B. Lippincott, 1867. See Wright American Fiction 1851-1875. <http://www.letrs.indiana.edu/web/wright2/> (accessed May 10, 2008).

---. *Gertie's Sacrifice; or, Glimpses of Two Lives.* Utica. Temperance Patriot Office, 1869. Reprinted Philadelphia: J. B. Lippincott, 1869. See Wright American Fiction 1851-1875. <http://www.letrs.indiana.edu/web/w/wright2/> (accessed May 10, 2008).

---. *Poems.* Philadelphia: J. B. Lippincott, 1867.

---. *Steps Upward.* Utica: Temperance Patriot Office, 1870. Reprinted Philadelphia: J. B. Lippincott, 1871. See Wright American Fiction 1851-1875. <http://www.letrs.indiana.edu/web/w/wright2/> (accessed May 10, 2008).

Frances Gage Articles

Gage, Frances. "Address of Frances D. Gage." Opening Session of the First Anniversary Meeting of the American Equal Rights Association, May 9, 1867; "Address of Frances D. Gage" Evening Session, May 10, 1867; American Equal Rights Association,1866-1869, 64-66, in *Proceedings of the First Anniversary of the American Equal Rights Association held at the Church of the Puritans* New York: Robert J. Johnston, Printer, 1867.

___. "Address to Woman's Rights Convention, Akron, Ohio, May 28, 1851." In *A Sweet, Separate Intimacy: Woman Writers of the American frontier, 1800-192*. Ed. Susan Cummins Miller, 32-34. Salt Lake City: University of Utah Press, 2000.

---. "Address." *Anti-Slavery Bugle*. Salem, Ohio. 23, April 1850.

___. "The Apple Dumpling." *Aunt Fanny's Story Book.* New York: D. Appleton and Company, 1850.

___. "Aunt Fanny in the Garden." *Ohio Farmer* 14, no. 31 (Aug. 5, 1865): 241.

___. "Aunt Fanny's Greeting." *Ohio Cultivator* 17, no. 1 (Jan. 1, 1851): 24.

___. "Aunt Fanny's Removal to the West—First Impressions of St. Louis." *Ohio Cultivator* 9, no. 2 (Jan 15, 1853): 20.

___. "Aunt Hanna's Quilt." *The Herald of Truth* 3 (Feb. 1, 1848): 141.

___. "The Autobiography of Frances D. Gage." *Woman's Journal* (March 31, 1883): 1

___. "The Black Soldiers of South Carolina." *Liberator* 32, no. 51 (Dec. 19, 1862): 1.

___. "Chapter about the Fourth of July." *Ohio Cultivator* 10, no. 15 (Aug. 1, 1854): 124.

___. "Correspondence with Clara Barton, General Correspondence, Library of Congress, Box 68, Reel 55." Lilly (Martin) Spencer Papers. Archives of American Art, Smithsonian Institution, Washington, D. C.

___. "The Doctor That Was Not a Humbug." *Water-Cure Journal* 19, no. 6 (June 1855): 130.

___. "The East Seen From the West." *Ohio Cultivator* 14, no. 16 (Aug. 15, 1858), 254.

___. "Excellent." *Boston Evening Transcript* (Aug. 4, 1856); rpt. *American Phrenological Journal* 25, no. 4: 82.

___. "A Few Thoughts About the War." *National Anti-Slavery Standard* 20, (Aug. 1, 1863): 2.

___. "Fourth of July at the House That Jeff Built." *Liberator* 34, no. 31 (July 29, 1864): 1.

___. "Frances D. Gage's Reply to Gerrit Smith." *History of Woman Suffrage* 1.

Elizabeth Cady Stanton, Susan B. Anthony, and Matilda Joslyn Gage, 842-844. New York: Fowler and Wells Publishers, 1861.

___. "Gage to Janney May 11, 1855." In Janney Family Papers. Mss. 142, Box 4/5. Columbus: Ohio Historical Society.

___. "Good Templars—Hog Cholera—Ohio History." *Ohio Cultivator* 13, no. 8 (April 14, 1857): 124.

———. "Greetings." *Field Notes* 1 (Jan. 3, 1861): 4.
———. "Home Miscellany, Mrs. Gage on Her Way to the West Indies." *Ohio Cultivator* 15, no. 6 (March 15, 1859): 93
———. "Home Miscellany, Glimpses About New York." *Ohio Cultivator* 14, 11 (June 1, 1858): 173.
———. "How Fares Our Cause." *Una* (June 1854): 282.
———. "How to Treat the Sick." *Herald of Health* 15, no. 2 (Feb. 1870): 86-88.
———. "The Indian Summer of Life." *Ohio Cultivator* 14, no. 18 (Sept. 15, 1858): *286.*
———. "Last Moments of General Mitchell," *National Anti-Slavery Standard* 19, no. 22 (Nov. 15, 1862): 3.
———. "Letter." *The Lily* 3 (May 6, 1851).
———. "Letter." *The Lily* 3 (June 1, 1851).
———. "Letter." *The Herald of Truth* 3 (Feb. 1, 1848): 141.
———. "Letter." *The Ohio State Journal* (August 1850), 177.
———. "Letter from Aunt Fanny," *Pittsburgh Saturday Visiter* (Nov. 16, 1850): 174.
———. "Letter to Charlotte Barker." In Collection of Jerry Devol. Devol: Ohio. n.d.
———. "A Letter from Mrs. Frances D. Gage." *Water-Cure Journal* 14, no. 3 (September 1852): 60.
———"Letter from Frances D. Gage." *The Women's Advocate* vol. 3 (Jan. 1870), n.p. Emory Women Writers Resource Project, <http://www.bingle.nu/results/php?type=www&query=Fraces Gage, Poems>
———. "Letter from Frances D. Gage to Matilda Joslyn Gage," *History* 1, 117-118.
———. "Letter from Mrs. Frances D. Gage, the Swedish Movement Cure." *Ohio Farmer* 17, 1 (Jan. 4, 1868): 10.
———. "Letter from Mrs. Gage." *The Lily* 4 (August 1852): 66.
———. "Letter from Mrs. Gage." *The Lily* 5 (Jan. 28, 1853): 174.
———. "Letter from Mrs. Gage." *The Lily* 6 (July 15, 1854): 104.
———. "Letter from Mrs. Gage." *The Lily* 7 (April 14, 1855), 41.
———. "Letter from Mrs. Gage." *Ohio Cultivator* 8, no. 23, (Dec. 1, 1852): 366.

___. "Letter from Mrs. Gage." *Ohio Cultivator* 9, no. 6 (April 1, 1853): 109.

___. "Letter from Mrs. Gage." *Ohio Cultivator* 9, no. 17 (Sept. 1, 1853): 286.

___. "Letter from Mrs. Gage." *Ohio Cultivator* 10, no. 8 (April 15, 1854), 216.

___. "Letter from Mrs. Gage." *Ohio Cultivator*, 10, no. 12 (June 15, 1854): 188.

___. "Letter from Mrs. Gage." *Ohio Cultivator*, 15, no. 6 (March 4, 1859): 142.

___. "Letter from Mrs. Gage." *Ohio Cultivator* 16, no, 1 (Jan. 1, 1860): 173.

___. "Letter from Mrs. Gage." *New York Tribune* (Aug. 29, 1863).

___. "Letter from Mrs. Gage," *New York Tribune* (October 16, 1863).

___. "Letter from Mrs. Gage: A Chapter for the 4th of July." *Ohio Cultivator* 9, no. 16 (Aug. 1, 1853): 237.

----. "Letter from Mrs. Gage: Visit to Antioch College." *Ohio Farmer* 6, no. 2 (Jan. 10, 1857): 6.

___. "Letter from Frances D. Gage May 10, 1870." *History* 2, 769.

___. "Letter from Mrs. F. D. Gage." *Ohio Cultivator* 15, no. 44 (October 29, 1859): 350.

---. "Letter from Mrs. Gage." *National Anti-Slavery Standard* 21, no. 20 (Oct. 22, 1864) 3.

___. "Letter from Mrs. Gage." *Ohio Farmer* 8 no. 25 (June 18, 1859): 198.

___. "Letter from Mrs. Gage." *Ohio Farmer* 8, no. 44 (Oct. 29, 1859): 350.

___. "Letter from Mrs. Gage," *Ohio Farmer* 13, no. 1 (Jan. 5, 1864).

___. "Letter from Mrs. Gage, The Swedish Movement Cure." *Ohio Farmer* 17, no. 1 (June 1868).

___. "Letter from Mrs. Gage: Visit to Antioch College." *Ohio Farmer* 23, no. 6 (Jan. 10, 1857): 6.

___. "Letter from Mrs. Gage," *Ohio Farmer* 14, no. 17 (August 1865).

___. "Letter from Mrs. Frances D. Gage." *Ohio Farmer* 17, no. 1 (Jan. 4, 1868): 10.

___. "Letter from Mrs. Frances D. Gage." *Liberator* 29, no. 11 (March 18, 1859): 44.
___. "Letter from Mrs. Frances D. Gage," *Liberator*, 29, no. 12 (April 1, 1859): 57.
___. "Letter from Mrs. Frances D. Gage." *Liberator* 32, no. 35 (Aug. 29, 1862): 140.
___. "Letter from Mrs. Frances D. Gage." *Liberator* 32, no. 51 (Dec. 19, 1862): 1.
___. "Letter from Mrs. Frances D. Gage." *Liberator* 33, no. 12 (March 20, 1863): 46.
___. "Letter from the West." *Water-Cure Journal* 17, no. 2 (Feb. 1854): 15.
___. "Letter from Frances D. Gage to the American Woman Suffrage Association."(Jan. 1869). Emory University, Women's Advocacy Collection. <http://www.bingle.nu/results.php?type=www&query=Frances Gage Poems>
___. "Letter from Mrs. Frances D. Gage to Dr. Jackson." *Water Cure Journal* 14, no. 3 (1852): 54, 57.
___. "Letter to Salem Women's Rights Convention, April 1850."
___. "Letter to the *Woman's Advocate.*" Reprinted in *American Phrenological Journal* 25, no. 4 (April 1857), 82.
___. "Letter of Frances Dana Gage to Frederick Douglas." *History* 1, 843.
___. "Looking Back." *The Woman's Advocate*. Vol. 1 (January 1869): 1-6. <http://womenwriters.library.emory.edu/content.hp?level=div&id=advocate>
___. "Market Woman." *Una* (May 1854).
___. "Masculine Women." *Liberator* 15, no. 3 (January 1858): 12.
___. "Memoir of Frances Dana Barker." In Janney Family Papers, Mss. 142, Box 3/7. Columbus: Ohio Historical Society.
___. "Mrs. Gage at Home." *Ohio Farmer* 8, no. 26 (June 25, 1859): 208.
___. "Mrs. Gage at Home Again." *Ohio Cultivator* 15. no. 13 (July 1, 1859): 206.
___. "Mrs. Jones Experience," *Ohio Cultivator* 3, no. 23 (December 1850): 132.
___. "New Year's Letter from Aunt Fanny." *The Ohio Cultivator* 8, no. 1 (Jan. 1, 1852): 12.

___. "Notes." *Ohio Farmer* 15, no. 421 (Oct. 20, 1866): 329.

___. "Personal." *The Independent* 19, no. 977 (Aug. 22, 1867): 4.

___. "A Remembrance of Abraham Lincoln." *The Independent* 18, no. 915 (June 14, 1860): 6.

___. "Reminiscences of Childhood." *Daily True Democrat* 4 (Sept. 19, 1850): 2.

___. "Reminiscences by Frances D. Gage of Sojourner Truth, 1851." *History* 2, 541.

___. "Relics of Andersonville; Clara Barton, and Her Works of Mercy." *Independent* 18, no. 895 (Jan. 25, 1866): 1.

___. "Response." Morning Session June 3, Woman's Rights Convention, 1852. Philadelphia, Pa.: Merrihew and Thompson, Printers, 1852: 30-31.

___. "Results of Emancipation in Santa Cruz." *National Anti-Slavery Standard*, 16, no. 13 (June 11, 1859): 204.

___. 'The Russet Apple Story, How Mischief Punishes Itself.'" *The Independent* 18, no. 921 (July 16, 1866): 6.

___. "Sigersons." *Valley Farmer* 5, no 7 (July 1853): 264.

___. "Sojourner Truth, *Independent* 18, no. 897 (Feb. 8, 1866): 2; *History* 1, 115-117.

___. "Speech." *Proceedings of the National Women's Rights Convention.* Cleveland, 1853), 6.

___. "Speech of Frances D. Gage." In *Proceedings of the Eleventh National Women's Rights Convention, Held at the Church of the Puritans, New York, May 10, 1866* by the National Woman's Rights Convention, 43-45. New York: Robert J. Johnston, Printer, 1866.

___. "Speech by Frances D. Gage." May 10, 1867. *History of Woman Suffrage* 2, 223-224.

___. "Speech of Mrs. Frances D. Gage." *Liberator* 34, no. 4 (Jan. 22, 1864): 1.

___. "Speech at New York Woman's Temperance Convention." *The Lily* 4 (May 1852).

___. "Tales of Truth," *The Lily*, 4, no. 5 (Jan. 1852). 2-3. Reprinted in *Water Drops from Women Writers: A Temperance Reader*. Ed. Carol Mattingly. 216-247; 260-267. Carbondale: Southern Illinois Press, 2001.

___. "Thoughts on the War." *National Anti-Slavery Standard* 32, no. 51 (Dec. 19, l863): 3.
___. "To Miss Alice Carey, 'The Dissatisfied.'" *National Era* 4, no. 50 (Dec. 13, 1849): 197.
___. "Untitled." *The Lily* 7 (Dec. 15, 1855): 181.
___. "Woman and the Press." *Liberator* 32, no. 24. (Jan. 13, 1862).
___. "Woman's Sphere." *Pittsburg Saturday Visiter* (1850); *The Lily* 4, no. 3 (March 1851).
___. "Woman's Sphere and Duty." *Ohio Farmer* 17, no. 35 (Aug. 29, 1868): 555.
___. "Woman's Sphere—What Mrs. Jones Said About It." *Ohio Cultivator* 71, no. 1 (Jan 1, 1851): 15.

Nineteenth-Century Sources Cited

Alcott, Louisa May. "The Brothers" or "My Contraband." *Atlantic Monthly* 12, no. 73 (Nov. 1863): 584-595.
Annual Review of the Commerce of St. Louis, for the Year 1854. (St. Louis, 1855): 33.
Ansell, J. W. ""Reminiscences of Morris Island." *National Tribune* (July 21, 188). GAR Museum, Philadelphia, Penn.
"Aunt Fanny's Husband," *Ohio Cultivator* 9, no. 5 (May 1, 1853): 74.
Barker, Catharine. "Written by Hand." Autobiography Ms. B. 57, vols. 1-3. Dawes Library Special Collections, Marietta College, Ohio.
_____. Collection, Iowa State Historical Dept., Div. of Historical Museums and Archives, Historical Library in Anti-Slavery Ms. Div., Boston Public Library and Schlesinger Library, Radcliffe College.
Barker, Joseph. *Recollections of the First Settlement of Ohio.* Ed. George Jordan Blazier. Marietta College, Marietta, Ohio, 1958.
"Barnyard Rhymes." New York: G. and C. Carvill and Company, 1838.

Barton, Clara. *Papers: General Correspondence 1863-1884 with Frances Gage*. Box 68, reel 55; *Letter book*. Ms. Div. Library of Congress, Washington, D. C.

___. "Letter of Clara Barton to Lucy Stone," In H*istory of Woman Suffrage*, Vol. 4: 1883-1900. Eds. Susan B. Anthony and Ida Husted Harper: 429. Rochester: Privately Published, 1902.

___. "Letter book." Box 68, reel 55; Ms. Div., Library of Congress, Washington, D. C.

Beecher, Henry Ward. "Letter to the Editor of the *New York Tribune*, Feb. 1860." *History*, 1, 678.

Brockett, L. P. and Mary C. Vaughan. *Woman's Work in the Civil War*. Boston, R. H. Curran, 1867.

Brown, Antoinette. "Letter to Lucy Stone," *Friends and Sisters: Letters between Lucy Stone and Antoinette Brown Blackwell*, editors Carol Lasser and Marlene Deahl Merrill. (Urbana: University of Illinois Press, 1987).

Burleigh, Celia. "Eulogy for Frances Dana Gage." *Proceedings* (1884): 26.

___. "People Worth Knowing" *National Anti-Slavery Standard* 24, no. 18 (August 24, 1867): 2.

Cary, Alice. "Hero of Fort Wagner," *The Poetical Works of Alice and Phoebe Cary."* Cambridge: The Riverside Press, 1880: 401.

Chamberlain, Norman H. *The Civil War Diary of Norman H. Chamberlain, 62nd Ohio Volunteer Infantry, Oct. 1861-July 1863."* In Archives, Lewis and Clark College. Portland, Oregon, 1974.

Child, Lydia Maria. "An Appeal in Favor of That Class of Americans Called Africans," Anti-Slavery Tract. Boston, American Anti-Slavery Society, 1833.

___. "The Duty of Disobedience to the Fugitive Slave Act," Boston, American Anti-Slavery Society, 1850.

"Civil War Archive," Union Regimental Histories. <www.civilwararchive.com.unionoh.htm.>

Coggeshall, W. T. "Frances Dana Gage." *The Poets and Poetry of the West*. New York: Arno Press, 1975: 393-98.

Coleman, Julia, *The Temperance Handbook for Speakers and Workers*. New York, National Temperance Society and Publication House, 1859.

Columbus Directory, City Guide and Business Mirror. Columbus, Ohio: J. H. Riley & Co. 1862: 114.

Corner Mary T. "Letter to Amelia Jenks Bloomer, Nov. 14, 1876." *History* 1, 123.

Cowan, Rep. "Suffrage in the District," U. S. Senate
    Congressional Hearing, (Dec. 11, 1866.) *History* 2, 116.
Cutler, Hannah Tracy. "Eulogy," *Woman's Journal* (Dec. 13, 1884): 4.
Cutler, Julia P. "Letter from Mrs. Cutler, Visit to St.
    Louis," *Ohio Cultivator* 11, no. 11 (June 15, 1855): 190.
Dacus, J. A. *Battling with the Demon.* Saint Louis:
    Scammell & Co., 1877.
Davis, Paulina Wright. *A History of the National Women's Rights Movement for Twenty Years, from 1850 to 1870.* New York: Journeyman Printers' Cooperative Associates, 1871.
DeTocqueville, Alexis. *Democracy in America.* Eds. Harvey Mansfield and Delba Winthrop. Chicago: University of Chicago Press, 2000.
Dickens, Charles. *"A Jaunt," American Notes,* Ch.13.
    London: Chapman and Hall, 1842.
"E." "Some Entertaining Reminiscences of the Siege of Morris Island." *National Tribune*
    (June 28, 1883). Philadelphia: Grand Army of the Republic Museum.
"Elsie Magoon." *American Phrenological Journal* 46, no. 2 (1867): 73.
"Elsie Magoon." *Christian Union* (1867): 102.
"Elsie Magoon." *Prairie Farmer* 42, no. 1 (1867): 5.
Executive Committee, "The Anti-Slavery History of the John Brown Year, Twenty Seventh Annual Report of the American Anti-Slavery Society, 1861."
"First Annual Circular of the Western Homeopathic College for the Session 1850-1851." *Morgan Bibliography of Ohio Imprints, 1760-1850.*
Forten, Charlotte. *The Journal of Charlotte L. Forten.* Ed. Ray Billington. New York: Dryden Press, 1953; "Life on the Sea Islands." *Atlantic Monthly* (May 1864, and June 1864): 666-676 and 587-596.
"Frances D. Gage." *Eminent Women of the Age.* Ed. James Parton et al., 382-86. Hartford, Conn.: S. M. Betts & Company, 1868.
Gage, John. "Autobiographical Notes." Vineland, New Jersey: Vineland Historical Society Archives, n.d.
___. "Vineland Letter to Clara Barton, Nov. 20, 1911." Vineland, New Jersey Historical Society Archives.

Gage, James L. "American Iron for Rail Roads." *Missouri Republican* (Sept. 3, 1854); *American Railway Times* 6, 30 (July 27, 1854): 1.

___. "Iron Mountain Region." *Western Journal and Civilian,* 14, No. 2 (July 1855): 124.

___. *Land Records.* "James L. Gage." 20 June 1826; document #1024, Serial #540_034. Cash entry sale, 80.0000 acres; Meridian on Watershed-12 sq. miles." http://www.RootsWeb

___. "A Letter from Illinois." *National Anti-Slavery Standard* 23 (March 13, 1863).

Gallagher, William D. *Facts and Conditions of Progress in the North-West.* Cincinnati: H. W. Derby, 1850.

___. "A Brief History," *The Hesperian,* vol. 3, no. 4 (1833): 268.

Griswold, Rufus. *The Female Poets of America.* Philadelphia, Carey and Hart, 1848.

The Harbinger, 3.10 (Aug. 15, 1846): 145.

Harper, Ida Husted, *The Life and Works of Susan B. Anthony.* Vols. 1-3. Indianapolis: Bower-Merrill Company, 1898.

Hay, John. *Complete War Diary of John Hay.* Eds. Michael Burlingame and John T. Ettlinger. Carbondale: Southern Illinois University Press, 1999.

Higginson, Thomas Wentworth. *Army Life in a Black Regiment.* New York: W. W. Norton and Company, 1984.

___. "Letter to Mother," *H. W. Higginson, the Story of His Life,* ed. Mary Thatcher Higginson. Boston: Houghton Mifflin, 1914.

Hildreth, Samuel Prescott. "Joseph Barker," *Pioneer History: Being an Account of the First Examinations of the Ohio Valley.* Cincinnati: Historical Society. Cincinnati: H. W. Derby & Co., 1848: 433-463.

Hood, Rodney. "Genealogy and Biography of Joseph Barker," "Introduction to Joseph Barker, *Recollections of the First Settlement of Ohio* ed. George Blazier. Marietta College Archives, Marietta, Ohio. 1958.

Hooker, John. "Letter to Isabella Beecher Hooker, Oct. 31, 1871." Isabella Beecher Hooker Project, "Letters and Papers" in Hartford, Conn.: Harriet Beecher Stowe Center.

Hudson, E. D. "Report from Mt. Pleasant," *The National Anti-Slavery Standard* 3, no. 13 (June 17, 1841): 6.

Hunt, William E. *Historical Collection of Coshocton County*. Cincinnati: E. Clarke & Co., 1876: 152.
Janney Family Papers. Collection Ms. no. 142, JBNox 4/5. Ohio Historical Society. Columbus, Ohio.
Johnson, Oliver. "Obituary." *The New York Tribune*. (Nov. 13, 1884): 5.
Jones, J. Elizabeth. "Report, May 16, 1861," *History* 1, 169.
Just Government League. "Our Enemy." In Western Reserve Historical Society. Cleveland, Ohio. nd.
Kennedy, Robert V. *St. Louis City Directory*. St. Louis: R. V. Kennedy, 1857.
Kimball, Charles A. *Life of Luther C. Ladd."* "The Great Naval and Land Battle. By an Eye Witness." Concord, N. Y. 1862: 33-40. <http://galenet.galegroup.com.libpac.leegov.com:2048/servlet/CivilWar?af=RN&ae=03800628287&srchtp=a&ste=14>
"Literary Notes." *The Independent* 19, no. 977 (Aug. 22, 1867): 4.
Livermore, Mary. *Union Signal* (Dec. 29, 1883): 7-9.
"McConnelsville Ordinance." *Historical Collection of Coshocton County*. Cincinnati: R. Clarke & Co., 1876: 152.
Martineau, Harriet. *Society in America*. Garden City: Doubleday Anchor Books, 1961.
Montagu, William L. *The St. Louis Business Directory*. St. Louis: E. A. Lewis Printer, 1853.
Moore, Frank, ed. *The Rebellion Record*. Vol. 6. New York: D. Van Nostrand, 1869.
Mott, Lucretia. "Letter to Cousin Mary, Oct. 16, 1855." *James and Lucretia Mott's Life and Letters*, Ed. Anna Davis Hallowell. Cambridge: Houghton and Mifflin, Co., 1884.
___ and James. *Life and Letters*. Ed. Anna Davis Hallowell. Cambridge: Houghton & Mifflin Co., 1884.
___. "Slavery and the Woman Question, Lucretia Mott's Diary of her Visit to Great Britain." Ed. Frederick B.Tolles. Supplement No. 23, *Journal of the Friends' Historical Society* (Haverford and London, 1952).

"Our Authors." *The Literary World*. Cincinnati, 1850.
Parton, James, et al., "Frances D. Gage," "The Woman's Rights Movement and Its Champions in the United States," *Eminent Women of the Age*. Ed. E. C. Stanton, Hartford: S. M. Betts & Co., 1868: 382-386.
Pierce, Edward. "The Contrabands of Fortress Monroe," *Atlantic Monthly* (Nov. 1861): 626-640.
___. "The Negroes at Port Royal, South Carolina." *Atlantic Monthly* (Sept 1863): 291-315; Boston: R. F. Wallcut, 1862.
___. "The Freedmen at Port Royal." *North American Review* 101, no. 208 (July 1865): 1-28. <http:www.beaufortonline.com> (accessed May 10, 2008).
Poe, Edgar Allen. "Review." *Democratic Review* 17, no. 89 (Nov. 1845).
Robertson, Charles. *History of Morgan County, Ohio with Portraits and Biographical Sketches of some of its Pioneers and Prominent Men*. L. H. Watkins and Co., Chicago: 1886.
Robinson, Marius. "Akron Women's Rights Convention," *Salem Anti-Slavery Bugle*, (June 21, 1851): 1.
Saxton, Rufus. *The War of the Rebellion: Official Records*, Series 3, vol. 4, serial 125 Washington, D. C.: Government Printing Office, 1880.
Shurz, Carl and Ulysses S. Grant. "Report on the Joint Committee on Reconstruction, Executive Document #2, 39th Congress, 1st Session." Part II, 233; Part III, 35. <http://www.genenberg.org/world/read-file?fk_files=207167> (28 Jan. 2010).
Siebert, Wilber H. "Routes of the Underground Railroad, 1830-1865." New York: The MacMillan Company, 1899.
Stanton, Elizabeth Cady. *Eighty Years and More, Reminiscences, 1815-1897*. New York: Schocken Books, 1971.
___. "Letter to Susan B. Anthony." (Jan. 31, 1871). In Elizabeth Cady Stanton Collection. Library of Congress, Washington, D. C.
___. *The Papers of Elizabeth Cady Stanton and Susan B. Anthony*. Ed. Patricia G. Holland and Ann D. Gordon. Reel 7:817. Wilmington: DE Scholarly Resources, Inc. 1990.
___. "The Woman Rights Movement and Its Champions in

the United States," Eminent *Women of the Age,* eds. James Parton, Horace Greeley, H. W. Higginson, et al. Hartford: S. M. Betts & Co., 1871: 312-404.

------ Matilda Joslyn Gage, eds. *History of Woman Suffrage. 1881-1902.* vols. 1-4. New York: Schocken Books, 1971.

Stowe, Harriet Beecher. "Sojourner Truth: The Libyan Sybil." *Atlantic Monthly* (March 1863): 473.

Stone, Lucy. "Letters," *Friends and Sisters: Letters Between Lucy Stone and Antoinette Brown Blackwell, 1846-1893.* Eds. Carol Lasser and Marlene Deahl Merrill. Urbana: University of Illinois Press, 1987.

___. "Woman Suffrage in New Jersey." Address to N. J. Legislators, March 6, 1867. Boston: C. H. Simonds & Co. Publishers.

Swisshelm, Jane. "Bloomers and Woman's Rights Conventions," *Half a Century,* New York: Source book, 1970.

Tilton, Theodore. "Address," *Proceedings of the Eleventh National Woman's Rights Convention, May 10, 1866.*

___. "Mrs. Elizabeth Cady Stanton," Hartford: S.M. Betts & Co., 1871.

Venable, W. H. *Beginnings of Literary Culture of the Ohio Valley. Historical and Biographical Sketches.* New York: Peter Smith, 1949.

Waters, Wilson. *History of St. Luke's Episcopal Church.* Marietta, Ohio, 1884.

Wilcox, Lucinda S. "To the Ladies of Vineland." Bentley Historical Library, University of Michigan. Ann Arbor: Michigan.

Wilson Waters. *History of St. Luke's Episcopal Church* (Marietta, Ohio, 1884).

Whitelaw, Reid. *Ohio in the War.* Vol. 1 Cincinnati: Wilstach, Baldwin & Co., 1871.

"The Woman Speaking," *Missouri Republican* (April 7, 1855): 3.

"Women of the Period," *Cincinnati Daily Gazette* (Nov. 26, 1869).

Twentieth Century Sources Cited

Aaron, Daniel, *How the West was Lost.* St. Pete: University of South Florida, 1999.

_____. *The Unwritten War.* Madison: University of Wisconsin Press, 1987.

Aaronson, Amy B., *Taking Liberties: Early American Women's Magazines and Their Readers.* West Port, Conn.: Praeger Publishers, 2002.

Adams, George W., "Caring for the Men." www.civil-warhome.com/medicinehistory.htm

Andrews, Martin R., *History of Marietta and Washington Counties.* Chicago: Biographical, 1902.

Ash, Stephen V., *Firebrand of Liberty.* New York: W. W. Norton, 2008.

Banning, Lance and Marvin Mayers, *The Jeffersonian Persuasion.* Ithaca: Cornell University Press, 1980.

Barnhart, Terry A., "The Partisan, William Davis Gallagher and the Cause of Western Literature." *Ohio History* 115 (2008): 101-120.

"Barnum on the Democratic Party and Temperance." <http:www.chm.gmu.edu/lostmuseum/lm/44/7> (accessed May 10, 2008).

Barton, William E., *The Life of Clara Barton.* Vols. 1 and 2. Boston: Houghton and Mifflin, 1922.

Baym, Nina, *Woman Writers of the American West, 1880-1927.* Urbana, University of Illinois Press, 2011.

Becher, Matthew E., "A Forgotten Industry." <http://www.ohioarchaeology.org> (accessed May 10, 2008).

Bernikow, Louise, *The World Split Open, Four Centuries of Women Poets in England and America.* New York: Random House, Inc., 1974.

Blackwell, Alice Stone, *Lucy Stone: Pioneer of Woman's Rights.* Boston: Brown and Little, 1930.

Blocker, Jack S. Jr., *American Temperance Movements.* Boston: Twayne Publishing Co., 1989.

_____. "Give to the Winds Thy Fears." *The Women's Temperance Crusade, 1873-874.* Westport, Conn.: Greenwood Press, 1985.

Bloomer, Dexter C., *The Life and Writings of Amelia Bloomer.* New York: Schocken Books, 1975.

Bordin, Ruth, "A Baptism of Power and Liberty, the Women's Crusade of 1873-1874." *Ohio History* 87, no. 4 (1978): 393-404.

Boynton, Henry Walcott, *Annals of American Bookselling, 1638-1850.* New York: John Wiley & Sons, Inc. 1932.

Brockett, L. P. and Mary C. Vaughan, *Woman's Work in the Civil War.* Philadelphia: Zeigler, McCurdy and Co., 1867.

Bruce, Norma J., "A Commitment to Women--*The Ohio Cultivator* and the *Ohio Farmer* of the Nineteenth Century." *The Serials Librarian* 37, no. 2 (1999): 13-31.

Brown, Olympia, *Acquaintances Old and New Among Reformers.* Milwaukee, Wisconsin: S. E. Tate, 1911.

Buhle, Mari Jo and Paul, Eds. *The Concise History of Woman Suffrage.* Urbana: University of Illinois Press, 1978.

Burghardt, Dubois, "The Freedmen's Bureau," *Atlantic Monthly 97 (1901): 354-363.*

Burke, Michael, "A Chronicle of the Life of Harmon Blennerhasset," *West Virginia Historical Society Quarterly* 13, no. 1 (Jan. 1999), 1. <http://www.wvculture.org/hiStory/wvhs1312.html>

Burlingame, Michael and John Ettlinger, *Complete War Diaries of John Hay*, Carbondale: Southern Illinois University Press, 1999.

Cantrell, Edna Pearl, *Temperance, Justice to the Negro, Justice to Women: Frances Dana Gage and the Triune Cause.* MA: Ohio University, 1987.

Cayton, Andrew R. L. and Peter S. Onuf, *The Midwest and the Nation: Rethinking the History of an American Region.* Bloomington: University of Indiana Press, 1990, 123-126.

Chambers-Schiller, Virginia Lee, *Liberty, a Better Husband.* New Haven: Yale University Press, 1984.

Clifford, Kate, *Bound for the Promised Land: Harriet Tubman, Portrait of an American Hero,* New York: Ballantine Books, 2004.

Colvin, David Leigh, *Prohibition in the United States.* New York: George H. Doran Co., 1926.

Cone, Helen Grey, "Women in American Literature." *Century* 40, no. 6 (Oct. 1890): 920-930.
Conrad, Susan Phinney, *Perish the Thought: Intellectual Women in Romantic America, 1830-1860*. New York: Oxford University Press, 1976.
Dannenbaum, Jed, *Drink and Disorder, Temperance Reform in Cincinnati, from the Washingtonian Revival to the WCTU*. Urbana: University of Illinois Press, 1984.
Dougan, Nettie H., *McConnelsville, Ohio, 1817-1967 Sesquicentennial*. 1967. Morgan County Historical Society, McConnelsville, Ohio. 1967.
DuBois, W. E. Burghardt, "The Freedmen's Bureau." *Atlantic Monthly* 87 (1901): 354-365.
Edelstein, Tilden G., *Strange Enthusiasm*. New York: Norton Co., Inc. 1967.
Epstein, Barbara Leslie, *The Politics of Domesticity: Women, Evangelism, and Temperance in Nineteenth-Century America*. Middletown, Conn.: Wesleyan University Press, 1981.
Etcheson, Nicolle, "Manliness and the Political Culture of the Old Northwest, 1790-1860." *Journal of the Early Republic,"* 15 (Spring 1995): 59-77.
Faragher, John Mack, "History from the Inside Out: Writing the History of Women in Rural America," *American Quarterly* 33, (1981): 537-557.
_____, *Sugar Creek, Life on the Prairie*. New Haven, Yale University Press, 1988.
Flexnor, Eleanor, *Century of Struggle*. Cambridge: Harvard University Press, 1959.
"Frances Gage," *The Feminist Companion to English Literature*. Eds. Virginia Blaine, Patricia Clement, Isobel Grundy: 406. New Haven: Yale University Press, 1990.
"Frances Dana Barker Gage," *Ohio Authors and Their Books*. Ed. William Coyle. Cleveland: World Publishing Company, 1962: 23.
Friedman, Laurence, *A History of the Law*. New York: Simon and Schuster, 1973.
Gaylord, James M. and Charles Robertson, *Historical Reminiscences of Morgan County*. Morgan County Historical Society: McConnelsville, Ohio, 1932.

Giele, Janet Zollinger, *Two Paths to Woman's Equality, Temperance, Suffrage and the Origins of Modern Feminism.* New York: Twayne Press, 1995.

Ginzberg, Lori D., *Elizabeth Cady Stanton: an American Life.* New York: Hill and Wang, 2009.

Goldsmith, Barbara, *Other Powers, The Age of Suffrage, Spiritualism, and the Scandalous Victoria Woodhull.* New York: Harper Collins, 1999.

Griffith, Elisabeth, *In Her Own Right: The Life of Elizabeth Cady Stanton.* New York: Oxford University Press, 1984.

Gusfield, Joseph R., *Symbolic Crusade: Status Politics and the American Temperance Society.* Urbana: University of Illinois Press, 1963.

Hays, Elinor Rice, *Morning Star, Biography of Lucy Stone, 1818-1897.* New York: Octagon Books, 1961.

Hayward, Michele H. and Mark A. Steinback, et al., *Research Design: Phase I Cultural Resources of Civil War and Postbellum Sites (1862-1892).* Marine Corps Recruit Depot, Parris Island, South Carolina. Pan American Consultants, Inc., Depew, New York, 1997.

Henery, Nettie T., "Aunt Fanny Gage: The Story of a Famous McConnelsville Woman." Typescript written for the *Morgan County Herald* (Dec. 28, 1937): 6. In Simpson Morgan County Public Library, McConnelsville, Ohio.

Hersch, Blanche Glassman, *The Slavery of Sex: Feminist Abolitionists in America.*Urbana: University of Illinois Press, 1978.

Hill, Patricia R., "Writing Out the War: Harriet Beecher Stowe's Averted Gaze." *Divided Houses, Gender and the Civil War.* Eds. Catharine Clinton and Nina Silber: 260-283. New York: Oxford University Press, 1992.

The History of Morgan County, Ohio 1980. McConnelsville, Ohio: Morgan County Historical Society, 1980.

Holland, Patricia G. and Ann D. Gordon, eds. *The Papers of Elizabeth Cady Stanton and Susan B. Anthony.* Reel 7: 817.Wilmington: DE: Scholarly Resources Inc., 1990.

Hood, Rodney, "Genealogy and Biography of Joseph Barker." *Joseph Barker, Recollections of the First Settlement of Ohio.* Ed. George Jordan Blazier. Marietta, Ohio: College Archives, Marietta College.

Holtzman, Clara C. *Frances Gage.* MA. Thesis, Ohio State University, 1931.

Howard, Oliver Otis, *Autobiography*, 2 New York: The
 Baker & Taylor Company, 1907.
Isetts, Charles A., "The Women's Christian Temperance Crusade of
 Ohio." M.A. Thesis Miami University, 1971.
Jabour, Anya, *Marriage in the Early Republic*. Baltimore: Johns
 Hopkins University Press, 1998.
James, Edward T., ed. "Frances D. Gage." *Notable
 American Women, 1607-1950*. Vol.1. Cambridge: Mass.
 Belknap Press, 1971.
Jeffrey, Julie Roy, *Frontier Women, the Trans-Mississippi West,
 1840-1880*. New York: Hill and Wang, 1979.
Jordan, Philip D. and Carl Wittke, *Ohio Comes of Age*. Columbus: Ohio Archaeological and Historical Society, 1938.
Kayes, Frances W., "The Ladies Department of the *Ohio Cultivator*, 1845-1855: A Feminist Forum." *Agricultural History* 50 (April 1976): 414-423.
Kerr, Andrea Moore, "White Women's Rights, Black
 Men's Wrongs." In *One Woman, One Vote*. Ed. Marjorie
 Spruill Wheeler. Troutdale, Oregon: New Sage Press, 1995.
Kilcup, Karen L., "Anthologizing Matters. The Poetry and Prose of
 Recovery Work." *Symploke* 8, no. 1-2 (Winter-Spring
 2000).
___., *Nineteenth Century Women Writers: a Critical Reader*. Athens: Ohio University Press, 1977.
Knepper, George, *Ohio and Its People*. Kent: Kent State
 University Press, 2003.
Kolodny, Annette, *The Land Before Us*, Fantasy and
 Experience of the American Frontiers, 1830-1860. Chapel
 Hill: University of North Carolina Press, 1975.
Larson, Kate Clifford, *Harriet Tubman, Portrait of an
 American Hero*. New York: Ballantine Books,
 2004.
Lasser, Carol and Marlene Merrill, *Friends and Sisters:
 Letters Between Lucy Stone and Antoinette Brown, 1846-1893*. Champaign: University of Illinois Press, 1987.
Leach, William, *True Love and Perfect Union*. New York:
 Basic Books, 1980.
Lender, Mark Edward, "Frances Dana Barker Gage."
 Dictionary of American Temperance Biography. Westport:
 Greenwood Press, 1894: 183-184.

Loeffelholz, Mary, "Subversion and Genre: The Postwar Fiction of Frances Dana Gage." *Legacy* 5.2 (Fall 1988): 19-32.

Looby, Christopher, Ed. *The Complete Civil War Journal and Selected Letters of Thomas Wentworth Higginson.* Chicago: University of Chicago Press, 2002.

Mabee, Carleton and Susan Whitehouse, *Sojourner Truth: Slave, Prophet, Legend.* New York: New York University Press, 1993.

Mason, Jeffrey D., *Melodrama and the Myth of America.* Bloomington: Indiana University Press, 1993.

Mattingly, Carol, *Well-Tempered Women: Nineteenth-Century Temperance Rhetoric.* Carbondale: Southern Illinois University Press, 1998.

Miller, Susan Cummins, *A Sweet, Separate Intimacy, Women Writers of the American Frontier, 1800-1922.* Salt Lake City: University of Utah Press, 2000.

Mills, Robert, *Statistics of South Carolina.* Spartanburg: The Reprint Company, 1986.

Mintz, Steven, *Moralists and Modernizers.* Baltimore: Johns Hopkins University Press, 1995.

Morantz-Sanchez, Regina, *Sympathy and Science, Women Physicians in American Medicine.* New York: Oxford University Press, 1985.

Moody, Linda, "Frances Dana Gage," 4 <http://www.janushead.org/JHSumm99/moody.cfm>

"Mrs. Frances Dana Gage," *Women of the Century.* Eds. Frances E. Willard and Mary Livermore, 308-309. Buffalo: Charles Wells Moulton, 1893.

Mott, Lucretia, *James and Lucretia Mott's Life and Letters*, ed. Anna Davis-Hallowell. Cambridge: Houghton & Mifflin Co., 1884.

___. "Sketches of the Anti-Slavery Convention." *The Liberator* (Oct. 23, 1840).

Murdock, Catharine Gilbert, *Domesticating Drink: Women, Men, and Alcohol in America, 1870-1940.* Baltimore: Johns Hopkins University Press, 1998.

Oates, Stephen B., *A Woman of Valor: Clara Barton and the Civil War.* New York: Free Press, 1994.

Oberhohzer, Ellis Paxson, *The Literary History of Philadelphia.* Philadelphia: Gordon W. Jacobs and Co., 1906.

O'Connor, Lillian, *Pioneer Woman Orators.* New York: Columbia University Press, 1954: 91-93.

"Ohio Women's Hall of Fame."
   http://www.odjfs.state.oh.us/women/Halloffame/bio.asp?ID=96
"Order of Good Templars," *Templar History Magazine* 2 (Dec. 21, 2002).
Painter, Nel Irvine, *Sojourner Truth, a Life, a Symbol*. New York: W. W. Norton, 1996.
Papashvily, Helen Waite, *All the Happy Endings*. Port Washington: Kennikat Press, 1956.
Parker, Gail, "Introduction." *Elizabeth Cady Stanton, Eighty Years and More, Reminiscences 1815-1897*. New York: Schocken Books, 1971.
Parker, Sandra, "Frances Dana Barker Gage." <www25.uua.org/articles/francesgage.html> (accessed May 10, 2008).
"Parris Island Mile History Tour." Parris Island Museum. Marine Corps Recruiting Depot, Parris Island, South Carolina. www.pimuseum.us/
Painter, Nell Irvin, *Sojourner Truth, a Life, a Symbol*. New York: W. W. Nortonand Company, 1996.
_____, "Difference, Slavery and Memory, Sojourner Truth in Feminist Abolition." *The Abolition Sisterhood, Women's Political Culture in Antebellum America, Sojourner Truth in Feminist Abolition*. Eds. Jean Fagan Yellin and John C. Van Horne, Ithaca: Cornell University Press, 1994: 129-158.
Phinney, Susan Conrad, *Perish the Thought*. New York: Oxford University Press, 1976.
Porter, Lorle, *A People Set Apart*. Zanesville: New Concord Press, 1998.
Povenmire, Kenneth Willett, *The Temperance Movement in Ohio, 1845-1860*. M.A. Thesis. The Ohio State University, 1933.
Pryor, Elizabeth Brown, *Clara Barton, Professional Angel*. Philadelphia: University of Pennsylvania Press, 1987.
Reid, Whitelaw, *Ohio in the War, 1861-1865*. Cincinnati: Moore, Wilstach and Baldwin, 1868.
Reynolds, David S., "Black Cats and Delirium Tremens." *Serpent in the Cup*. Eds. David S. Reynolds and Debra J. Rosenthal: 22-59. Amherst: University of Massachusetts Press, 1997.

Rorabaugh, W. J., *The Alcoholic Republic: An American Tradition*. New York: Oxford University Press, 1981.

___. "Review of Jack S. Blocker's "Give to the Wind Thy Fears,*" Ohio History* 87, no. 4 (1978).

Rose, Willie Lee, *Rehearsal for Reconstruction: The Port Royal Experiment*. New York: Vintage Books, Random House, 1964.

Roseboom, Eugene H., "Frances Dana Gage." In *Notable American Women, 1607-195*. Vol. 2, Ed. Edward T. James: 2-4. Cambridge: Belknap Press, 1971.

Rosenberg, Carol Smith, *Disorderly Conduct: Visions of Gender in Victorian America*. New York: Alfred A. Knopf, 1985.

Rosengarten, Theodore, *Tombee: Portrait of a Cotton Planter*. New York: William Morrow & Co., Inc., 1986.

Rosenthall, Debra J., "Introduction," *Serpent in the Cup, Temperance in American Literature*, editors David S. Reynolds and Debra J. Rosenthall, Amherst: University of Mass. Press, 1997.

Rowland, Lawrence S., *The History of Beaufort County, South Carolina, 1514-1861*. Columbia: University of South Carolina Press, 1996.

Russo, Ann and Cherri Kramarae, *Radical Women's Press of the 1850's*. New York: Routledge, 1991.

Rugemer, Edward Bartlett, *The Problem of Emancipation, The Caribbean Roots of the American Civil War*. Baton Rouge: Louisiana State University Press, 2008.

Showalter, Elaine, *A Jury of Her Peers*. New York: Alfred A. Knopf, 2009.

Shumpert, Catherine Leigh, "The Eighteenth and Nineteenth Century Plantation Components on Parris Island, South Carolina." M.A. Thesis, University of South Carolina, 2001.

___. *Reminiscences*. 4 vols. New York: Doubleday, Page, & Company, 1909.

Sigerman, Harriet, "Frances Dana Gage. *The American National Biography*, Vol. 8. Eds. John Garraty and Mark C. Carnes: 605-606. New York: Oxford Univ. Press, 1999.

"Sites on the Civil War Discovery Trail." Parris Island Museum. South Carolina.<http://www,civilwardiscoverytrail.org/location_detail.php?SiteID=14>

Smith, Jeffrey E., "Frances Dana Gage: Turning the World Upside Down," *Feminist Frontiers, Women Who Shaped the Midwest*. Ed. Yvonne Johnson. Kirksville: Missouri, Truman State University Press, 2010.

Squire. Belle, *The Woman Movement in America*. Chicago: A. C. McClurg and Co., 1911.

Squier, Harriet, "Women in Nineteenth Century Medicine. *The Journal of Medical Humanities* 16 no. 2 (1995): 121-131.

Stegh, Leslie, "Wet and Dry Battles in the Cradle State of Prohibition." Ph.D. diss., Kent State University, 1975.

Steinhagen, Carol. "The Two Lives of Frances Dana Gage." *Ohio History* 107 (Winter-Spring 1998): 22-38.

Stevens, Larry, "62nd Ohio Infantry." <http://www.ohiocivilwar.com/cw62.html>

Stewart, James Brewer, *Holy Warriors, The Abolitionists and American Slavery*. New York: Hill & Wang, 1996.

Stewart, George, "Western Writings." *Regional Approach to Literature*. Ed. Gerald Haslan. Albuquerque: University of New Mexico Press, 1948: 47.

Swick, Ray, "An Island Called Eden." *West Virginia Social Quarterly* 13, no. 1 (Jan. 1999).

Swint, Henry Lee, *The Northern Teacher in the South, 1862-1870*. New York: Octagon Books, Inc., 1967.

Terzian, Barbara A., "Frances Dana Gage and Northern Women's Reform Activities in the Nineteenth Century." *Builders of Ohio*. Eds. Warren Van Tine and Michael Pierce: 109-120. Columbus: Ohio State University Press, 2003.

"A Thumbnail Sketch of Robert Smalls." National Park Service Dept. of the Interior. <http://www.robertsmalls.org/about.htm>

Tompkins, Jane, *Sensational Designs, the Cultural Work of American Fiction 1790-1860*. New York: Ohio University Press, 1985.

Tonkovich, Longworth, "The Postwar Fiction of Frances Dana Gage." *Legacy* 5, no. 2 (1988): 19-32.

Tyrell, Ian R., *Sobering Up: From Temperance to Prohibition in Antebellum America, 1800-1860*. Westport, Conn.: Greenwood Press, 1979.

Turner, Frederick Jackson, "The Significance of the Frontier in American History," *The Frontier in American History*, New York: Henry Holt & Co., 1921.

"U. S. Colored Troops." July 1, 2005. <http://www.ohiohistorycentral.org/entry,php?rec=2139>

Utter, William T., "The Frontier State, 1803-1825." Vol. II *History of the State of Ohio*. Ed. Carl Wittke. Columbus: Ohio Society of Archaeology and History Society, 1942.

Watts, Liz, "Lydia Maria Child: Editor of the *National Anti-Slavery Standard*," 41-41. <http://findarticles.com/p/atiles/mi_7647/is2000904/ai_b32327853/tag=content; col1>

Webster, Laura Josephine, "The Operation of the Freedmen's Bureau in South Carolina." *Smith College Studies in History* 1, no. 2-3 (January 1916): 66-163.

Whitaker, Francis, M., "A History of Ohio's W.C.T.U, 1874-1920." Ph.D. diss., The Ohio State University, 1971.

Wilson, Edmund, *Patriotic Gore: Studies in the Literature of the American Civil War*. New York: W. W. Norton and Company, 1994.

Wise, Stephen, *Gate of Hell, Campaign for Charleston Harbor, 1863*. Columbia: University of South Carolina Press, 1994.

____."Teaching Freedom: Frances Gage on Parris Island." *Parris Island Museum Newsletter* (Spring 2007) http://www.pimuseum.us/

"Women's Hall of Fame, Frances Dana Gage." <http://odjfs.state.oh.us/women/Halloffame/bio.asp?ID=96>

Wolley, Robert S., "Clara Barton: A Biographical Sketch." *The Annual Journal of the Universalist Historical Society* 1 (1959): 20-21.

W.R.W., "Frances Dana Barker Gage," *Dictionary of American Biography*, Vol. 7. Ed. L. G. Wickham Legg: 84-85. New York: Charles Scribner' Sons, 1931.

Yellin, Jean Fagan and John C. Van Horne, "Difference, Slavery and Memory, Sojourner Truth in Feminist Abolition," *The Abolitionist Sisterhood, Women's Political Culture in Antebellum America*. Ithaca: Cornell University Press, 1994.

Young, Elizabeth, *Disarming the Nation, Women's Writing, and the American Civil War.*Chicago: University of Chicago Press, 1999.

Made in the USA
Coppell, TX
31 October 2019